DATE DUE

GAYLORD			PRINTED IN U.S.A.

Academic Work

SRHE and Open University Press Imprint
General Editor: Heather Eggins

Current titles include:

Ronald Barnett: *Improving Higher Education*
Ronald Barnett: *Learning to Effect*
Ronald Barnett: *The Limits of Competence*
Ronald Barnett: *The Idea of Higher Education*
Tony Becher: *Governments and Professional Education*
Robert Bell and Malcolm Tight: *Open Universities: A British Tradition?*
Hazel Bines and David Watson: *Developing Professional Education*
Jean Bocock and David Watson: *Managing the Curriculum*
David Boud *et al.*: *Using Experience for Learning*
John Earwaker: *Helping and Supporting Students*
Roger Ellis: *Quality Assurance for University Teaching*
Gavin J. Fairbairn and Christopher Winch: *Reading, Writing and Reasoning: A Guide for Students*
Shirley Fisher: *Stress in Academic Life*
Diana Green: *What is Quality in Higher Education?*
Susanne Haselgrove: *The Student Experience*
Jill Johnes and Jim Taylor: *Performance Indicators in Higher Education*
Ian McNay: *Visions of Post-compulsory Education*
Robin Middlehurst: *Leading Academics*
Henry Miller: *The Management of Change in Universities*
Jennifer Nias: *The Human Nature of Learning: Selections from the Work of M.L.J. Abercrombie*
Keith Noble: *Changing Doctoral Degrees*
Gillian Pascall and Roger Cox: *Women Returning to Higher Education*
Graham Peeke: *Mission and Change*
Moira Peelo: *Helping Students with Study Problems*
Kjell Raaheim *et al.*: *Helping Students to Learn*
Tom Schuller: *The Future of Higher Education*
Michael Shattock: *The UGC and the Management of British Universities*
John Smyth: *Academic Work*
Geoffrey Squires: *First Degree*
Ted Tapper and Brian Salter: *Oxford, Cambridge and the Changing Idea of the University*
Kim Thomas: *Gender and Subject in Higher Education*
Malcolm Tight: *Higher Education: A Part-time Perspective*
David Warner and Gordon Kelly: *Managing Educational Property*
David Warner and Charles Leonard: *The Income Generation Handbook*
Sue Wheeler and Jan Birtle: *A Handbook for Personal Tutors*
Thomas G. Whiston and Roger L. Geiger: *Research and Higher Education*
Gareth Williams: *Changing Patterns of Finance in Higher Education*
John Wyatt: *Commitment to Higher Education*

Academic Work

The Changing Labour Process in Higher Education

Edited by
John Smyth

Society for Research into Higher Education
& Open University Press

Published by SRHE and
Open University Press
Celtic Court
22 Ballmoor
Buckingham
MK18 1XW

and 1900 Frost Road, Suite 101
Bristol, PA 19007, USA

First published 1995

A catalogue record of this book is available from the British Library

ISBN 0 335 19022 7 (hbk)

Library of Congress Cataloging-in-Publication Data

Academic work: the changing labour process in higher education / John
   Smyth, editor.
      p.   cm.
   Includes bibliographical references and index.
   ISBN 1–335–19022–7
   1. College teaching. 2. Research. 3. Education, Higher—Economic
aspects. 4. Division of labor. 5. Educational change. I. Smyth,
John, 1944– .
LB2331.A297   1994
372.1'25—dc20   94–3577
                                                          CIP

Typeset by Graphicraft Typesetters, Hong Kong
Printed in Great Britain by St Edmundsbury Press Limited,
Bury St Edmunds, Suffolk

Contents

Contributors

Kerry Barlow teaches at University of Sydney and is a frequent contributor to educational policy literature and critic of many of the emerging trends.

Clyde W. Barrow is Associate Professor of political science at the University of Massachusetts – Dartmouth and a senior research associate at the Institution's Center for Policy Analysis. His most recent work is *Universities and the Capitalist State: Corporate Liberalism and the Reconstruction of American Higher Education 1894–1928* (University of Wisconsin Press).

Howard Buchbinder is Professor and Chair, Social Sciences Department, Atkinson College, York University, Toronto. His research interests are in the politics of higher education with a particular focus on corporate and market-oriented linkages. Among his published works is (with Janice Newsom) *The University Means Business* (Network Basic Books).

Mick Campion is Deputy Director of External Studies at Murdoch University and author of several articles on distance education and open learning policy and practice from a sociological perspective.

Jan Currie is Associate Professor, School of Education, Murdoch University. Her research interests include the sociology of work, higher education policy and Aboriginal education.

Larry Leslie is a member of the Center for the Study of Higher Education, University of Arizona, Tucson.

Simon Marginson is a Senior Lecturer in the Centre for the Study of Higher Education, University of Melbourne. His most recent book is *Education and Public Policy in Australia* (Cambridge University Press).

Henry Miller teaches Sociology and Management at Aston Business School, Aston University. Among his recently published books are (with Geoffrey Walford) *City Technology College* (Open University Press) and *The Management of Change in Universities* (Open University Press).

P. Rajagopal is Professor of Mathematics and Computer Science at Atkinson College, York University, Toronto. His interests are in mathematics and the academic workplace, its funding and governance.

William Renner at the time of writing his contribution was a Research Assistant at Murdoch University. He is about to commence doctoral studies on telecommunications policy for distance education at Monash University.

Robert A. Rhoads is a Research Associate and post-doctoral scholar in the Center for the Study of Higher Education at The Pennsylvania State University. He has recently published *Coming Out in College: the Struggle for a Queer Identity*.

Wesley Shumar holds joint positions at Shippensburgh University and Swarthmore College and recently completed a doctoral dissertation entitled 'College for Sale: An Ethnographic Analysis of the Commoditization of Higher Education' at Temple University.

Sheila Slaughter is Professor in the Center for the Study of Higher Education, University of Arizona, Tucson. She has published extensively in the higher education literature and among her recent works is: *The Higher Learning and High Technology; Dynamics of Higher Education Policy Formation* (State University of New York Press).

John Smyth is Foundation Professor of Teacher Education at The Flinders University of South Australia and Director of the Flinders Institute for the Study of Teaching. His most recent published books are an edited collection *A Socially Critical View of the Self-Managing School* (Falmer Press) and *Teachers as Collaborative Learners* (Open University Press).

William G. Tierney is Professor and senior scientist in the Center for the Study of Higher Education at The Pennsylvania State University. His most recent book is *Building Communities of Difference: Higher Education in the 21st Century* (Bergin & Garvey).

Richard Winter is Professor of Education at Anglia Polytechnic University with interests in alternative versions of competence-based education. Among his recent published works are *Action Research and the Nature of Social Inquiry* (Gower) and *Learning from Experience: Principles and Practice in Action Research* (Falmer Press).

Roger Woock formerly Deputy Dean, is currently Head of the Department of Social and Educational Studies, Institute of Education, The University of Melbourne.

Anna Yeatman is Professor of Sociology at Macquarie University in Sydney. Her most recent books are *Postmodern Revisionings of the Political* (Routledge) and co-edited with Sneja Gunew *Feminism and the Politics of Difference* (Allen & Unwin).

Introduction

John Smyth

It is so obvious it hardly even deserves a mention: higher education around the world is undergoing massive and unprecedented changes, and herein lies its major problem! Most of what is happening is going ahead largely unexamined, and certainly unopposed, and it is not that academics are unaware of these changes, for they clearly are – such changes impact daily on the quality of their work. What is most surprising, given the nature of the 'animal', is that there are so few attempts to document systematically what is happening to it, or to explain it theoretically. This is curious given the predisposition of academics towards working on and explaining other people's lives and worlds. That we devote so little time to analysing what it is we do, and how others are increasingly coming to shape that work, must be one of the great unexplained educational issues of our times.

There could be several possible explanations for this. One that comes readily to mind is that as academics we are not by nature a very reflexive lot. We tend to take occurrences surrounding our own work very much for granted, preferring instead to focus our intellectual and analytical skills on investigating and theorizing the problems and issues of others. Perhaps this is in part to avoid being labelled self-indulgent, but equally, it may be that we just don't see things happening close to us as being interesting enough to warrant investigation – besides, who would be interested? There are far more exotic phenomena worth investigating in other people's patches.

Another possible explanation is that governments are not likely to be wildly enthusiastic about funding research of this kind. After all, if you want to bring about radical change, one of the last things you would want to foster is minds that are likely to ask questions about 'what's happening here'. The consequence is that many of the extensive changes being visited upon universities around the world are occurring in contexts which themselves are far from subject to intense and rigorous intellectual analysis and scrutiny.

The fundamental purpose of this book is to bring the issue of academic work out of the closet and to subject it to the kind of discussion, analysis and debate it so desperately deserves. Unless we do this, a decade or so down the road, we are going to look back and find that many of the uneasy feelings we had about what is happening to our work have come to pass, and that the situation is irretrievable. In doing this we need to lay aside many of the common myths of academic work, such as its being an easy worklife, the flexibility of the work hours attaching to the job and the appearance of what might seem to outsiders as a short academic year (McInnis 1992), and concentrate instead on what academics do *as a work process* and how that is changing dramatically with the fiscal crises being experienced by most governments around the world. What is important, above all, is the labour process of academic work; that is to say, how the work is organized, how it is enacted, in whose interests and with what ultimate effects. These are not so much questions of self-interest, but rather matters that go to the very heart of how knowledge is produced, construed and conveyed.

There is no shortage of commentary on the widespread nature of the changes that have occurred to higher education over the past decade or so – indeed there is remarkably widespread agreement. But there is considerable confusion over how to characterize these changes, why they are occurring now, the underlying mechanisms at work and the policy implications of this for the various stakeholders.

One way of tackling this conceptual confusion and lack of consensus is to adopt a particular theoretical stance or approach, and to use that as a way of unravelling what appear to be some remarkably similar trends. In particular, we need to analyse recent higher education reforms and the changes they appear to have brought to academic work, in ways that situate and locate them in the context of the wider international and global economic and political imperatives that have given rise to them in the first place.

Without approaching it in anything like a prescriptive manner, many of the contributors to this volume had a broad conception and understanding of how we might approach this project differently. The work of Harry Braverman (1974), entitled *Labor and Monopoly Capital*, and the notions of the 'labour process', 'deskilling' and 'proletarianization' provided a convenient canvas on which to sketch something of what was happening in higher education in a number of parts of the world. We were all aware, to some degree at least, of the controversies, prospects, possibilities, pitfalls and limitations of 'Bravermania' (Littler and Salaman 1982), but notwithstanding these, we felt that the broad direction and the interpretive scope that it offered us was well worth the risk-taking. The focus, then, is broadly speaking on how control of higher education is undergoing some major shifts (Smyth 1989) and, in the process, some quite dramatic changes are occurring in the nature of academic work. Some of these changes are welcome, even overdue – but others hold the potential to be quite damaging to the institution of higher education, and likely to produce degradation and alienation of the workers involved.

First, however, it may be useful to highlight briefly some of the changes that have been occurring and to provide a way of conceptualizing them.

Neave (1990: 106) provides a useful approach to this when he claims that over the past decade or so, higher education has passed through three distinct phases. The first, which corresponded roughly to the first half of the 1980s, witnessed 'the reduction of government spending on higher education as part of the welfare state'. The second corresponded with the 'setting up of new mechanisms of public control over output [and] the cost and performance of individual institutions'. It was during this phase, Neave says, that 'the powers of central control increased amazingly, though the interventionist state was pleased to present itself as the "Evaluative State" in the name of system reform'. The third involved a reinforcement of these trends even though it was sometimes presented as the 'withdrawal of the state'. In point of fact, it is more accurately portrayed as a 'divestiture of certain of its functions – primarily in the area of financing, and secondly in the degree of control assigned to the institutional level'. But, while there are elements of continuity here, there are also ruptures and disjunctures, particularly the new developments 'designed to extend financial partnerships beyond those of the collectivity, and to place at the disposal of higher education an array of sources of support other than simply the state budget'.

There are various ways of describing what is happening, some more colourful than others. What Neave (1988) prefers to label as the 'cultivation of quality, efficiency and enterprise' and as 'preparing for markets' (Neave 1990) in the inevitable shift to 'market forces' (Howarth 1991), others regard indignantly as a blatant case of 'privatizing state workers' (O'Brien 1990) and as a conversion of 'academic labour *for* and *as* commodity production' (Marginson 1990). What some regard as the 'internationalization' of higher education (Seidel 1991) and as a source of challenge, others regard as an incursion and the reaching of a new low point in the move from 'cloister to market' (Marginson n.d.).

The origins of what is occurring in the restructuring of higher education in Western countries can be traced back to (or is ideologically warehoused, at least in its most recent manifestations, in) various proclamations by the OECD and its decidedly 'human capital' view of higher education in particular. According to the OECD, the rightful role of education lies squarely in the contribution it can make to international economic reconstruction and competitiveness, through:

- producing more 'flexible' and 'responsive' forms of labour;
- fostering greater participation by the private sector in higher education, especially through research;
- requiring that higher education operate more like the private market.

But these are responses more than they are penetrating explanations of deeper causes, and if we want a more robust explanation then we have to turn to what Neave (1982) terms the 'changing boundary between the state and higher education'. The tension, while by no means new, is closely tied up with the need to maintain a crucial balance, 'on the one hand, the necessary independence from bureaucratic intervention that constitutes the

sine qua non of scholarship, and on the other, the requirement that the
state have some measure of control over those professions. . .termed "value
allocating bodies in society" – in effect, law, theology and medicine' (Neave
1982: 231). As Neave (1984: 111) argues elsewhere, while it has been 'fashionable to describe the more spectacular developments in higher education
in terms of crises, watersheds, climacterics and turning points', such por-
trayals give a false impression of the past having 'a golden hue of tranquil-
lity, even a retrospective benign nature'. What Neave points to is the ending
or cessation of a 'settlement' or 'consensus' – the end of what he terms 'the
neo-Keynesian consensus' in social policy. Briefly, he sees three elements to
this:

> The first is economic. It sees higher education as an instrument by
> which the resource development of a country may be advanced by
> public investment in it. The second element is social. From this par-
> ticular standpoint the role of higher education is to act in a distributory
> manner by providing the opportunity and the facilities for those duly
> qualified to study, irrespective of income or background. The third
> element, which may be seen as a corollary to the second, is political.
> It sees higher education as a good to be broadcast among as many as
> are qualified or who need to avail themselves of the opportunity as a
> means of raising the overall level of the population in general.
>
> (Neave 1984: 112)

The backdrop against which higher educational reform is occurring is,
therefore, clearly one of delivering major policy changes in a context of
massive structural adjustment occurring in capitalism. It is clear that as
national sovereignty comes to mean less and less (Camilleri and Falk 1992)
in terms of control over national resources, there is an increasing tendency
by the state to try to ameliorate the worst effects of the pendulum-like
actions of the business cycle, through technical/rational planning. We need
to focus on the contradictory dual processes of capital 'accumulation' and
democratic 'legitimation' afflicting Western economies – that is to say, the
desire of the state to promote the infrastructure and climate necessary to
reproduce labour power of the right kind to serve the requirements of
capital, while at the same time devizing ways of maximizing and maintaining mass support, particularly in terms of the flexibility, creativity and the
understandings workers bring to the work process, in this case, higher
education (Smyth 1991). There is an inherent contradiction involved here.
Held (1982) maintains that 'the capitalist state must act to support the
accumulation process and at the same time act, if it is to protect its image
as fair and just, to conceal what it is doing'. The irony, as Habermas (1976)
notes, is that the more the state intervenes in seeking to provide rational,
technical and scientific administrative solutions (in the process generating
a '*rationality*' *crisis*), the more it is required to listen to and acknowledge the
cultural norms and interests of widely disparate groups, and, concomitantly,
the greater the risk it runs of losing credibility because of its ultimate

inability to deliver promised solutions in a situation of complex decision-overload (which is to say, a *'legitimation'* crisis). According to Habermas (1976), it is these two interlocking crises (the growing inability of the state to bring about widespread and equitable social change because of insufficiency of resources, coupled with the incapacity of large bureaucracies to make increasingly complex decisions) that in turn gives rise to a *crisis of 'motivation'* characterized by individuals' growing sense of powerlessness, alienation, loss of meaning and general feelings of exclusion from discourse about the resolution of these issues.

We can see the evidence of these crises and the international restructuring of capitalism in the 'new round of global integration and intense competition' (Bastian *et al.* 1985: 40) that has emerged out of the prolonged contraction and structural changes set off by the oil crises of the 1970s. What has emerged has been an 'accelerated displacement of labour', but in a context typified by a 'shortage of jobs in a wide range of skills' (not a shortage of qualified and motivated workers, as frequently alleged). The jewel in this economic reconstructionist crown has been various forms of educational reform that are touted as holding the supposed key to 'reversing economic decline by restoring educational productivity' (Bastian *et al.* 1985: 34), something conservatives argue occurred because of the decline in educational achievement owing to earlier misguided permissive egalitarian policies.

Essentially, the New Right argues that this situation has emerged because the working class have made substantial gains in social wages which have caused capital accumulation to decline, and that, therefore, the solution is clear – cut wages and reduce the services of government. This argument has particular relevance for education because, as well as appearing to attend to the improvement of skills, this approach is neatly coupled with a view of human nature that regards individuals as being maximizers of their own advantage and as pursuing self-interest, 'primarily toward the acquisition of wealth, status and power' (Lauder 1987: 5). In this situation of social Darwinism, there is a diminution of state support, an attempt to reduce solidarity among workers, and a linking of individualism to competition 'under conditions of unrestrained free market capitalism [that] leads to the survival of the fittest' (p. 5). The influence of the state, because it is interventionist, must be reduced, it is argued. The consequence for education, as noted by Nash (1989), is that there have been significant restructurings of educational systems worldwide in ways that enable the state to acquire even greater control over essential functions (especially the power to determine policy and control resources), while simultaneously withdrawing from intervention in areas where it demonstrably cannot be successful (such as, equality of educational opportunity and equality of educational provision). As Nash (1989: 117) put it:

Strategic withdrawal is an attractive response to the general crisis of legitimation. The essential machinery of control is strengthened while new institutions take responsibility for the most contested frontal sites and buffer the central state apparatus from whole areas of criticism. The rationale for lobbying is weakened and the potential of state institutions themselves to become internally contested arenas is reduced.

The major hallmark of the style of governance being used to grapple with these issues is what Kickert (1993) calls 'steering at a distance': that is to say, dispensing with close and direct forms of surveillance and governance through such means as legislation, prohibition and regulation, and moving instead towards the delegation of autonomy and responsibility to institutions, regulated by the operation of 'market forces'.

The intrusion of market forces is taken up by several of the contributors, but Marginson (in Chapter 1 of this volume) in particular argues that what happens in the 'marketization' process is that education increasingly takes on the qualities of a 'positional good' capable of providing relative advantage to those who acquire it in the competition for shrinking high skill jobs, income and social status. This takes the form, he says, of competition between institutions, the growth of fee-based courses, overseas marketing of courses and fee-for-service research. The effect can be seen in a fragmentation into marketable and non-marketable aspects of university activity as emphasis shifts from 'is it true' to 'is it saleable' and 'is it efficient'? There is a growing tension in the separation between those aspects of teaching and research that are marketable and those that are not, with the former being separated off into specialist centres able to respond more effectively to market demands. Marginson concludes that this is a recipe for the atomization of students and the standardization of 'product' that is more easily controlled by entrepreneurial management.

While many of the changes in the direction of producing 'flexible workers' through higher education, as alluded to by the contributors to this book, may be desirable and inevitable given what many would argue has been too long a separation of universities from the 'real world', there can be no doubt that the increasing intervention by the state that has accompanied this process of knowledge generation, production and dissemination is considered to be a central plank to the restoration of competitive economies. The contributors to this book show how the changes that are occurring to the core of academic work (broadly conceived of as research and teaching), and the way these are designed, organized and produced (Tancred-Sheriff 1985: 370), are not unconnected to the academic labour process itself – that is to say, the physical and social location of workers in relation to each other (Tancred-Sheriff 1985: 373).

The argument is that the work of academics is increasingly becoming fractured and fragmented, as Miller (in Chapter 2) argues, with more and more of the intellectual planning function being progressively removed from academic practitioners and placed in the hands of corporate-executive style managers and strategic planning groups. But, as Miller argues, this has not come about in a straightforward way; nor have academics lost complete control. Rather, it has happened through academics becoming increasingly constrained, monitored and documented via their performance, while colluding in the construction of their own fate. As Wilson (1991: 259) cogently expressed it: 'Control is gained not by engineering responsible autonomy but by conceding it.' On the point of whether or not academic labour is becoming proletarianized in countries like the UK, Australia and Canada, Miller is much less coy than some other commentators. He sees senior academic management, in the way it has chosen to respond to the problems of the state and the economy, as producing a marked impact which, while it may not represent the kind of deskilling and degradation of manual labour evident in nineteenth-century manual workers, it certainly represents increasing managerial control through the separation and appropriation of the mental planning of the work. Miller points to the 1973 oil crisis as the starting point of the prolonged crisis in all three countries that has produced a growing intervention by the state based on claims that knowledge generation and dissemination are central to the development of competitive industries. On how universities have responded to this, Miller finds a remarkably uniform positive response: increasing access to students, reining in expenditure and adopting measures purportedly designed to maintain quality; all in the context of belt-tightening, downward-spiralling government funding, and the incessant search for new ways of doing things. But this has not been without noticeable effects, characterized by a move away from collegial to managerial forms of decision-making, the development of a 'them versus us' mentality and more and more strategic decisions being made by central management teams in universities. While these are apparently rational responses to the increasing pressures, Miller asks to what extent they represent a degradation and a deskilling for ordinary academics. He makes it clear that while it is not possible to 'demonstrate a full version of the proletarianization thesis' (Braverman 1974), the direction of responding to the market economy is moving higher education inevitably into that quarter. He sees academics as still retaining 'technical control' over their work, while losing 'ideological control'. This is evidenced in three interrelated factors: (a) policy pressures from governments that research and the production of skilled labour meet the needs of increased international competitiveness; (b) that the reduction in state funding be met by funds from corporate sources (a situation in which the older and bigger institutions are better positioned to respond); and (c) the promulgation among senior academics of a corporate management style.

Buchbinder and Rajagopal (Chapter 3) describe a not unfamiliar context of fiscal cutbacks, followed by a number of options available to universities in a Canadian context. As in Australia, the situation in Canada amounts to a shift in governance structures and patterns, but it produces along with it increased unionization and a set of quite adversarial relationships. This analysis of a single Canadian university produced, in the words of Buchbinder and Rajagopal, 'a veritable cornucopia of plans' of a technical-rational kind that responded to government priorities by corporatizing the research of faculty departments, and by-passing faculty decision-making through the creation of institutes and centres. The self-fulfilling nature of the problem becomes clear: universities are exhorted (even required) to respond to external economic agenda; those who are well positioned (or predisposed) to the industry agenda come aboard, while others ignore the problem hoping it will go away; relationships become fractured along adversarial lines as control moves increasingly to centralized management, and as unions are seen as a block to efficiency; the university becomes increasingly vulnerable to market forces, as what was 'public knowledge' is converted to 'private' ends, and as 'training' agendas take over business-centred orientations; questions arise as to the real purpose of the university as staff lose control over the organization of academic work; faculties become restructured along lines of part-time (untenured) teachers and full-time (permanent) researchers, while students are unwilling to buy into the deteriorating conditions of their learning, adopting instead a 'let us get on with our careers' mentality. Buchbinder and Rajagopal deal harshly with their colleagues, who, they claim, have become complicit through their own inaction, and have knowingly contributed (without so much as a whimper) to the progressive 'fragmentation', 'stratification' and 'alienation' of academic work.

Campion and Renner (in Chapter 4) provide a particular illustration of what they see as 'the domestication of the university' through 'half hearted uncritiqued imported managerial tools from industry'. To make their case, Campion and Renner draw on the historical parallel of engineers in the USA at the turn of the century, who were forced from small craft-like shops into becoming wage labourers in large corporations. In their quest to carve out more autonomy for themselves the engineers eagerly embraced scientific management in much the way many academics are buying into technical-rational approaches at the moment. Campion and Renner claim that there is an uncanny resemblance in the 'loss of proprietorship', 'the loss of autonomy' and the 'loss of status' in both cases. The parallel, they say, is in terms of the way instructional designers are being used to commodify knowledge into foolproof curriculum packages according to tightly stated objectives, methodologies and outcome measures, with closed feedback loops. Evidence for this can be seen in moves to standardize learning procedures, in instrumental goal-setting and in the deeply cut divisions of labour between small elite groups of instructional designers (especially in 'distance education') and the teaching pools of tutor grade staff. The net effect is that academics who become co-opted as free-thinkers become replaced by those who operate instrumentally, and forms of research arise that are driven by 'national priorities', with a displacement of personal goals of scholarship and enquiry by national efficiency and productivity. This is something that is rapidly becoming increasingly widespread.

Shumar (in Chapter 5) offers an alternative analysis of what has happened to higher education that focuses on what he describes as the 'binary nature of the public image of the university' – either a medieval community of scholars, or the university as a knowledge-producing factory staffed by proletarianized scholars labouring under oppressive management. Neither of these is accurate, he says, and in the manner of most over-simplified caricatures, they 'gloss over the more complex dialectical reality'. The reality Shumar refers to is a long history of the state and corporate capitalism being entwined in the USA, collectively to dominate the university. He proposes as an alternative the notion of 'commoditization' (a selling of a product to stay financially solvent) as an explanation of how universities (as other-than-profit organizations) responded with instrumental market-based responses to the increasing fiscal crisis confronting them. This fiscal and legitimacy crisis encountered by universities, far from being a recent phenomenon, has its origins in the early part of this century. Commoditization, as a recent response, is part of a much larger transition from large-scale Fordist forms of state-regulated monopoly capitalism to post-Fordist, decentralized, flexible, globalized and temporary workforces, where capital is much more complex and difficult to regulate, and where national and international boundaries are coming to mean less and less.

As Shumar shows, the corporatization of US universities started in the early part of this century with businessmen and business leaders replacing the clergy and other professionals on boards of trustees. Universities, as a consequence, began to produce social scientists capable of managing workers in the workplace, and professionals able to manage consumption through advertising and marketing. In effect, corporations in the USA came to have an early vested interest in extracting as much as possible from research and technological innovation in universities. In the boom that followed the Second World War universities, far from being places of high knowledge, became instead 'the holding tanks for workers to allow slower integration into the workforce', and when this inevitably became intolerable because of a public loss of confidence in higher education, universities managed the 'invented', 'imagined' and 'structured' crisis by resort to scientific rationality, technical-rational planning, corporate management and dramatic increases in the numbers of administrators to manage the image-producing function of universities. They hired out research expertise, stimulated enrolments, cut costs, remained poised to act and generally began to treat education as something to be sold. The effect, Shumar argues, is that 'crisis became the norm' as permanent flexibility meant that staff became 'proletarianized and stratified into temporary part-time workers, permanent teachers and permanent researchers' stitched into a network of universities and corporations that constituted the 'entrepreneurial university'. The cumulative effect of the state operating in concert with corporations on universities was an increasing series of instrumental market-driven responses to fiscal and legitimacy crises that resulted in universities suffering a total loss of democratic and participatory forms of education. The irony in all of this, Shumar says, is that the Fordist production models that have been imposed on higher education are precisely the ones that are currently decaying and giving way to flexible forms of specialization outside universities.

Tierney and Rhoads (in Chapter 6) take the specific case of how assessment in this era of higher education as human capital is increasingly being used as an expression that higher education should be more 'accountable'. What counts as quality needs to be calibrated, standardized and measured in order that student markets can be captured and retained, so that 'consumers' can be told how 'their product differed or was better than that of their competitors'. Education thus becomes a 'product' to be unashamedly haggled over in the marketplace and eventually sold to 'consumers', with 'excellence' being the gold standard upon which measurable performance is grounded and according to which staff are seen to be simultaneously central to the troubles as well as the solution. Tierney and Rhoads show how through crisis, change and control such situations hinge not on whether or not something of integrity and worth is being created, but on whether the product is accurately measured and value is added. Assessment becomes a lever of control, as management of learning is reduced to increasingly segmented activities in which staff lose sight of the whole job of teaching, and the skills of meaningful assessment and evaluation atrophy. Tierney and Rhoads argue, furthermore, that what are required in higher education to arrest this are forms of assessment that move away from abstract standards producing sharper divisions between managers and academic workers, and instead restore democratic notions of assessment that engage students and staff in discussions of theories of power, theories of community and, in turn, theories of assessment, in which students as learners are architects rather than passive recipients in learning.

Slaughter and Leslie (in Chapter 7) sketch out the by now all too familiar fiscal crisis in universities in the USA, UK, Canada and Australia, in which university management has created an environment which not only actively encourages, but demands, 'that staff act as entrepreneurs, raising monies to fund their units and departments'. Slaughter and Leslie report on two studies they did in ten Australian universities over six months, employing two quite different theoretical traditions: neo-classical economics (focused on entrepreneurialism across universities) and neo-Marxist sociology (focusing on the generation of intellectual property in universities). In both cases, the attempt was to explore how staff were responding to these changes, broadly defined as 'activities undertaken with a view to capitalizing on university research or academic expertise through contracts or grants with business or government agencies'. In the first study, it was found that senior academic staff (from the applied sciences) regarded the activity favourably. As well as the direct beneficial effect of enhanced funding, Slaughter and Leslie found support for the indirect 'spillover effects' of working with industry on the vitality of academic life that tended to accompany the funding as new relationships were established with outside bodies. For these staff, the benefits considerably outweighed the costs. As to the second study, on the development of intellectual property, staff saw this as a natural activity in a context of global international competitiveness and as a sensible response to securing market share. They saw it as a 'local and inevitable extension of the applied work in which they had always engaged'. It seemed that both applied and social scientists were 'unhappy with commercial norms, but were committed to engaging in the development of intellectual property to sustain their careers', even though they felt that pursuing contracts, keeping clients happy and ensuring the next contract undermined their academic independence and created substantial dilemmas for them.

Slaughter and Leslie's studies generated some light, but they also produced a host of potentially intractable questions, like:

- How far can entrepreneurial activities proceed before they become the central routine activity of academic units?
- How much can academics do of this before they become heads of small firms?
- At what point do differences between the privileged and non-privileged become exacerbated?
- At what point does division occur in the wider university?
- Will entrepreneurial activity solve system-wide financial problems, or will it simply substitute for government monies?
- Will such activities enable countries to compete more successfully in global markets, or will they turn university research towards safe national niche markets?
- When academics work with multinational firms, how much profit will really be repatriated?

Winter (in Chapter 8) explores a somewhat more optimistic side of the crisis of confidence alluded to by other contributors to this volume, and in it finds that at the heart is a fundamental and complex shift from craftwork to industrialized production in higher education. From his vantage point, the public institutions of higher education are no longer able to operate according to 'institutionalized expert authority' as they have in the past, because cultural authority has been projected on to the market with matters of priority adjudicated by the forces of supply and demand within a managerial ideology which is itself replete with contestable notions of power. In other words, it is not a simple case in higher education of 'educational values' being obliterated by the monolithic dogma of 'economic development'. There is a contestation and a working out of educational possibilities within innovative spaces created inside a competitive profitability ethos and the 'inherent developmental logic of capitalism'. It is true, Winter says, that the commodified market-logic view of education does produce government initiatives like 'competency-based vocational education', where objectives are established by consortia of employers, where the role of the teacher becomes that of support tutor and purveyor of knowledge within a knowledge supermarket, and where university courses are increasingly cast as 'integrated systems of modular units' with overall responsibility residing with 'academic managers'. But notwithstanding all of this, there are still manifold contradictions as management struggles, because of its inability to exercise more than partial control, owing to the need to maintain consent and creativity from academic workers. Besides, management has yet to learn with any degree of certainty how to measure (or even clearly conceptualize) objectives/performance in line with proxy notions of profitability. Currently fashionable notions like total quality management (TQM), which are ostensibly designed as an alternative to reductionist forms of Taylorism, amount in Winter's view to looking mournfully in the rear view mirror for a return to some 'golden age' that never really existed. His claim is that rather than capitulating completely to notions of commodification, academic workers need to grasp the educational possibilities presented in such notions, and reformulate them as an 'intellectual critique' capable of 'political challenge'. He sees hope and possibility in the capacity of scholarship to challenge and disrupt the limitations of market decision-making, and to offer the possibility of an alternative range of understandings. In large measure, this will come, he says, when those who emerge from higher education institutions do so with the capacities of reflexivity, self-monitoring, meta-communication and the ability to see problematic justifications in what they do. Finally, and fundamentally, it is within the 'educative workplace' itself, not in current sterile conceptions of objectives and competencies, that the greatest hope lies in reintroducing educational approaches that endorse critical reflections on values.

Currie and Woock (in Chapter 9) provide a specific case analysis of how this push to reconfigure academic work along the lines of 'entrepreneurialism' has occurred in Australia through the vehicle of award restructuring. Behind moves to streamline academic labour through notions like corporate management and the application of so-called scientific principles of performance measurement is an attempt to rank institutions against one another. The basis of this ranking is the demonstrable capacity of institutions to be mission-oriented and to prove themselves capable of producing commercial returns, in contexts in which the institutions themselves are able to rearrange their resources so as to conform with notions of research concentration and selectivity based on national priorities. Currie and Woock claim that the effect of these economic rationalist moves is to produce leaner organizations in the short term, the devolution of responsibility through single line budgets, funding according to profiles, targets, benchmarks and performance indicators, *but* at the substantial cost of generating adversarial/confrontationist styles of operation in which organizations drift from professional/collegial forms of decision-making (without over-romanticizing the prevalence of these) to centralized forms of management control. It is, they say, these 'sharp, local, adversarial, confrontational relationships', and the unionized responses they spurn, that most of all characterize restructuring.

Barrow (in Chapter 10) provides an extensive and detailed analysis of how in the USA the funding crisis in higher education is producing and will continue to produce the 'flexiversity', with a restructuring of academic labour around the three principles of selective excellence, flexible specialization and workforce dualization. He provides a history of how the various waves of this crisis have come about, and how the responses adopted may prove counterproductive in the long run, depending on how they are received and acted upon. Barrow sees these three routes as not necessarily being anti-educational, but that will depend on the extent to which staff are prepared to embrace them as educational opportunities (a point made by Winter as well).

Barlow (in Chapter 11) tackles the issue of the changes to academic work from the point of view of the crisis in mass production techniques and the difficulties being experienced in producing changes through macroeconomic policies. She shows how governments are resorting more and more to microeconomic reform, and restructuring of higher education in particular, as the means by which to eliminate what are regarded as rigidities in the production of labour. The particular form this 'adjustment' (to use an OECD term) has taken in Australia has been the restructuring of industrial awards for academics, aimed at changing the nature of academic work through the preparation and certification of post-Fordist employees equipped with the flexibility to bring about the desired overall increases in economic productivity. Increases in academic pay and conditions are, therefore, conditional upon demonstrated increases in productivity in higher education, measured through performance indicators aimed at gauging the production of flexible multiskilled workers. The danger with this, Barlow argues, is that 'teachers are responsible for things over which they have no real control', and the consequent reconfiguration of academic work involves regarding curriculum content as 'modules', teaching methods as 'delivery systems' and assessment as 'credentialling'. Moves towards 'competency standards frameworks', which are meant to be the method by which these adjustments are to be made, fall a long way short of being able to deliver on their extravagant promises. Expertise under these circumstances comes to be defined in terms of preparing tasks, their delivery and assessment of outcomes. Control becomes vested in 'economic entrepreneurs' in the upper ranks of academics and administrators of universities, with judgements hinging on the extent to which those lower down deliver on notions of efficiency and productivity as defined by industry. Commodification and market-driven approaches of this kind are not accompanied by efficacious ways of measuring efficiency and productivity gains, and treating education as if it were any other commodity is unlikely to produce the result desired.

The difficulty, as Yeatman portrays it (in Chapter 12), with the direction described by Barlow and others in this book is that restructuring of higher education along the lines indicated by the various contributors involves more than the economic and the managerial – there is a value-oriented agenda as well. She draws on affirmative action legislation in New Zealand as an illustration of how the 'brokering of complexities' that accompanies changes of the type being experienced amounts to a fundamental challenge to the core values of the university. She demonstrates how, in her own institution, white middle-class males were unable to grapple with a critique of values. The preferred direction in higher education in New

Zealand, as elsewhere, involves: a lowering of costs per student; staffing by academics whose qualifications place them low on the pecking order; and decision-making by executive fiat, rather than collegial discussion and debate. Yeatman says that while there is some evidence that Australia and New Zealand have adapted the restructuring agenda to fit the needs and the culture of the university, this has been at a high cost: decisions made by small groups of academic managers; small groups of academics who improve their positions and status by commercialization; and a large group of semi-proletarianized workers for whom there is little scope. In this kind of context, an 'equity-oriented vision for academic development' is unlikely to come from traditional leaders and managers because women's work (mostly teaching) is accorded lower status than that of staff who have gained commercial opportunities through buying themselves out of lower-level teaching. Marketable research also becomes the new patriarchal heartland of the university, with middle management becoming increasingly feminized as women are 'used' to give 'an institutional breath of fresh air'. The challenge is to move women who are regarded as 'front-runner equity change agents' from their current vulnerable position in universities, something that is unlikely to occur with the current established male culture of doing things.

What the contributors to this volume have not done is prove or disprove Braverman's (1974) proletarianization thesis as it might or might not apply to academic labour in higher education – that would have been too grand a goal and, besides, is probably impossible. They have, however, collectively and fairly consistently highlighted a number of well advanced, disturbing and worrying tendencies, namely that:

- there is a growing separation in higher education between those who conceptualize the work and those who execute the work;
- the quest for increased managerial control is well advanced, and occurs under the guise of restoring intentional competitiveness and enabling higher education institutions to respond better to national priorities;
- there is evidence of reduced worker autonomy, particularly among the growing peripheral workforce of untenured (and largely female) staff who operate in the teaching areas not regarded as being commercially viable;
- the skills of being an academic are increasingly becoming isolated and fragmented in contexts in which the paramount requirement is to make the work more explicit, so that it can be more easily codified and measured by performance indicators;
- institutional drift is tending increasingly to take the form of greater ideological control over the work of academics as they are vested with technical control in contexts that are framed by the norms and values of business and industry;
- despite the increased rhetoric about devolution, self-management, autonomy and single-line budgets, the reality is that the important decisions

in higher education are made further and further away from the work, in elite policy-making units.

References

Bastian, A., Fruchter, N., Gittell, M. and Greer, C. (1985) Choosing equality: the case for democratic schooling, *Social Policy*, Spring, 34–51.

Braverman, H. (1974) *Labor and Monopoly Capital: the Degradation of Work in the Twentieth Century*. New York, Monthly Review Press.

Camilleri, J. and Falk, J. (1992) *The End of Sovreignty? The Politics of a Shrinking and Fragmenting World*. Pyrmont, New South Wales, Gower.

Habermas, J. (1976) *Legitimation Crisis*. London, Heinemann.

Held, D. (1982) Crisis tendencies, legitimation and the state, in J. Thompson and D. Held (eds) *Habermas: Critical Debates*. London, Macmillan.

Howarth, A. (1991) Market forces in higher education, *Higher Education Quarterly*, 45(1), 5–13.

Kickert, W. (1993) Steering at a distance: a new paradigm of public goverance in Dutch higher education. Unpublished manuscript, Department of Public Administration, Erasmus University, Rotterdam.

Lauder, H. (1987) The New Right and educational policy in New Zealand, *New Zealand Journal of Educational Studies*, 22(1), 3–23.

Littler, G. and Salaman, G. (1982) Bravermania and beyond: recent theories of the labour process, *Sociology*, 16(2), 251–69.

Marginson, S. (n.d.) From cloister to market: the new era in higher education. Unpublished manuscript, Melbourne University.

Marginson, S. (1990) The culture of the White Paper: academic labour for and as commodity production, *Discourse*, 10(2), 22–35.

McInnis, C. (1992) Changes in the nature of academic work, *Australian Universities' Review*, 35(2), 9–12.

Nash, R. (1989) Tomorrow's schools: state power and parent participation, *New Zealand Journal of Educational Studies*, 24(2), 113–28.

Neave, G. (1982) The changing boundary between the state and higher education, *European Journal of Education*, 17(3), 231–41.

Neave, G. (1984) On the road to Silicon Valley? The changing relationship between higher education and government in Western Europe, *European Journal of Education*, 19(2), 111–29.

Neave, G. (1988) On the cultivation of quality, efficiency and enterprise: an overview of recent trends in higher education in Western Europe 1986–8, *European Journal of Education*, 23(1 and 2), 7–23.

Neave, G. (1990) On preparing for markets: trends in higher education in Western Europe 1988–90, *European Journal of Education*, 25(2), 105–22.

O'Brien, J. (1990) Privatising state workers: the case of academics, *Australian Universities' Review*, 33(1 and 2), 30–7.

Seidel, H. (1991) Internationalisation: a new challenge for universities, *Higher Education*, 21(3), 289–96.

Smyth, J. (1989) Collegiality as a counter discourse to the intrusion of corporate management into higher education, *Journal of Tertiary Educational Administration*, 11(2), 143–55.

Smyth, J. (1991) Theories of the state and recent policy reforms in Australian higher education, *Discourse*, 11(2), 48–69.

Tancred-Sheriff, P. (1985) Craft hierarchy and bureaucracy: modes of control of the academic labour process, *Canadian Journal of Sociology*, 10(4), 369–90.

Wilson, T. (1991) The proletarianisation of academic labour, *Industrial Relations Journal*, 22(4), 250–62.

1

Markets in Higher Education: Australia

Simon Marginson

This chapter is about the development of markets in higher education, with reference to the case of Australia.[1]

There are three main sections. The first summarizes a theoretical position on the nature of markets in higher education. The second employs these concepts to describe the growing role of, and diversification of, higher education markets in Australia since the mid-1980s. 'Markets' include positional competition between institutions, overseas marketing, the growth of fee-based courses, and commercial research and consultancy. The final section draws out some general conclusions about the changing labour process in higher education.

Markets in higher education

Full knowledge is impossible to attain. Any issue may be approached 'from a variety of starting points, using a range of partial analyses in order to build up a picture' (Dow 1990: 146). Political economy, sociology and social theory all have something to tell us about the contemporary development of markets in education and other human services.

Production in education is complex. The product or 'output' of education is many sided, and some aspects elude measurement. Further, insofar as production in education is an economic phenomenon, this production can only be understood in its social and political context. More than most social sectors, practices in education are affected by public policy and politics. Thus part of the explanation for markets in education lies in the rising importance of neo-classical economic discourse in public policy, although these markets have a longer history than does 'economic rationalism' and the new right (Marginson 1992a, b, c, 1993).

The production of education may take either market or non-market forms and, often, a mixture of both. Market production is constituted by three interdependent elements. First, there is production of a scarce *commodity* or commodities, where the product has a dual nature. At one and the same time it has a use value or values for the consumer, and an exchange value in money terms for the producer (Marx 1976: 125–77). Second, there is a system of competitive production, with market exchange between buyers and sellers of education services. Third, practices in education becomes influenced, if not governed, by the attitudes (subjectivities) and actions required to be successful under competitive market conditions. People take on some of the characteristics defined in the neo-classical economic abstraction of 'economic man': they maximize their individual economic returns and minimize their individual economic costs; they compete against each other; they attempt to secure the best possible deal for themselves at the expense of all others (unequal exchange). These 'economic identities' are not fixed human natures, but products of their context and 'ultimately precarious and unstable' (Daly 1991: 83, 93).

Market production in education sometimes takes the fully capitalist form, in which all three features of markets are mature, and the object of production is the accumulation of money for its own sake. More often, the particular education institution or system is a 'mixed economy' in which non-individualized or non-economic objectives (the provision of academic learning or moral security, the reproduction of cultural traditions, the creation of equality of opportunity, etc.) jostle for attention alongside private economic objectives. Market production takes the form of 'simple commodity production' rather than 'the circulation of money as capital', with the expansionary dynamic of classical capitalism:

> The simple circulation of commodities – selling in order to buy – is a means to a final goal which lies outside circulation, namely the appropriation of use values, the satisfaction of needs. As against this, the circulation of money as capital is an end in itself, for the valorisation of value takes place only within this constantly renewed movement. The movement of capital is therefore limitless.
>
> (Marx 1976: 253)

Market production may take place either in the public higher education sector or in private institutions. The market/non-market distinction is not the same as the public/private distinction, and cuts across it, despite the claims made by orthodox economists using Samuelson's (1954) definition of 'public goods'.[2] Commercial activity occurs in the public sector as well as the private sector: for example, public airlines or telecommunications companies, or full-fee overseas marketing in higher education. Likewise, the private sector produces goods and services on a non-market basis, ranging from backyard production of agricultural goods to open access private schooling in some Catholic systemic institutions, where fees are often very low and waived altogether for certain students.

Nevertheless, private ownership tends to be fertile ground for the development of markets, being more compatible than public ownership with the production of scarce, alienable (privately appropriated) commodities without regard to access or equal rights. While government services have a history of favouring the affluent and the powerful, they are also subject to broader democratic considerations, and must be credible in the public realm. Those education systems where the private sector plays a major role – such as the Japanese and American higher education systems and the Australian system of secondary schooling – tend also to be those systems where commodity production is most highly developed.

There are two main forms of commodity produced in education. These can be described as positional goods and knowledge goods.

Positional goods

Positional goods are places in education which provide students (or more strictly, are *seen* to provide students) with relative advantage in the competition for jobs, income, social standing and prestige. Places in elite private schools, and the professional faculties of the leading universities, are the most desired form of positional good; but many forms of participation in education are associated with a more modest competitive advantage. Purchase of prestigious positional goods in education has both a consumption effect and an investment effect: such education confers social standing in the present, as well as the promise of future social advantage. Positional value is ultimately signified by the credentials assigned at the end of each course, which operate as portable 'signs' of position able to be exchanged in the labour markets. In Baudrillard's words, what is consumed in education 'is not simply a material object. . .but a symbolic meaning in which the consumer places himself [*sic*] in a communication structure where an exchange occurs' (Baudrillard 1975: 9).[3]

The main distinguishing characteristic of positional goods is that they are not only scarce (like all commodities) but scarce *in absolute terms*. At any given time, there are a limited number of positions of economic and social leadership. If there is significant growth in the number of students in exclusive schools or university courses, there is a 'crowd out' effect which reduces the value of the average place. With a fixed number of positional goods, one person can gain positional advantage only at another's expense. As Fred Hirsch put it in *Social Limits to Growth*:

> By positional competition is meant competition that is fundamentally for a higher place within some explicit or implicit hierarchy and that thereby yields gains for some only by dint of loss for others. Positional competition, in the language of game theory, is a zero sum game: what winners win, losers lose.
>
> (Hirsch 1976: 52)

Thus there is always a hierarchy in the possession of positional goods. There cannot be equality of positional outcomes, and there certainly cannot be universality in positional outcomes in education, except in the polar case when education is produced entirely on a non-market basis and has no positional value at all. Positional goods only exist under conditions of market competition. In the absence of competition and a hierarchy of outcomes, positional goods as such disappear. There cannot be an abundance of positional goods, which evaporates the positional market and abolishes the exchange value of education, leaving only use values (unless knowledge goods are also being produced). But when education of a particular type becomes scarce, a positional market may readily develop, even in the absence of some market features such as tuition fees.

One of the consequences is that, by definition, demand for education as a positional good can never be satisfied. The more demand expands, the more social resources are absorbed in the positional competition, and the less new consumers can achieve satisfaction. Even as the new layers of the population obtain access to higher education, the individual benefits fade mysteriously. Positional competition has the reverse effect to those attributed by Adam Smith to the 'invisible hand'. Instead of competition between individuals leading to the maximization of the overall outcome, what happens is that the overall outcome falls short of the apparent individual utilities, taken separately. This gap tends to increase over time.

It can be seen that not all places in education, or all the credentials gained through education, provide positional advantage. With near universal retention to year 11 in Australian secondary schools, a year 11 place as such no longer constitutes a positional good, and retains market value only in a minority of schools. All places in higher education retain some positional value. But again, not all places or all credentials are equal in positional terms, and mass higher education has devalued the average value of each individual positional good. The modern growth of higher education has led to a large, complex and vertically differentiated market of institutions and courses. Within the mass system, some traditional forms of participation have retained their positional value by imposing severe limits on access. The United States' Ivy League institutions have grown much more slowly than has the total system of higher education. In Australia, the 914 medical graduates of 1953 represented 24.9 per cent of all university graduates. By 1984 there were 2534 medicine graduates, but these now represented only 3.6 per cent of the total number of graduates in all courses.

Because it is inherently non-expansionary, and often mingles economic and non-economic objectives (e.g. in the elite private schools), the production of goods for the positional market tends to take the form of 'the simple circulation of commodities' rather than 'the circulation of money as capital'. There are two important exceptions to this generalization. One results from credentialism, i.e. extension of the levels of credentials that are required in particular occupations. Credentialism opens up new positional markets and producers are able freely to expand the number of places, at least until the market becomes 'crowded'. The other exception is overseas marketing. In terms of a national system of education, at least, there is no limit to the number of places that are offered to international students.

The limits are set globally rather than nationally, and to the extent that an international education is becoming a desired positional commodity in most countries, there is far to go before those limits are reached. Thus overseas marketing and vocational training in newly credentialled areas can operate as 'islands' of fully capitalist education within systems in which 'simple circulation' of positional commodities holds sway. To anticipate the later argument, this is the situation in Australian higher education today.

Knowledge goods

The dynamics of knowledge goods are different. They are not subject to absolute scarcity and the expansion of production of these goods does not necessarily reduce their value. There is no obstacle to knowledge goods becoming subject to fully capitalist production. At the other extreme, the absence of market conditions does not cause knowledge goods to disappear. Production may take the non-market form. In these respects knowledge goods are unlike positional goods and akin to more conventional economic outputs in manufacturing and agriculture.

There are two forms of knowledge good. First are artefacts of knowledge, as defined by the laws governing intellectual property (copyright, patents, trademarks, etc.). These include the conventional artefacts – books and periodicals, research reports, videos, films, sound recordings, works of art, computer software, information systems, etc. – and also discrete bodies of knowledge or 'know how', now a recognized form of intellectual property. Second, there is knowledge in the form of self-transformation or *savoir*.

The development of knowledge markets has been facilitated by two important cultural changes. First, there is a spreading understanding (associated in social theory with post-modernism) that knowledge is constructed, rather than 'discovered', and that an infinite plurality of knowledges, knowledge languages and knowledge goods is possible. This plurality is not necessarily tied to market economic practices, but parts can feed into the growth of market activity.[4] One corollary is the realization that research reports, research teams or even new academic sub-disciplines may be *constructed* according to predetermined economic ends. The second change is the interaction of technological change with the growing markets in information and education. The effects of this change are comparable to the effects of the generalization of printing at an earlier time.[5] Lyotard notes that 'the miniaturisation and commercialisation of machines is already changing the way in which learning is acquired, classified, made available and exploited.' Only learning which 'is translated into direct quantities of information' is readily adaptable to market exchange, and increasingly 'the direction of new research will be dictated by the possibility of its eventual results being translatable into computer language' (Lyotard 1984: 3–4). The development of information technologies is expanding the diversity and range of tradeable artefacts of knowledge.

Various new media, information and communications technologies, in particular broadcasting, publishing and modern computing and tele-communications are converging to increasingly become integral to the operations of many education (and other) markets. Evident here is a striking new and unfamiliar nexus between education, the market and information technology... Because of their increasing use of various information and communications technologies, educational institutions are providing an expanding market... Fierce competition developed in schools at all levels, when the first commercially available microcom-puters appeared. Schools were identified as the key sites in the com-mercial contests between computer vendors... And, on the other hand, educational institutions are using their relationships to information technologies in their own marketing enterprises. Some institutions are seeking to promote themselves on the basis of their use of such tech-nologies in the curriculum and others are using such technologies to offer new forms of pedagogy which increase their market reach both nationally and internationally. A key example in this respect is distance education, a field which is, to some extent, at the cutting edge of the nexus of formal education, the new information technologies and the market.

(Kenway *et al.* 1992: 5)

Foucault describes artefacts of knowledge good in terms of *connaissance*, meaning 'the multiplication of knowable objects' within given knowledge systems in which the subject of knowledge (the knower, i.e. the researcher or student) remains unchanged. But he also identifies a different form of knowledge good in *savoir*, through which the subject of knowledge under-goes a personal transformation in the process of developing or acquiring the knowledge. 'The transformation of contemporary man [*sic*] is in rela-tion to his sense of self' (Foucault 1991: 69–70, 42). *Savoir* has roots in the liberal educational tradition, with its shaping of minds and its discovery of the 'essence' of the individual, but in *savoir* the self (like knowledge) is not discovered, but constructed. Education provides the technologies for this self-transformation. Often, *savoir* is the main object of the consumer of educational services. Baudrillard talks about 'the production of oneself' as pervasive: 'it is no longer a question of "being" oneself but of "producing" oneself...man [*sic*] becomes his own signified for himself and enjoys him-self as the content of value and meaning in a process of self-expression and self-accumulation' (Baudrillard 1975: 19–20).

When students invest in their own 'human capital', as well as purchasing education in the form of a positional good they are often purchasing *savoir*. In the process of (as they hope) securing access to the labour markets, they are also turning themselves into more skilful and economically competent individuals. But the two commodities, positional good and *savoir*, are not always coexistent. It is possible to purchase a credential without regard to any personal transformation, and people often purchase *savoir* for non-vocational ends, enrolling in education to explore the possibilities of becoming a different person. Thus *savoir* may also be produced and consumed on a non-market basis. It cannot be a commodity unless its production is governed by scarcity and market exchange.

The case of Australia

Positional markets and fees

Between 1974 and 1986 there were no tuition charges in Australian higher education, with the exception of fees paid by international students from 1980 onwards (see below). Public education was dominant – there were only three small private institutions, all of them in receipt of government funding – but places were scarce. The number of students was limited by Commonwealth government regulation, and student selection was governed by quotas and academic competition. The supply of places was not determined by market supply and demand, but was affected by macroeconomic policy, particularly in relation to aggregate costs and assumptions about national needs. In certain professional courses, the professions themselves supported restrictions on numbers. Higher education as such was no longer as exclusive as it had been. In 1939 only 1 per cent of the relevant age cohort reached university (McCallum 1990: 114); by the mid-1980s higher education in Australia had become a mass system. Even so, fewer than one in five young people enrolled in higher education within a year of leaving school, and the elite professional faculties were beyond most people's reach. In 1980 more than half of the first year medicine students at the Universities of Monash, Melbourne, Western Australia and Tasmania were drawn from the non-Catholic private schools, although these schools comprised less than 15 per cent of the student population in the final year of schooling (Williams 1982: 19, 23). This was a positional market without exchange, but characterized by competition between producers, in which the longest established universities and, within them, professional training in medicine, dentistry and law were at the top of the positional hierarchy. Within the system, the greater the degree of scarcity and competition, the more the market characteristics became apparent.

In terms of the markets in positional goods, the main trends since the mid-1980s have been the emergence of fees (including full fee, profit-based sub-markets), growth in the relative scarcity of higher education as demand for places has outstripped supply, increasing competitiveness in relations between institutions and what appears to be a steepening of the positional hierarchy. It is likely that in association with the growth of credentialism, these trends have strengthened the relative importance of positional characteristics within higher education.

Between 1985 and 1991 the number of enrolled students in higher

Table 1.1   Cut-off scores at the University of Sydney

Course	1982	1983	1984	1985	1986	1987	1988	1989	1990
Medicine	425	425	439	429	440	445	448	447	453
Law	397	407	406	422	421	433	435	439	446
Economics	322	332	352	363	368	371	373	390	393

Source: Susskind (1990: 2)

education increased from 370 016 to 534 538 (44.5 per cent). Nevertheless, over the same time period the retention of students to the final year of secondary schooling rose from 46.4 to 71.3 per cent (Australian Bureau of Statistics 1992), and demand for entry into higher education increased faster than the number of places. 'Unmet demand' among qualified school-leavers had been low in the early 1980s but by 1992, despite rapid growth in enrolments during the previous half decade, an estimated 34 000–49 700 eligible applicants were unable to secure places in higher education. This does not include additional unmet demand for entry by mature age students, on the basis of non-conventional entry criteria (Trinca 1992). This is a record level of unmet demand. Within the growing student population, competition for places in the most sought-after courses and institutions has become more intense. Table 1.1 shows the rising year 12 cut-off scores for entry into three faculties at the University of Sydney.

Amid increasing pressure for the reintroduction of fees, both from within government and from economic commentators in the media (Marginson 1993: 181–2), the Commonwealth government introduced a $250 per annum Higher Education Administration Charge from 1987, generating $105.4 million in revenue in the first year. In 1988 it was decided to introduce the Higher Education Contribution Scheme (HECS), in the form of a 'graduate tax'. Under the HECS arrangements all students, aside from a small proportion of exemptions, are liable to pay a tuition fee fixed at an estimated average 20 per cent of course costs, $1800 for full-time students during the first year of the HECS in 1989. The HECS can be paid either at the point of enrolment, in which case a 15 per cent discount applies, or through the tax system at a later date. Repayments can be deferred until annual income reaches a certain level ($22 000 in 1989). Students whose income is already at that level are required to pay during the year of study. Part-timers pay on a pro-rata basis. The level of HECS, the repayment thresholds and the accumulated HECS debt are all indexed.

The HECS established the principle of 'user charges' for higher education. In conjunction with the government's argument that higher education was a process of individual self-investment (Wran 1988), this provided political conditions for the establishment of other fee-based arrangements, as well as reliance on student loans rather than grants as the source of additional student support (Chapman 1992).[6]

Competition between institutions

The HECS itself is not a fully fledged market reform: it does not vary by institution or course, and HECS receipts go to the government, not the institution. There is no direct exchange between producer and consumer, nor is there any necessary competition between producers, additional to that which was prior to the HECS.

The federal opposition parties have proposed the introduction of voucher-based funding, along with the deregulation of fee levels – allowing institutions to determine their own level of fees – and the deregulation of enrolment numbers (Liberal and National Parties 1991).[7] This would enable a fully developed positional market to emerge. Institutions would be able to set market-based fees and offer full fee places to those students not eligible for vouchers (to be known as 'National Education Awards'), allowing an open-ended expansion to take place. The value of the different positional goods would be reflected in their price, with the most sought after places now subject to financial barriers as well as academic entry. The government would no longer be obliged to maintain resources and quality levels across the whole system, and institutions, now placed in direct competition with each other in every respect, would be responsible for their own survival and growth. The government would be able to retain influence over higher education through the terms governing the vouchers.

Certain funding systems introduced in the late 1980s already encourage a greater element of competition between institutions. Competitive bidding arrangements govern part of the operating grants received by institutions, as well as funding for new enrolments, the improvement of teaching, the enhancement of quality, and research projects and centres. The use of competitive funding is now common to many systems in the OECD region. Increasingly, as Williams notes, governments are encouraging corporate autonomy and market forms. In this policy framework there is no contradiction between market development and government intervention:

> There has been a growing interest world-wide in the introduction of market incentives and forms of organisation. Governments are seeing financial incentives as a more effective way of influencing the pattern of activities in higher education institutions than administrative intervention. Changes in public funding have aimed both to increase the financial autonomy of universities and to concentrate funds more sharply on national priorities. In Britain as in some other countries national funding agencies now see themselves as 'buying services' from universities and colleges on a contractual basis, rather than subsidising them. . .Relatively small amounts of expenditure can exert powerful leverage on the system if they are used strategically.
>
> (Williams 1992: 136, 151)

Williams also notes that institutions 'are being encouraged to seek an increasing proportion of their finance from non-traditional sources' (Williams

1992: 125–6). In Australia, before the mid-1980s, governments restricted the capacity of institutions to raise money through market activity. They are now encouraged to compete freely with each other for commercial research funding, the corporate training dollar, and in overseas marketing and fee-based postgraduate courses. The opposition parties have suggested that a part of funding for basic research be made conditional on the level of income from commercial research (LNP 1991: 45, 52–4).

Fee-based postgraduate courses

In late 1987 it was announced that higher education institutions would be able to charge up front fees to students in vocational postgraduate courses, subject to some restrictions. Each fee-based course required the personal approval of the Commonwealth Minister for Employment, Education and Training, John Dawkins. Nine institutions began 18 fee-based courses in 1988, including the University of Melbourne's Executive Master of Business Administration ($22 000), the University of Wollongong's Master of Science in Cellular and Molecular Biology ($18 000) and the Chisholm Institute of Technology Graduate Diploma in Computing ($11 500).

Fee-based courses grew rapidly. The Minister's approval proved to be easy to obtain. Students enrolled in these courses did not have to pay the HECS, and their fees went to the institution rather than the government. Unlike HECS payments, these fees were tax deductible. Thus both students and the institutions had incentives to support fee-based education, although the incentive for students was reduced when the government stipulated that from 1990 the minimum fee should be at least twice the level of the HECS. In 1989 the University of Melbourne offered 31 fee-based postgraduate courses and, in 1990, 39 courses. By 1993 the number of courses had risen to 76, including the Executive MBA at $36 000, the Master of Management (Technology) at $15 800 and the Postgraduate Diploma in Management Studies at $14 580 (University of Melbourne Postgraduate Association 1992: 1, 7). Across all institutions, most of the fee-based courses are in business education, the technologies, computing and advanced training in law and medicine.

In business training, where there has always been an established full-fee international market, the development of fee-based courses is associated with new forms of corporate sponsorship. In 1989 the University of Melbourne announced the formation of a Graduate School of Management, in the form of a private company, although one that was formally subject to the University Act. Half the initial governing board was drawn from the sponsoring companies, including Elders IXL, Pacific-Dunlop, BTR Nylex, CRA and BHP. The board was to be consulted in relation to course content. Some $12 million was raised in the form of corporate donations, enabling a doubling of the school's capacity in 1990 (Kirby and Doman 1989; White 1990).

Overseas marketing

The most dramatic growth has been in overseas marketing, where, as noted, higher education has yet to reach the limits governing the number of positional advantages which can be produced, and there have been no inhibitions to the fully capitalist approach.

International students have long been a significant minority in Australian higher education. As a proportion of total enrolments they peaked at 11.2 per cent in 1962. From the 1950s to the 1970s international student policy was treated primarily as an aspect of foreign aid. International students were required to pay the same fees as domestic students, until all fees were abolished in 1974, but many were sponsored by either their home country governments or the Australian government (Australian Universities Commission 1975: 188–9). In the 1979–80 Commonwealth budget an Overseas Student Charge was introduced, fixed at approximately one-third of course costs. Sponsored students were exempt, but during the 1980s both the cost and the incidence of the charge were increased, and the role of sponsorship began to decline. By 1988 the charge was fixed at 55 per cent for commencing students, and had been extended to international students studying in technical and further education (TAFE) and secondary schools. Meanwhile, more explicitly market-based arrangements were developing.

The government's 1984 Jackson Committee found that 'international trade in Australian education services had potential as a significant new industry for Australia', that a deregulated industry would maximize competitiveness and that existing student subsidies constituted a form of industry protection and should be abandoned (National Board of Employment, Education and Training, NBEET 1990: 1–2). A 1985 government mission to Hong Kong and South East Asia estimated the potential market at $100 million per annum (Australian Department of Trade 1985). The same year, Education Minister Susan Ryan announced guidelines for full-fee marketing. In 1988 it was announced that the main purpose of international student policy would henceforth be overseas marketing, not foreign aid, and the subsidized programme would be phased out. The fees of some students would still be covered on an aid basis, but henceforth full cost arrangements would be the norm for policy purposes (NBEET 1990). Institutions have received strong incentives to expand overseas marketing. Places offered to full-fee international students are additional to government-funded places and 'outside the quota arrangements', so there is no limit on numbers. The standard fees are set at profit-making levels, so institutions can use overseas marketing to subsidize other needs, including additional salaries. Initially, the minimum fees in university courses in business studies were set at 82 per cent above marginal cost. University fees in engineering and computer science were set at 36 per cent above marginal cost (Commonwealth Tertiary Education Commission 1987: 36).

The number of full-fee students has grown very rapidly, with the main source countries being Malaysia, Hong Kong, Singapore and Indonesia. In

Table 1.2   Full-fee international students in Australian education

Year	Number of full-fee students	
	Higher education	*Total*
1987	622	7 131
1988	2 393	21 128
1989	6 130	32 198
1990	14 379	47 065
1991	20 219	47 882

Source: Dwyer (1992)

1987 there were only 622 full-fee international students in Australian higher education. By 1991 there were 20 219. Enrolments in English language training grew almost as rapidly until 1990, when a number of colleges in this unregulated sector collapsed, wiping out students' fees. Table 1.2 shows the trends.

Income from all forms of overseas marketing reached $100 million as early as 1988. The Australian Bureau of Statistics has estimated that in 1990–1 full-fee programmes generated $392 million in direct sales of educational services and another $270 million in the sale of other goods and services to full-fee students. By 1991 six higher education institutions were listed among Australia's top 500 exporters and in 1992 Monash University earned $40 million from international students, one-eighth of its total revenue. The International Development Program, whose role was to coordinate marketing by individual institutions, estimated that by the year 2000 there could be 50 000 full-fee students in Australian higher education (ABS 1991; Lewis 1991; Dwyer 1992; Hutchinson 1992).

There are increasing reports that the aggressive expansion of overseas marketing, with little attention to the quality of services offered, or to educational rather than financial objectives, has generated resentment in South East Asian countries. A study of the market in Singapore found that 'Singaporeans hold widely to the view that we treat overseas students as a "money making racket"; their reverence for education clashes with our treatment of it as a commodity item' (Laurie 1992: 43; see also Hutchinson 1992). This is the consequence of production based on the circulation of money as capital as an end in itself, in the context of a global market in the early stages of development, in which the positional hierarchies between institutions and between national systems are still in relative flux.

Private institutions

As noted, private institutions have played a negligible role in the development of Australian higher education. In the late 1940s a private Catholic university was planned for Sydney. The site was purchased but there was considerable opposition inside and outside the Church, and eventually the plans were dropped (Franke 1991: 296). The contemporary Australian Catholic university is a private institution mainly devoted to teacher training, but is fully government funded and is little different to a public institution. A more independent Catholic university, Notre Dame University in Western Australia, is beginning to take shape. The Western Australian government assisted through the provision of land, but in the absence of Commonwealth funding for operating costs, Notre Dame's development is necessarily slow. The same limitation has dogged the other established private university, Bond University on the Gold Coast. Some $195 million was spent on the site but after three years the university was enrolling little more than 1000 students and its graduate school of science and technology had already closed.

The Bond University charges fees of $6000 per semester. In Australia the basic economic conditions have been unfavourable to private education institutions; they are competing against public institutions charging a deferred fee of just over $1000 per semester. Moreover, the public institutions have been able to capture most of the international student market and the developing market in fee-based postgraduate courses. Successive Labor governments have refused to provide operating funds, despite intensive lobbying. The Commonwealth government has deliberately encouraged the development of a 'mixed economy' in public education, with islands of fully capitalist activity, rather than a dual public/private system of higher education akin to the dual system of schooling, or the North American higher education system. As the Minister for Education put the matter at a conference on privatization in 1987:

> Public institutions are increasingly geared to attract private sector research funding, to take full cost overseas students, to export consultancies, teaching and other education services and to provide, on a profitable basis, many of the technical and managerial skills sought by industry. Given these developments, there is no need for the development of so called private universities.
>
> (Ryan 1987: 3–4)

A Liberal/National Party government would change the environment fundamentally, by providing vouchers to students whether enrolled in public or private institutions. 'National Education Awards would be tenurable for their full value at accredited private institutions' (LNP 1991: 48). In conjunction with the establishment of high fees in some of the most popular courses in public universities, the result would be the rapid development of the private sector, intensifying positional competition. The remaining constraints on the development of the private sector would be the process of government accreditation and the cost of capital works.

Knowledge goods

The development of market-based research and consultancy has been facilitated by changes in research policies and in the arrangements governing intellectual property. United States' research by Slaughter on the annual Congressional testimony of the leaders of American science shows that during the Reagan era in the 1980s the principal public justification for government support of science shifted from 'veneration of fundamental research to promotion of entrepreneurial science', so that academic participation in product innovation became 'key to economic prosperity' (Slaughter and Rhoades 1990: 359; Rhoades and Slaughter 1991: 10; Slaughter 1991: 5, 18):

> The changes in the president's testimony about science policy coincide with broad legal, political and economic changes that shape the conditions under which science is done. These changes involve academic science in the privatisation of intellectual property, the deregulation of institutional rules governing academic science, and the commercialisation of scientific output. Whether or not academic scientists generally engage in entrepreneurial science, the institutional opportunities are now available, and some scientists are making the most of them.
>
> (Slaughter 1991: 7–8)

There is no equivalent study of research practices in Australia, but similar trends have been apparent since at least the late 1980s. Official policies focus on the industrial application of research. The main new programme, that of the Cooperative Research Centres (announced in 1990), is designed to reward collaboration between academic researchers, the government laboratories (CSIRO) and industry research. Following the 1988 decision to transfer a proportion of institutions' operating funds to the centrally based Australian Research Council, a growing proportion of publicly funded research now takes the form of limited life projects with prefigured outcomes. This has moved the norm of public research effort closer to the model of commercial research. As in other OECD countries, in some disciplines project-based applied research is becoming pragmatic, rather than open-ended programmes of basic research (OECD 1987: 101). In project-based research, whether public or commercial, the relationship between researcher and funding agency is that of supplier and client.

Morris-Suzuki (1984: 113) has pointed out that the property arrangements governing intellectual and artistic works are crucial to the production of knowledge goods. 'The special properties of knowledge (its lack of material substance; the ease with which it can be copied and transmitted) mean that it can only acquire exchange value where institutional arrangements confer a degree of monopoly power on its owner.' Intellectual property law allows these commodities to be defined, alienated, stored and exchanged. Slaughter argues that in the United States the commercial development of science, and the corporatization of the universities, was facilitated by an important 1980 change in the arrangements governing patents. The ownership of intellectual property arising from federally funded research projects was transferred from the federal government to the individual universities. This allowed the universities 'to engage in privatization of intellectual property on an unprecedented scale', and established the corporate university, rather than the individual academic, as the producer of research (Slaughter 1991: 21–2). In Australia universities are moving to secure a similar outcome by claiming *prima facie* ownership of all copyright and patents through the employer–employee relationship, as specified in the relevant Acts, while cementing the claim through broad ownership provisions in individual contracts. The object is to strengthen corporate university ownership against both academics and the commercial companies which employ those academies in market research and consultancy. The respective ownership rights of universities, academics and commercial clients have yet to be fully tested (Marginson 1990). What is clear is that formal intellectual property arrangements are being extended to previously informal areas, where knowledge was able to circulate freely, such as books, journal articles and research by students.[8]

Slaughter shows how in the United States the trade in knowledge goods, and the emergence of entrepreneurial universities, has been associated with a proliferation of new agencies in the zone between the universities and private industry, whose object is to secure for the universities part of the benefits of commercial product development. Affiliation to 'arms length foundations and centres aligned with for-profit corporations around production of specific pieces of university-owned intellectual property blurred the boundaries between private and public sector, between science and commerce, between the university and the corporate world' (Slaughter 1991: 20–31). In Australia the sale of research and consultancy services has a long history, but they grew considerably from the early 1980s, exemplified by the mushrooming of subsidiary commercial companies attached to the universities. By 1985 there were at least 30 such companies (CTEC 1985: 36) and by 1989 they had a combined turnover of at least $100 million, including $15.2 million at ANU Tech Pty Ltd (Maloney 1990: 15). More recent figures are not available, but there has been a substantial increase in commercial research since then, assisted by a 150 per cent tax write-off for corporate research, and the emergence of research and development 'parks', specific sectors set aside for commercial research and university–industry interaction (Harley 1990a, b). More research on these trends is needed.

Changes in the labour process

The markets in knowledge goods, the intensification of positional competition, the spread of fee-based courses (especially in business education) and the adoption of quasi-market forms in public funding and government–institution relations are all implicated in the more corporatized form of university that is now emerging. Slaughter (1991) finds that as the presidents of the elite research universities move their institutions closer to the the private sector, 'they become effectively indistinguishable from the CEOs of large corporations'. Even while partially dependent on government funding, these universities share with the private sector a common anti-statist discourse. But governments' primary concerns about economic efficiency and functionality (Lyotard 1984: 51)[9] are understood in terms of neo-classical, market-based models. In this context even the anti-statism has policy uses. Policy-makers now want institutions that are market-autonomous and proactive, run by a professional, entrepreneurial management (Dawkins 1988; Williams 1992).

The changes are uneven, by institution and by faculty – those sectors with direct market dealings are usually the first to adopt the new mode – but the overall trend is apparent (see, for example, Yeatman 1991). The majority of academics do not sell teaching and research, but they are employed within universities engaged in the production of positional goods, and they are inevitably affected by changes at the 'cutting edge' of academic labour.

Ambiguities of academic labour

In the context of the more corporatized university, what, then, are the labour implications of the growing role of market production? Non-market academic labour produces only use values. But commodity-producing academic labour has a dual character: it creates use values *and* is expressed in the form of exchange values (Marx 1976: 131–2, 166). Thus production for use and production for exchange are simultaneous. They are also contradictory. When the production of education takes the market form, this does not mean it ceases to have use value, but the nature and diversity of use values are constrained by the requirements of the market. Collective academic labour is a mix of production for use and production for exchange: different types of labour are often present in the same department, and even the same individual. But market/non-market also serves as a dividing line between different branches of higher education. Where market-generated income is essential for normal operations in research or teaching, it leaves its mark on systems of management and modes of labour. The growth of markets means that within the overall mix of academic labour, production for exchange is becoming more important, and more often dominant.

To complicate matters further, there is more than one type of commodity-producing labour. In his analysis of cultural production, Williams (1981: 44–53) distinguished between market professionalism and corporate professionalism. The market professional is an entrepreneurial, self-employed producer who relates to an organized professional market, for example in art or literature. Market professionals define their own work, but production for the market takes priority over any other purpose. Some producers effectively ignore market trends. The corporate professional is the salaried employee of a corporation producing education or culture, albeit one who may also receive royalties. Compared with the market professional, the corporate professional has less control over her or his work. The work tends to be commissioned by the corporation itself. Thus academic labour is pulled in three directions, between market professionalism (especially in commercial research and consultancy), corporate professionalism (for example in full-fee marketing programmes) and non-market labour, ranging from individualized tuition to large-scale government-financed teaching and research. 'The academic' is a hybrid in which all three elements may be combined in the same department or even the same person. It is not surprising that Slaughter (1991: 3) found that scientists are characterized by 'shifting allegiances'.

The growth of corporate-style market activity means that the once-individualized relationships between academics and the market tend to become centralized. The university–industry relationship shifts from the terrain of market professionalism to that of corporate professionalism. Within the general shift from non-market production to market activity, there is a further displacement from fee-for-service professionalism to salaried employment. The result is a crisis of traditional academic autonomy, twice over. But here the ambiguity of 'academic freedom' becomes apparent. It draws on two not always compatible elements: the liberal economic freedom characteristic of the self-employed market professional, and the democratic claims of state-sector intellectuals about freely circulating scientific research and social criticism as public goods. The two approaches are more compatible than this first suggests, because non-market academic practice is competitive and often possessive of fields of knowledge. It has its own form of 'exchange value', based on professional authority and standing. Nevertheless, the agreement about professional autonomy is precarious. It rests on contradictory notions of professionalism, and is riven by the market/non-market divide. To what extent should market requirements be allowed to dictate the research agenda? Do such requirements constitute a *prima facie* loss of autonomy? Slaughter and Rhoades (1990: 351–3) note that the capacity of scientific researchers to oppose the corporatization of research is compromised by their desire to retain individual commercial links, and their in-principle support for entrepreneurial science (see also Rhoades and Slaughter 1991: 2, 25). There is no easy way of sorting this out: 'the contrast between market-originated and producer-originated work cannot be made absolute. . .producers often internalise known or possible market relationships, and this is a very complex process indeed, ranging from obvious production for the market which is still the work the producer "always wanted to do", through all the possible compromises between the market demand and the producer's intention' (Williams 1981: 105).

Fragmentation of traditional practices

In those departments, courses and research institutes where market production is dominant, academic labour which does *not* produce any exchange
values can only be sustained by the additional effort of the individual producer, whose energy is already largely absorbed by the demands of the
market. The more market activity grows in importance, the more the space
for non-market activity is reduced. The transition to corporate professionalism means that the requirements of the market are managed more efficiently – there is less individual autonomy and more surveillance – and the
remaining non-market practices become still more difficult to sustain. Thus
the ambiguities of academic labour start to be resolved in favour of the
market. The final culmination is reached when the only use values produced are those that secure exchange values in the market. This is a very
different sort of academic practice to either of the traditional models. The
result is the fragmentation of the academic profession along the market/
non-market continuum. Those outside the circle of market activity share
neither the constraints nor the uneven, sometimes lucrative, benefits. The
formal equality between the different disciplines is weakened. In Australia,
this formal equality has long underpinned the regulated national academic
salary scale, but academics working in areas able to attract significant non-
government funding may now receive salary loadings or relocation allow-
ances, and are more likely to be promoted quickly. The capacity to raise
market funds is increasingly important when appointments are made, especially at senior levels.

Another consequence is the weakening of traditional liberal academic
discourse, at least as a *universalizing* discourse common to all fields of scholarship. 'The old principle that the acquisition of knowledge is indissociable
from the training (*Bildung*) of minds, or even of individuals, is becoming
obsolete and will become ever more so', declares Lyotard. 'The relationship
of the suppliers and users of knowledge to the knowledge they supply and
use is now tending, and will increasingly tend, to assume the form already
taken by the relationship of commodity producers and consumers to the
commodities they produce and consume – that is, the form of value'. The
academic question is no longer 'is it true?' It is 'is it saleable?' and 'is it
efficient?' (Lyotard 1984: 4, 51). This is too sweeping, but the tendency is
there. Williams identifies a crisis of traditional non-market cultural authority in the arts, broadcasting and education, as market forms become more
pervasive. Conservatives may support a regulated positional market in education but fear the unregulated fecundity of knowledge goods (Williams
1981: 100–3; 1983: 129, 134–5).

Within the organization of universities there are growing tensions in the
traditional nexus between teaching and research (Lyotard 1984: 39, 50).
The production of knowledge goods is not always compatible with the
production of positional goods. Much of the market-based research is separ-
ating from the teaching function into specialist centres, or moving outside

the academic frame altogether, in order to concentrate research resources and respond more effectively to market demands. Science policy now favours specialist centres. In social research, the example of the private sector 'think tanks', which outperformed the universities during the 1970s, has been much imitated. The proliferation of knowledge goods and specialist vocational training is also dividing the universities more sharply between undergraduate education, where the main focus is on production of positional goods and the market is substantially modified by public policy requirements, and postgraduate education/research, where knowledge goods play a more important role, corporate involvement in both training and research is profound and markets have developed more freely.

Atomized individuals, standardized product

Hirsch makes the point that when a product is supplied through commercial markets, rather than 'informal exchange, mutual obligation, altruism or love, or feelings of service or obligation', this changes the nature of the product itself. The market economy focuses on the wants of the individual in her or his 'isolated capacity'. Atomized 'individualistic maximization' is crucial to the market process. But 'it is precisely this maximization that makes individuals underproduce the amount of sociability they want':

> It is important to be clear that the distortion with which we are here concerned arises from the essence of the market process itself. The market framework, as has been well established in response to a widespread popular misunderstanding, permits in principle altruistic or communally directed objectives to be pursued so long as they are held by individuals and can be affected by their own actions. It is individual action to optimise individual objectives that is the crux. But there is one objective that the market mechanism cannot optimise. That objective is the altruistic concern for the partner in the market transaction – what Wicksteed called tu-ism.
>
> (Hirsch 1976: 81)

Thus market exchange creates an antagonism between teacher and student (and researcher and client) which is not necessary to most forms of non-market production, but *is* necessary to markets. The dual nature of the commodity is expressed in the tension between buyer and seller, whose relationship is formally understood as one of contractual equality, but whose ends are different and incommensurate. The buyer seeks use values and the maximization of production. The seller only wants exchange values, and from a minimum of producer effort. While production is at the level of 'the simple circulation of commodities', this tension remains benign. But when production takes the fully capitalist form, as in the case of overseas marketing, there is the relentless drive to maximize the number of 'consumers' and minimize unit costs by standardizing the product, eliminating difference in teaching and research. Marx's critique of market relations has two strands. On the one hand, markets foster a particular form of atomized individuality in which individuals seem independent, but 'this is an independence which is at bottom merely an illusion, and it is more correctly called indifference.' Atomized individualism conceals the real social interdependence. On the other hand, the objectifying, standardizing character of markets extinguishes qualitative differences between people: 'exchange value is a generality, in which all individuality and peculiarity are negated and extinguished' (Marx 1973: 157, 163; 1976: 165).

Thus, in market production, the overriding importance of exchange values places limits on diversity and innovation. This may not be so important in the production of rivets, or potatoes, but becomes very significant in education. In positional markets, the pressures of competition enforce uniform market norms to which all competing institutions must aspire. These norms are set by the practices of the exemplary institutions (leading universities, their departments, their feeder schools). Deviations from the norm are punished in positional terms. Experiment only comes easily in educational institutions like A. S. Neill's Summerhill, which has opted out of the positional race. It is too risky for other institutions, unless they are at the bottom of the ladder and have nothing to lose. This form of standardization is as rigid as any government regulation – even though, in formal terms, market-based institutions are free to enforce their own 'voluntary' compliance. Likewise, in research, 'though the market is always sensitive to innovations, and must in part of its production promote them, the great bulk of market production is solidly based on known forms and minor variants of known forms' (Williams 1981: 106–7). Even when innovation is the quality that is being purchased, the direction and extent of innovation is mostly predetermined by the client. Further, commercial ownership of intellectual property tends to slow the rate of diffusion of new discoveries, compared to research that is based on free public circulation.

'Whereas labour positing exchange values is abstract universal and uniform labour, labour positing use-value is concrete and distinctive labour, comprising infinitely varying kinds of labour as regards its form and the material to which it is applied' (Marx 1970: 36). In market-based systems the limitless variety of pedagogies, systems of thought and objects of knowledge, imagined in theories of the post-modern, remains elusive. There is proliferation of a sort, as any and every market avenue is quickly exploited, but the 'plurality' of positional goods and knowledge goods is confined to a narrow band within which exchange values can be realized.

Notes

1. The chapter is drawn from doctoral work on the development of markets in Australian education.
2. Essentially, Samuelson's famous 1954 essay defined public goods as goods that were unable to be produced on a market basis, because of their characteristics

of non-rivalry and non-excludability. It was assumed that all other goods were inherently 'private' goods, subject to private appropriation and alienation. Thus market production was seen as the norm: the public sector was assigned to a residual role, and it was assumed that private sector production was necessarily market production. These assumptions do not hold, and they are particularly problematic in areas like education, which is capable of being produced on either a market or a non-market basis. The choice between the two is determined not by the inherent characteristics of the good/service, as Samuelson implied, but by political considerations.

3. In a blueprint for the wholesale market reform of Australian education, Fane (1984) proposed direct trade in positional goods. He suggested the establishment of a market in university places ('tickets'), whereby students successful in gaining entry would be able to sell their place to students whose marks had been insufficient: 'the market price of a ticket would be the value of a college place to the marginal student' (Fane 1984: 68–73).

4. Jameson conceives of post-modernism as a 'unified system of differentiation' based on the 'latest systematic mutation' of capitalist economies, associated with the further extension of markets in the cultural and intellectual realms (Jameson 1989: 33–5).

5. With printing 'what had been technically and socially achieved was not only extended distribution but that inherent mobility of cultural objects which is crucial to regular market relations' (Williams 1981: 97–8).

6. In 1992–3 the government announced that an interest-free student loans scheme would be introduced. Students awarded grants under the government's AUSTUDY scheme would be able to 'trade' the value of these grants for up to twice as much in loans. The loans were to be repaid through the tax system, as with the HECS.

7. However, under a Liberal/National Party Government, enrolments in medicine would *not* be deregulated, enabling the positional value of a medical degree to be preserved (LNP 1991: 49). Note that the opposition parties would retain the HECS in order to offset some of the budgetary costs of government funding of higher education. Many students would have to pay two fees: the HECS and the difference between the institution's fee and the value of the voucher, which would be based on a standard cost-based schedule of fees.

8. At the end of 1992, draft copyright policy under consideration at the University of Melbourne required that in the case of books – previously outside intellectual property arrangements – academics would negotiate specifically with the university if royalties from any one item were likely to exceed 5 per cent of the base professorial salary (about $4000). In the case of computer programs, 'ownership is claimed by the university', although the inventor would share in any royalty payments (Larkins 1992: 3–4).

9. Productivity has become 'a discourse of total reference' (Baudrillard 1975: 18).

References

Australian Bureau of Statistics (1991) *Balance of Payments, 1990–91, Australia.* Catalogue No. 5303.0, Canberra, ABS.

Australian Bureau of Statistics (1992) *Schools, Australia, 1991.* Catalogue No. 4221.0, Canberra, ABS.

Australian Department of Trade (1985) *Report of the Australian Government Education Mission to South-East Asia and Hong Kong.* Canberra, Australian Government Publishing Service.

Australian Universities Commission (1975) *Sixth Report.* Canberra, Australian Government Publishing Service.

Baudrillard, J. (1975) *The Mirror of Production,* translated by Mark Poster. St Louis, Telos Press.

Chapman, B. (1992) *AUSTUDY: towards a More Flexible Approach – an Options Paper.* Canberra, Australian Government Publishing Service.

Commonwealth Tertiary Education Commission (1985) *Supplementary Report for 1986–87.* Canberra, Australian Government Publishing Service.

Commonwealth Tertiary Education Commission (1987) *Report for the 1988–90 Triennium; Volume 1, Part 1, Recommendations on Guidelines.* Canberra, Australian Government Publishing Service.

Daly, G. (1991) The discursive construction of economic space: logics of organisation and disorganisation, *Economy and Society,* 20(1), 79–102.

Dawkins, J., Commonwealth Minister for Employment, Education and Training (1988) *Higher Education: a Policy Statement.* Canberra, Australian Government Publishing Service.

Dow, S. (1990) Beyond dualism, *Cambridge Journal of Economics,* 14, 143–57.

Dwyer, M. (1992) Call to change approach to Aust education exports, *Australian Financial Review,* 18 February.

Fane, G. (1984) *Education Policy in Australia,* Economic Planning Advisory Council (EPAC) Discussion Paper 85/08. Canberra, EPAC.

Foucault, M. (1991) *Remarks on Marx,* translated by R.J. Goldstein and J. Cascaito. New York, Columbia University.

Franke, A. (1991) Private universities in Australia, *Minerva,* 29(3), 294–320.

Harley, R. (1990a) Uni proposes R & D park, *Australian Financial Review,* 20 June.

Harley, R. (1990b) The science park: now real estate's latest phenomenon, *Australian Financial Review,* 27 June.

Hickox, M. (1991) Review of Chubb and Moe's 'Politics, markets and America's schools', *British Journal of Sociology of Education,* 12(3), 393–6.

Hirsch, F. (1976) *Social Limits to Growth.* Cambridge, MA, Harvard University Press.

Hutchinson, J. (1992) Bid to keep tertiary students coming, *The Age,* 2 May, 23 and 25.

Jameson, F. (1989) Marxism and postmodernism, *New Left Review,* 176, 31–45.

Kenway, J., Bigum, C. and Fitzclarence, L. (1992) Marketing education in the postmodern age, paper delivered to the American Association for Research in Education Conference, San Francisco.

Kirby, J. and Doman, M. (1989) Elders is main Melb Uni donor, *Australian Financial Review,* 9 November.

Larkins, F. (1992) Some answers on intellectual property debate, *Uninews, University of Melbourne,* 1(21), 3–4.

Laurie, V. (1992) Learning to export, by degree, *The Bulletin,* 14 April, 42–4.

Lewis, S. (1991) Universities join the top 500 exporters, *Australian Financial Review,* 6 August, 28.

Liberal and National Parties (1991) Supplementary paper no. 4, World class schools, universities and training, in *Fightback! Supplementary Papers.* Melbourne, LNP.

Lyotard, J.-F. (1984) *The Post-modern Condition: a Report on Knowledge,* translated by G. Bessington and B. Massumi. Manchester, Manchester University Press.

Maloney, J. (1990) Time to shed myth of the ivory tower, *Australian Financial Review*, 14 August, 15.

Marginson, S. (1990) *Intellectual Property*. Report prepared for the annual meeting of the Federated Australian University Staff Association, Melbourne.

Marginson, S. (1992a) Productivity in the non-market services: issues and problems, *Labour Economics and Productivity*, 4(1), 53–71.

Marginson, S. (1992b) Education as a branch of economics: the universal claims of economic rationalism, *Melbourne Studies in Education*, 1–14.

Marginson, S. (1992c) *The Free Market*, Monograph No. 1. Sydney, University of New South Wales Public Sector Research Centre.

Marginson, S. (1993) *Education and Public Policy in Australia*. Sydney, Cambridge University Press.

Marx, K. (1970) *A Contribution to the Critique of Political Economy*, translated by S.W. Ryazanskaya. Moscow, Progress Publishers.

Marx, K. (1973) *Grundrisse*, translated by M. Nicolaus. Harmondsworth, Penguin.

Marx, K. (1976) *Capital, Volume 1*, translated by Ben Fowkes. Harmondsworth, Penguin.

McCallum, D. (1990) *The Social Production of Merit*. London, Falmer.

Morris-Suzuki, T. (1984) Robots and capitalism, *New Left Review*, 147, 109–21.

National Board of Employment, Education and Training (1990) Australian Government paper for the OECD/CERI conference on Higher education and the flow of foreign students: programs and policies, Hanover, 26–28 April. Canberra, NBEET.

Organisation for Economic Co-operation and Development (1987) *Structural Adjustment and Economic Performance*. Paris, OECD.

Rhoades, G. and Slaughter, S. (1991) Professors, administrators and patents: the negotiation of technology transfer, *Sociology of Education*, 64(2): 65–77.

Ryan, S., Commonwealth Minister for Education (1987) Address to conference on Private Initiatives in Higher Education, Australian National University, 22 May.

Samuelson, P. (1954) The pure theory of public expenditure, *Review of Economics and Statistics*, 36(4), 387–9.

Slaughter, S. (1991) *Beyond Basic Science: Research University Presidents' Narratives of Science Policy*. Tucson, University of Arizona.

Slaughter, S. and Rhoades, G. (1990) Renorming the social relations of academic science: technology transfer, *Educational Policy*, 4(4), 341–61.

Susskind, A. (1990) Law takes top marks at NSW, *Sydney Morning Herald*, 26 January, 2.

Trinca, H. (1992) Record shortfall in uni places, *The Australian*, 20 May, 1, 4.

University of Melbourne Postgraduate Association (1992) Fee-paying courses: 'still no rhyme or reason', *Melbourne Postgraduate*, 14(3), 1, 7.

White, A. (1990) Big business steps into funding breach, *Australian Financial Review*, 27 March.

Williams, C. (1982) *The Early Experiences of Students on Australian University Campuses*. Sydney, University of Sydney.

Williams, G. (1992) *Changing Patterns of Finance in Higher Education*. Buckingham, Open University Press.

Williams, R. (1981) *Culture*. Glasgow, Fontana.

Williams, R. (1983) *Towards 2000*. London, Chatto and Windus.

Wran, N., Chair of Committee (1988) *Report of the Committee on Higher Education Funding*. Canberra, Department of Employment, Education and Training.

Yeatman, A. (1991) Corporate managerialism: an overview, paper to a New South Wales Teachers' Federation Conference, 8–9 March.

2

States, Economies and the Changing Labour Process of Academics: Australia, Canada and the United Kingdom

Henry Miller

In this chapter I shall explore some aspects of the changing academic labour process of academics working in universities in three liberal capitalist democratic states, two federal, Australia and Canada, and one unitary, the United Kingdom. First, it is necessary to make some comments on what is meant by the academic labour process and how it relates to professionalism and proletarianization, the state and economy. Second, I shall outline some features of the Australian, Canadian and UK policies on higher education. Third, I shall provide some illustrations of how senior academics, increasingly identified as managers, react to and manage pressure from state and economy. Finally, I shall discuss the impact of state, economy and institutional management on the everyday work of ordinary academics.

A.H. Halsey (1992) characterizes a process which entails:

> The gradual proletarianisation of the academic professions – an erosion of their relative class and status advantages as the system of higher education is propelled towards a wider admission of those who survive beyond compulsory schooling. Managerialism gradually comes to dominate collegiate cooperation in the organisation of both teaching and research. Explicit vocationalism displaces implicit vocational preparation, as degree courses are adapted to the changing division of labour in the graduate market. Research endeavours are increasingly applied to the requirements of government or industrial demands. The don becomes increasingly a salaried or even a piece-work labourer in the service of an expanding middle class of administrators and technologists.
>
> (Halsey 1992: 13)

Halsey's analysis is founded on a careful historical account and the results of three surveys of academics, situations and attitudes (in 1964, 1976 and

1989). Similar processes with different speeds and political contexts are under way in Australia and Canada.

The OPEC oil price rise of 1973 marked a period of prolonged crisis and restructuring. Restrictions on the availability of public funds for higher education caused conditions of academic labour in general to deteriorate. Braverman's (1974) book *Labor and Monopoly Capitalism* began the labour process debate and argued that with the development of scientific management in twentieth-century capitalism labour was increasingly controlled and deskilled. Although Braverman's analysis is focused on the degradation and deskilling of male skilled manual workers in private productive industry, it does involve a more general analysis of the development of managerial control through the separation and appropriation of the mental planning of work. Smith and Willmott (1991) argue that with a broader Marxist framework which analyses the mutual contributions that different sorts of workers make to the collective enterprise of the production of goods and services for the state and society as well as private capital, it is possible to extend a labour process analysis to white collar workers in the public sector, such as academics (Miller 1991).

Some of the complexities of the context of academic labour are explored in the next section through an account of state policies for higher education in the three countries.

Higher education policies in Australia, the United Kingdom and Canada

Many academics move between universities in the United Kingdom, Australia and Canada, and the ideas that inform the dominant political discourses have much common ground. The economic analysis developed by Milton Friedman and the Chicago School, and the political example of the Reagan and Thatcher governments, all signified influences on Australian Labor government policy itself mediated by home grown New Right or corporate advocates. Pusey (1991) provides a good account of how new 'economic rationalist' policies and personnel penetrated the Australian Commonwealth state apparatus in the 1980s. These influential discourses are connected with the dynamics and problems that the economies of the United States, the United Kingdom, Canada and Australia have all experienced in similar but varying forms. Following the accounts and analysis given by Smart (1989) and by Robertson and Woock (1989), one can distinguish a number of stages of increasing involvement and control by the Commonwealth government in the shaping of the higher education system and the development of a discourse increasingly marked by a market and managerialist perspective.

The period in Australia from 1975 to 1989 was one of budgetary deficits, a faltering economy and consequent squeezing of public expenditure within which the higher education percentage of total Commonwealth budgetary outlay shrank from 4.5 to less than 3 per cent. This is paralleled by similar reductions in the United Kingdom and Canada. The cumulative effect of this neglect brought, as Smart (1989: 3) puts it succinctly, 'Serious deterioration in: capital buildings and research equipment provision and maintenance; student staff ratios; current student demand; and academic morale'.

From 1987, with the third Hawke Labor government, against a background of trade deficit and the influence of New Right free-market analysis, higher education entered a phase of increased Commonwealth intervention which attempted both to rationalize the system and to relate it to the needs of the economy. This was implemented in part by the creation of a new Ministry of Employment, Education and Training, headed by John Dawkins. Dawkins, previously Trade Minister, had already had a substantial impact on universities and colleges through his successful advocacy of legislation to encourage the development of programmes to recruit full-fee paying overseas students.

In 1987 the Tertiary Education Commission, an independent buffer body, was abolished. There followed a series of policy, green and white papers and legislation which, among other things, abolished the binary divide between universities and colleges of advanced education. Government-sponsored mergers reduced over 80 universities and colleges of advanced education to some 35 institutions by 1991. An Australian Research Council was established, and research was concentrated and orientated towards the needs of the economy. Funding was based on individual institutions negotiating directly with the ministry on the basis of their teaching and research profiles. Pressure was maintained to change university government from a collegial to a corporate managerial model.

There are clear historical differences between higher education in Australia, Canada and the United Kingdom, in particular the importance of the ancient collegial universities of Oxford and Cambridge which have dominated the UK system (Halsey 1992; Tapper and Salter 1992). The difference between imperial and colonial history, the contrast between unitary and federal structures and the precedent of Oxford and Cambridge have affected the character of university institutions, their government and the nature of academic work in profound ways. However, there has been increasing convergence between the Australian and United Kingdom systems since the end of the Second World War and in particular over the past two decades. To a lesser degree, this has also occurred with the Canadian system.

In all three countries the immediate post-Second World War period was marked by a rapid expansion of universities and teacher training colleges to meet the needs of returning ex-servicemen. The UK government intended there to be, as Simon (1991: 95) points out, 'a radical expansion in science and technology to meet the needs of the economy'. The 1950s and 1960s saw an expansion of university provision and student numbers in the UK, which grew from 85 000 in 1950 to 108 000 in 1960, with a further 61 000 students in teacher training and technical colleges. The Robbins Report of 1963 legitimated (Perkin 1972) the existing expansion and proposed more, so that by 1970 there were 443 000 students on degree or equivalent courses in universities, colleges of education or polytechnics, within a binary system, established in 1965, of 'autonomous' universities and 'public sector' polytechnics and colleges.

The pace of expansion slowed in the 1970s and higher education became subject to a pattern of cuts and delayed expansion which was to continue into the 1980s. The advent of the 1979 Thatcher government marked an increase in state intervention and the espousal of monetarist political economy, which entailed cut-backs in public expenditure, including higher education. By the mid-1980s the principles of a more managerialist approach to university governance, epitomized in the Jarrat Report (1985), had become apparent. The desirability of an increase in the participation rate and an expansion of student numbers to meet the needs of the economy more effectively was recognized in the White Paper *Higher Education: Meeting the Challenge* (DES 1987). The 1988 Education Reform Act removed polytechnics from local authority control and organized their funding under the Polytechnics and Colleges Funding Council (PCFC). The University Funding Council (UFC) replaced the Universities Grants Committee. The PCFC and UFC had similar constitutions and a greater representation of business interest than the former bodies. The Act also made provision for the revision of university charters to abolish tenure for academics. Funding arrangements changed, so that universities and polytechnics were encouraged to compete and increase overall student numbers while reducing per capita costs. Selectivity in research funding and its separation from student-related resources has been proceeding since 1986. The 1992 Higher Education Act abolished the binary divide and established one Higher Education Funding Council.

There are important similarities in the establishment of unified systems in Australia and the United Kingdom and in the likely effects on the nature and organization of academic work. In both cases the state's rationale is in part administrative convenience and in part the expectation of increased efficiency and cost-saving. In the Australian case there was strong pressure to establish large institutions through amalgamations, often over large distances, on the unargued principle that 'bigger is better'. In the United Kingdom this has not occurred, although some amalgamations are taking place under institutional initiatives where managements see advantages in competing for funds and students.

The development and reinforcement of new and old status hierarchies between institutions within a formally unified system seems likely. Although the conditions of funding and recruitment of students are now more equal, those universities with established research records and international reputations will in general be able to hold their own at the top of a status hierarchy. The crucial term in both countries is competition. The centralized control of funds for research at ministry, funding council or research council level and the increased emphasis on competition for these funds are likely to lead to a concentration of research funding in relatively few institutions, probably fewer than ten in Australia and around fifteen in the

United Kingdom. The continued importance of research at both institutional and academic career level means that there is pressure on academic staff in the former colleges and polytechnics to obtain PhDs and engage in research, despite the fact that many were recruited essentially as teachers. This is a change in the academic labour process which provides opportunities for some and increases stress for many.

These pressures are also present in Canada, which has a unified yet highly diversified university system, with significant status differences between an elite of research universities and other institutions. It is worth outlining some of the similarities and differences between the Canadian and United Kingdom and Australian systems to understand and compare the changes within academic work in the three countries.

The United Kingdom has a more devolved education system than Australia, and a more centralized one than Canada. Although Canada and Australia are both federal states their education systems are very different. Australia is a 'hard' federal state where the Commonwealth government in Canberra, through the exercise of financial, administrative and political power, has been able to take increasing control over universities and those who work in them. In the UK the traditional autonomy and diversity of universities (in particular Oxford and Cambridge), together with the differences of culture, history and educational arrangements in Scotland, Northern Ireland, Wales and England, has mitigated central control. For example, in 1992 a curious administrative semi-federal arrangement of separate funding councils for England, Wales and Scotland was established. However, that is some way short of the powers that some provincial governments of Canada can exercise *vis-à-vis* the federal government in Ottawa.

Canada is a federal state of ten provinces and two territories, whose constitution recognizes higher education as a matter of provincial jurisdiction and control. While Canada's federal nature and size are similar to Australia's, the balance of provincial/state influence as against federal/commonwealth is different. In part this is because of the historical and contemporary importance of French-speaking Catholic Quebec, where the education system, including higher education, has been important in protecting the language, culture, identity and material interests of the French-speaking majority in that province.

There has been a broadly similar pattern of developments to those in Australia and the United Kingdom. These included: the expansion of provision for Second World War veterans; increasing central government finance and control; and substantial increases in the numbers of students and universities. Students increased from 68 595 in 1959 to 294 000 by the end of the 1960s. However, the Federal Provincial Arrangement Act of 1967 provided that federal funds for post-secondary education should be channelled through the provinces rather than directly allotted to the institutions. Acts of Parliament in 1976 and 1984 ensured that this federal money for post-secondary education became part of 'block' funding, which included hospital insurance and medical care. While Ottawa makes specific calculations for post-secondary education, each province can distribute the overall money as it wishes. Health care has often squeezed the university budget and federal funds appear as provincial grants. In 1986 the federal government limited the growth of these transfer payments to 2 per cent below the rate of growth of the GNP. There is also direct federal support to universities through national research councils and research and consultancy for government departments. In 1988–9, 12.5 per cent of total income for universities came from direct federal funding, and 70.7 per cent from the provinces. The provincial control of university budgets, the wide variation in resources and changes in political control all mean different provincial patterns of cuts and expansion.

The organization of research funding has increasingly entailed competitive bidding for large projects. Research which involves cooperation between institutions, partnership with the private sector and a focus on topics considered to be of 'central importance to the country's development and well being', and with a 'discernible prospect for innovation and commercial exploitation' (Gregor 1991: 1020), has been favoured. Half of all federal research funds go to five large universities which account for about half the graduates and one-third of full-time staff in the country.

Dr Pedersen (1991), Vice-Chancellor of the University of Western Ontario, has pointed out that:

> Recent trends in Ministries of Higher Education across Canada are toward directing the universities' size, shape and orientation through the mechanism of 'targeted funding'. While enrolment accessibility incentives are a general instance of this, specific manipulation is often used directly at the program level. In several provinces, Alberta, British Columbia and Ontario in particular, financial steering of academic programmes is complemented by direct government involvement in programme review. Newly-proposed courses of study are evaluated not only on the bases of academic legitimacy, instructional and research support available within the institution, and compatibility with the academic aspirations of the particular university, but they are also scrutinised in terms of their likely immediate social impacts and potential for generating funding from business and industry. New programmes are required not only to address specific 'societal needs', but to offer at least the promise of entrepreneurial opportunities before they will be authorised for government funding support.
>
> (Pedersen 1991: 4)

Some of the characteristics of the Canadian system are similar to those of Australia and the United Kingdom. The pressure to develop research which is related to the needs of the economy, the increase in student numbers and the squeeze in government resources, with the consequent pressure on universities to attempt to raise funds from elsewhere, are similar. Two features appear to be different: the degree of provincial control and differentiation (which is especially significant in the case of Quebec); the absence of a large polytechnic or college of advanced education sector as in Britain up to 1992 and Australia up to 1989.

In all three countries the increasing intervention of the state in the organization of universities' research and teaching is partly justified by the view that knowledge creation and dissemination is central to the development of competitive industries. Three quotations from different sources stand for a much larger body of public statements which have come to dominate the discourse about the purpose and practice of universities.

In Australia, the 1988 White Paper (as Smyth 1991 points out) contains the rhetoric of equity, access, egalitarianism and meritocracy, but also a different and dominant economic rationale:

> The society we want cannot be achieved without a strong economic base. In Australia, this now requires a greatly increased export income, a far more favourable balance of trade and a considerable reduction in our external debt. Our industry is increasingly faced with rapidly changing international markets in which success depends on, among other things, the conceptual, creative and technical skills of the labour force and the ability to innovate and be entrepreneurial.
>
> (Dawkins 1988: 6)

In Canada there is a somewhat similar pronouncement from the Science Council of Canada (1987), addressed directly to the role of universities. It states:

> Teaching and basic research are major roles of the university and must remain so. But as knowledge replaces raw materials as the primer of the world economy, the universities' part in creating wealth – too often understated – becomes crucially important. The intellectual resources of the university are needed to help revitalise mature industries and generate the product ideas needed to create new ones. Canada's future prosperity increasingly depends on designing effective ways to integrate the university and the market place.

In the United Kingdom the 1987 White Paper entitled *Higher Education: Meeting the Challenge* states in its introduction on 'aims and purposes' that higher education should:

- serve the economy more efficiently;
- pursue basic scientific research and scholarship in the arts and humanities;
- have closer links with industry and commerce, and promote enterprise.

It goes on to elaborate:

> In higher education itself there is need to pursue reforms, both in the management and funding of the system and in the monitoring of the quality of its work, so that we can build on areas of excellence in the arts and sciences. But *above all* [my emphasis] there is an urgent need, in the interests of the nation as a whole, and therefore of

universities, polytechnics and colleges themselves, for higher education
to take increasing account of the economic requirements of the country.
(DES 1987: 1, 2)

The 1991 White Paper, *Higher Education: a New Framework*, notes that: 'There
has been an encouraging willingness on the part of higher education to
take account of the needs of industry and commerce by positive responses'
(DES 1991: 9). These include: the demand for part-time courses, the Enterprise in Higher Education initiative; the development of more enterprising
graduates; expansion of business studies; increases in private income from
research contracts; links with European higher education institutions; and
the widespread introduction of modern languages. It is interesting to see
how broadly the 'needs of industry and commerce' are defined, not only as
enterprise and research contracts but also as links with European universities and the featuring of modern languages.

How do these state policies on funding, research and governance affect
the institutions? I shall look at the response of some senior academics,
sometimes defined as managers, across the three countries. This material is
drawn from more than a hundred interviews conducted between February
and October 1991 in twenty universities and polytechnics in Australia, Canada
and the United Kingdom, as well as from public statements by senior academics. I shall seek to show how state and, more particularly, government
pressures, often articulating the assumed needs of the economy, affect the
way in which senior academics see their own role and managerial strategy.
This has implications for the nature of academic labour in general.

Pressures and management

In the United Kingdom, Professor Martin Harrison, Vice-Chancellor of Essex
University and Chairman of the CVCP, in an article entitled 'Crisis deepens
on Britain's campuses' (*Observer*, 10 November 1991), wrote: 'The central
problem springs from an attempt to achieve simultaneously three policy
objectives: to increase access to higher education, to constrain public expenditure severely and to maintain quality.' A dean at the University of Ulster
assessed the pressures from central government like this: 'The pressures will
continue to be of a conflicting kind, namely a desire for expansion of
student numbers and more industry-oriented research coupled with a continued unwillingness to pay for either.'

On the other hand, a central administrator in a polytechnic, admittedly
where student numbers had grown less than in most other polytechnics,
only 5 or 6 per cent a year, but with a dramatic increase of nearly 25 per
cent in the academic year starting in September 1991 through the takeover
of an adjoining college, said: 'We find we can manage on current funding
although it's a declining unit of resource by supplementing with short
courses, research and consultancy and overseas students.'

The range of developments of particular significance to a higher education institution are many and various. One Australian administrator listed the following current pressures: (a) unified national system; (b) adverse economic conditions; (c) lower priority to higher education; (d) demographic changes; (e) instrumentalist approach and pressures; (f) national industrial system; (g) state interference; (h) amalgamations; (i) industrial training.

A dean at a Western Australia university said that there had been a

continuing downward spiral of funding since 1975. We've had fifteen or more years of continuous belt tightening, we've well and truly pared away any fat that was there, we keep searching for new and more efficient ways of doing things and this has led into a range of administrative and teaching practices which are far from desirable. The major one is the gradual move away from a collegial model of decision making towards a more management dominated mode.

He thought that there might have been some time saved on committees but was unhappy about the effect on the quality of education and said that in the university:

There would be a strong perception that more and more of the important decisions have been taken out of the hands of the academics and placed in the hands of the central administration. So there has been an increasing development of a 'them and us' mentality. This has been exacerbated by a shift at national level to an employer employee relationship, from an academic salaries tribunal to an arbitration commission.

Here we can see the relationships and interactions between redirection of resources and the changes at both local and national level to a more managerial system of governance. A dean in a new university in New South Wales clearly saw the development of the unified national system and the three-way merger thus precipitated as the major recent development in his institution: 'Flowing from the new system was pressure for more staff to be more active in research and the need to generate our own funds. . .to engage in entrepreneurial activities and develop fee-paying courses.'

In another university in Western Australia, a member of central administration saw recent major developments in the following terms. First, the provision of facilities had fallen behind the growth of student numbers, graphically illustrated by his own position in a prefab! Second, the growth in his institution of distance learning. Third, the increased emphasis on working more closely with industry. As early as 1978 he had been granted study leave to explore the development of the university's links with industry; his own institution, he claimed, was the first to establish a technical park, in 1981. Since then it had established an innovation centre with a company to evaluate ideas and provide marketing skills, and had run courses in entrepreneurship for engineers and scientists.

In Canada, while most senior administrators saw pressure for increased student numbers and a provision of reduced units of resource, there was some significant variation between provinces and even between institutions in the same province. Some institutions, like Simon Fraser University in British Columbia, are now in a period of expansion, in marked contrast to the cuts experienced in the earlier 1980s (recorded by Harvey 1988), so that the full-time equivalent undergraduate and student body increased from 9858 in the academic year 1986–7 to 13 011 in 1990–1 and the budgeted staff complement from 482 to 571. The student/staff ratio has increased from 20.47 to 22.79. Thus a senior dean could say: 'Problems are to do with accommodating growth, not downsizing.'

In other Canadian universities and provinces the picture is different. For example, at the University of Alberta at Edmonton, in what to English eyes seems a very large and rich institution, there was considerable concern expressed about current budgetary cuts in the unit of resource and plans to cut some specific programmes. As early as 1986 in a university document, *The Next Decade and Beyond* (Holdaway and Meekison 1990), there were plans to stabilize the size of the student body at the then total of 25 000, but to increase the proportion of graduate students to 20 per cent. An academic administrator gave a pessimistic view of the situation, not one shared by all his senior colleagues, but significant nevertheless as a perception of the difficulties of a premier university in what has been one of the richer provinces: 'Erosion of quality. . .increased work loads for staff members. . . deterioration of equipment that can't even be repaired. . .deterioration in the library and a lack of addition of new things, basically physical plant and intellectual resources are in decline.' At Queens University in Ontario a professor saw the situation in the following way: 'Enrolments are going up – and resources down and down.'

Most of these perceptions share the view that there are formidable external pressures on universities and polytechnics in the shape of increased student numbers, reduced resources and an increasing commitment to research, all of which require more institutional management and planning. The Chair of the Committee of Vice-Chancellors and Principals (CVCP) in the United Kingdom comments: 'Most of those involved in the management of UK universities would not have made frequent use of the terms "cost-effectiveness", or "efficiency" before the start of the 1980s. Indeed, even the world "management" itself was generally avoided in the university context until fairly recently. . .during the 1960s and 1970s. . .the rhetoric was primarily that of "quality" and "academic freedom" rather than that of "management" and "efficiency" ' (Harrison 1991: 2).

In an extended quotation from an interview with an Australian central administrator we can see his view of the connections between the recent changes in ethos and institutional structure wrought by the establishment of a unified national system, in the production of a preferred managerial style which is in part at odds with the perception of an older type of administrative or collegial governance:

Traditional universities are not a good model for us. There are unsuccessful practices bordering on incompetence. I sense Dawkins is right,
he would want a stronger administrative leadership in Australian universities. You could have a better learning and academic environment
in which staff, academic autonomy at a discipline level is better preserved, because with some luck in selection of the Vice-Chancellor, the
Chief Executive Officer, you would have somebody that appreciates
that that is the environment in which most of the best academic enterprise occurs. That would be the best way to go rather than the hands
off, or hand in velvet glove, approach that perhaps traditional communities of scholars would think is appropriate. That's the ivory tower,
nineteenth century way of doing business. There are a number of
universities and Chief Executive Officers who are probably adopting a
more modern managerial role, they are entrepreneurial, they make
things happen, they break down barriers that staff would want to put
up and continue in some form of splendid isolation.

He hoped to have more Vice-Chancellors in this chief executive mode who
'Would force the universities to play in a different game, with different rules
and different teams. . .the scenario will change.'

Senior academic personnel saw themselves in a variety of administrative,
scholarly and research roles, but most emphasized their managerial function. A senior central administrator in one of the older Australian universities commented that there was 'Some pressure to become more managerial
to cope with external pressures and rising internal tensions. However, internal tensions and reactions are also leading to a reaction against the managerial model as a protest.' A person in a similar position in an English
polytechnic identified himself as '*a manager*'. His previous experience had
been in the Civil Service and he saw his job as managing a complex institution and delivering a service to customers. He argued that the essential
task would be the same whether or not the institution he was managing was
an academic one or not, and he did not identify himself as an academic
leader or scholar, which most of the other senior administrators I interviewed wished to do.

There is a range of difference in the degree of identification and commitment to a managerial mode. Nevertheless, increased student numbers,
funding which is not keeping pace with the expansion, and a consequently
lowered unit of resource per student, increased competition for research
and other funds and the pressures from the local and federal state make
planning the development of strategy and managerial procedures an increasingly dominant part of the culture of higher education institutions.

Laurens, himself a senior central administrator in Australia, points to
some of the tensions in the managerial role:

One outcome of academic administrative tension leading to anxiety,
other than implementation of the White Paper outcomes, is the increasing disparity between academic and administrative salaries. . .academics

are becoming increasingly critical of the number and remuneration of
equally hard pressed administrators.

(Laurens 1990: 229)

Despite the variations between the managerial cultures in different institutions of higher education in Australia, Canada and the United Kingdom,
there are common elements which relate to the structures of economy,
polity and language which affect all three countries.

In varying degrees in all three countries there has been a continuing
economic crisis and restructuring since the mid-1970s. In the main, this has
weakened manufacturing industry and not changed the traditional reluctance of business to invest in research or development, either on its own
account or through universities, in comparison with major industrial competitors in Germany, Japan or the United States. This economic crisis and
weakness has led governments to stress the importance of the development
of industry-related research in universities to meet the needs of the economy.
In at least this minimal sense there has been a strategy to manage the
universities to meet the needs of the state and the economy.

Changing academic labour

I have outlined the main pressures on universities. These are perceived by
senior academics to be primarily from the state insofar as they affect the
management of their own institutions. But what can we say about the changing conditions of academic work? Some have already been alluded to:
reduced resources, rising student numbers and higher expectations of research productivity. I shall give a brief sketch of the main material and
cultural factors affecting the day-to-day life of the ordinary academic, drawing predominantly on the UK experience, and consider how far this is a
degrading and deskilling process consistent with the proletarianization thesis.

In 1970–1 the university staff/student ratio in Great Britain was 1 to 8.5;
by 1980–1 it had risen to 1 to 9.5, in 1988–9 it was nearly 1 to 11.5 and in
1990–1 it was 1 to 12.3 (AUT 1990). The polytechnic and college average
was 1 to 15 in this same year, having increased from 1 to 13.5 in 1986. The
rise in university staff/student ratio has been exponential, at nearly 11 per
cent in the first half of the 1980s and 19 per cent in the second.

The higher rate in the polytechnics and colleges was partly owing to the
different subject mix in the two sectors. The 30 medical schools with low
staff/student ratios are all within the old university sector. In the early
1980s the UGC, when faced with government cutbacks, attempted to protect the unit of resource by limiting student intake and cutting staff, whereas
polytechnics expanded their student numbers. Expansion in student numbers in the early 1990s has been proceeding apace in both traditional universities and the ex-polytechnics. In the 1991–2 academic year, for example,
there were 30 000 more students in the old universities compared to the

previous year, equivalent to the creation of three new fair-sized universities of the 1980s.

In terms of teaching productivity, there have been substantial increases in throughput concomitant with increased class size. If we turn to the other main aspect of academic work, research, one measure of productivity is the number of publications per member of staff. Halsey's (1990) surveys show that the mean number of papers, articles or books staff reported published in the previous two years increased from 3.5 in 1976 to 6.6 in 1989 in universities and from 0.9 to 2.0 in polytechnics. The percentage of staff who had not published at all declined from 23 per cent in universities and 68 per cent in polytechnics in 1976 to 9 and 46 per cent respectively in 1989. Some commentators assume that institutional funding changes promoting research selectivity are producing a division between staff engaged in research and those who will solely teach. That may happen in the future, but the evidence so far suggests that increased competition has produced effective pressure on more academic staff in both sectors to publish. More research is being done with the same or scarcely increased resources, but it is difficult to assess if quality is being maintained.

Halsey's respondents reported that, in 1989, 13 per cent of those in universities felt they were under a lot of pressure to do research and 23 per cent a little pressure; the comparable figures in polytechnics were 7 and 27 per cent respectively. The main obstacle to research was identified as time spent in teaching and other commitments. Most staff in UK higher education institutions are torn by three-way pressures: teaching, administration and research. It is hardly surprising that Carroll and Cross (1989) reported that 77.2 per cent of their sample had become more stressed in recent years, with only 3.7 per cent less so; 62 per cent expected their posts to become even more stressful in the future and only 3 per cent expected to experience a reduction in job-related stress. In terms of job satisfaction, 48 per cent reported it less (33 per cent) or much less (15 per cent) in recent years, only 24 per cent indicating that they found it more satisfying.

Two important sources of job dissatisfaction mentioned frequently as important or moderately important were conflicting and increased job demands (both 65 per cent). They were exceeded only by inadequate salary (74 per cent) and inadequate resources (73 per cent). Other sources of dissatisfaction were: absence of promotion prospects (60 per cent); lack of public recognition of worth (55 per cent); job insecurity (47 per cent); lack of autonomy and control (44 per cent) and isolation from colleagues (28 per cent).

One of the features of the demands of administration is its density and complexity in many institutions. There is often an overlay of different structures and pressures. These coexist and compete. First, there is a departmental and faculty administrative system focused on heads of departments and deans, but with its own plethora of committees. Second, there is a more or less powerful collegial system of academic assemblies, senates and councils, with associated committees, minutes and papers. Third, there is a developing central management system with increasingly powerful vice-chancellors and administrators, with in some institutions appointed deans and *ad hoc* working parties, whose role only partly articulates with older administrative and collegial structures. There is evidence to suggest from both senior and junior staff that increasingly crucial strategic decisions, particularly financial ones, but flowing from these decisions around staffing, student recruitment and research profile, are being concentrated in a central management team. The Jarrat Report (1985) and government papers (Dawkins 1987, 1988) in Australia explicitly advocate this.

However, that does not mean that junior staff are left to get on with teaching and research freed from administrative responsibilities, much as many of them might like this. There are three pressures that exacerbate the situation. First, the increasing pressure from the state in terms of account-ability, planning and competition between institutions means that there are increasing demands on all staff to be involved at least at the level of providing data and consent in the processes of planning courses, ensuring quality, devising research strategies, raising money, etc. Second, the central management of the institution may be keen to devolve certain responsibil-ities, often financial, to the departmental level, thus relieving itself of having to face difficult political choices. Yeatman (1990: 172), commenting on this process in Australia, put it well, relating it to the discursive practice of policy makers at the state and institutional level:

> With regard to highly empowered discursive producers as in the case of the professional educators within...the higher, education system, the state...has embarked on subtle strategies of containment of the claims generated by these masters of discursive production. The gen-eral thrust has been in the direction of corporate management whereby, in the current general environment of declining public resources and services, and as legitimised by the discourse of decentralisation (letting the managers manage, etc.), the management of reduced budgets is given over to the units closest to the coal-face. The Commonwealth Government [devolves authority] to individual institutions of higher education; and, within the latter the central administration devolves the management of reduced budget to faculties. This means that claims and claimants are brokered much lower down the line, and it becomes all the more difficult for their advocates to elaborate them into gener-alised and generally visible discursive maps and claims.

Attempts to maintain general claims, not only about resources, curricula or research, and about the right through collegial processes to be involved in crucial decisions about, for example, staff reductions, do continue. Some-times this is through the defence of established collegial structures and processes, sometimes through increased union activity, and often through combinations of both. There are costs: when trusted union representatives are elected to senates or councils it means that, for a minority of active staff, there is the increased pressure of more meetings, minutes, newsletters, petition, lobbies and delegations (Miller and Wheeler 1989).

These processes relate an important aspect of the Braverman labour process theory: the concentration of intellectual planning functions in the hands of managers and their removal from the control of the practitioners. There have been largely successful attempts by the state with the (sometimes willing, sometimes unwilling) compliance of senior academics in universities to institute corporate executive styles of planning and management. Yet academics have by no means totally lost control of the organization of their work of teaching and research. It may be increasingly constrained, monitored and documented, but there are peculiar features of the academic labour process which make the forms of control, alienation and exploitation ones which often involve the individual academic in the construction of his or her own fate. There is often a curious collusion between management and academics on the terms of the effort bargain, whereby degrees of at least apparent control are retained by the individual on the implicit understanding that the targets of increased student numbers, more articles or more form-filling are met.

Wilson (1991: 259) draws on his experience as a union researcher to characterize the situation of some university academics:

> For them the absence of fixed laws of attendance requirements can be seen as an unspoken bargain. The price of autonomy is, say, the pressure to produce a book every two years. Even though ten years ago books were perhaps required only every four years the bargain may still be worthwhile for both management and academics. Control is gained not by engineering responsible autonomy but by conceding it.

In all three countries and in all three areas of work – teaching, research and administration – there seems to be an intensification of effort. But does this amount to a process of degradation and deskilling, as in Braverman's labour process thesis? In teaching, if the analogy with industrial production is to be pursued, the movement is perhaps best understood as craft workers moving from small batch to large batch production as lectures, seminars, laboratory classes and tutorials have all increased in size. There are certainly processes of the commodification and compartmentalization of knowledge in process, often through the development of module or credit systems. There is the increased use of technology. The overhead projector, tape–slide sequence, Xerox copier, TV programmes or computer-assisted learning of various sorts can be used to supplement or supplant direct staff–student interaction, but overall it would be an exaggeration to assert that higher education has yet moved to assembly line, mass production methods. Thus, while there may have been some degradation and deskilling in the teaching situation, particularly the opportunities to engage in small group teaching, some staff at least, not necessarily with enthusiasm or without pain and stress, have acquired the skills of the performer before large audiences.

The composition, funding and terms of contract of academic staff have been changing over the past decade. A greater proportion of staff are on untenured, short-term, part-time or temporary contracts. Among academic non-clinical staff in UK universities, between 1977–8 and 1987–8 the numbers of part-time staff more than doubled from 1501 to 3162, as did staff not wholly funded by the UGC, from 7015 to 14 315, whereas wholly funded staff actually dropped from 30 459 to 29 169 (AUT 1990). This is caused in part by the pressure to gain research or consultancy income, where the typical contract is for three years or less. However, many university managements are also turning to short-term contracts for full-time academic staff primarily engaged in teaching, as a means of increasing their flexibility and ability to respond to rapidly changing funding and market situations. The effect of the 1988 Education Reform Act was to remove the protection of tenure for staff appointed or promoted after 20 November 1988.

One of the most clear changes in the conditions of academic work has been the relative decline in pay. In the United Kingdom in the period from 1981–2 to 1989–90 university academics increased their salaries by 74 per cent, in a period when inflation was 72 per cent and police pay increased by 119 per cent, that of nurses by 112 per cent and that of teachers by 92 per cent. In a comparison with movements of average earnings between 1979–80 and 1987–8, UK academics gained only 76 per cent of the average UK increase, their Australian colleagues 77 per cent and those in Canada 99 per cent in their respective countries (AUT 1990). Taking 1980–1 as 100, the relative value of UK academic salaries as a proportion of US comparable salaries had declined to 86 per cent by 1989–90. Whereas the average for all categories (lecturers, senior lecturers and professors) in the UK was just over £20 000, in the USA for professors, associate professors and assistant professors in public and private funded institutions awarding doctoral degrees it was equivalent to approximately £28 000, using the average exchange rate between the currencies of £1 = \$1.61 in 1989 (*Academe* volume 76, no. 2, 1989).

The salary situation in the UK was not significantly improved by the 1989 or 1990 settlements and in these the government insisted on the imposition of discretionary pay awards to be used by university management to 'recruit or retain exceptionally scarce or valuable staff and reward exceptional performance'. By 1991–2 such performance-related pay amounted to 3 per cent of the pay bill. In 1992 the CVCP and AUT, having thought they had reached a 6 per cent settlement, a little over the rate of inflation, found the government vetoing the deal and insisting on a lower settlement with a greater discretionary element.

In the polytechnic sector in 1989–90 the National Association of Teachers in Further and Higher Education (NATFHE), the academic staff union, managed to retain national bargaining against pressure for local bargaining. However, it had to concede increased managerial control over hours, holidays, income from consultancy and presence at work. Wilson (1991: 256) argues that 'such controls were perceived as a fundamental attack on the high trust and discretion of academic work for staff in this sector'. In the future it is likely that negotiations will take place for all academic staff in the post-binary unified university sector in one forum and it will be within this that varying traditions of managerialism and collegiality in relation to pressure from the state will be played out. Currie (1991) has given an account of the award restructuring negotiating process in Australia, which took place from May 1990 to July 1991. Many of the same themes emerge as in the United Kingdom. Arguments about managerial authority and autonomy, appraisal, staff development and the criteria for pay awards as well as equity issues were important. However, already well-advanced processes of amalgamations of universities and colleges of advanced education, the more overt role of the Department of Employment, Education and Training (DEET) and the Australian Council of Trade Unions (ACTU) and the background of the accords between business, union and government on award restructuring and deskilling probably provided a context more favourable to the unions' positions than in the United Kingdom. In Canada there is much more devolution of salary negotiation to the provincial and institutional levels and variations in pay to professors in different disciplines depend on the relative strength of their market position. In short, there is a much more individualized and market-driven system, similar in some respects to that in the United States, with which many of the relevant comparisons are made.

Conclusions

Filson (1988) and Derber (1983) argue that a useful but limited analogy for understanding the processes of proletarianization is the way in which management in the market gained control of the work of craft workers in the nineteenth-century textile industry. There, the workers first remain as outworkers and retain some control over the work process, although the entrepreneur controls and owns the raw material, the product and at some stage the machinery. The industrialist controls the nature and quantity of the product. Only later are workers gathered together in factories where managerial control is gradually extended. Derber (1983) uses the term 'ideological' proletarianization to describe the first phase of extension of control, and 'technical' for the later stages. Clearly academics working in state universities are not like textile outworkers working on their own; nevertheless, there may be some force in the analogy. Through their command of discrete expertise, academics can still largely influence the processes of both their research and teaching, but the raw material (students or problems to be investigated) is increasingly determined by the combined influences of the state, institutional managers and the market. The outcomes of research and teaching are being similarly influenced. Academics, because of the nature of the relation of their expertise to the work process, can exercise more control than nineteenth-century textile workers, but, while they may retain quite high degrees of technical control, they can be seen to be losing 'ideological' control of their work.

A hard and extended version of the labour process theory and the associated thesis of proletarianization would demand that the extension of control over the process and outcome of work would need to be demonstrated, and that this was in the interests of capital. In the cases under consideration, we can show degrees of deskilling, degradation through loss of status and some loss of control. It is more difficult to show direct subordination to the needs of capital. The processes are more complex and, indeed, contested. In our review of some official policies and documents, and of the responses of university management and ordinary academics, we can see three ways in which academics are being pushed towards the needs of the market economy. There is a further analytical and empirical analysis needed to show that this is the same as the needs of capital or the needs of particular corporations.

The first of the three interrelated factors is the perception and policy and pressure from governments in their respective countries that universities, in terms of their research and the production of trained personnel, should meet the needs and increase the competitiveness of the economies of Australia, Canada and the United Kingdom. Second, partly because of monetarist ideologies, there has been over at least the past decade an effective reduction of state funds relative to the tasks of teaching and research required. This has meant, both at government behest and because university managements are anxious to maintain financial viability and institutional autonomy, that there have been renewed attempts to get corporate finance for research and endowments, and the marketing of courses to meet the managerial, professional and technical needs of the corporate sector. Because of the histories of the relation of industry to research and education and the relative weakness of industrial capital, it has by and large been universities approaching corporate capital rather than the other way round. The older, more prestigious, universities are better placed to raise corporate funds and thus the disparity of resource base available to different institutions within the three systems is likely to increase (Tapper and Salter 1992: 110).

The third feature is the promulgation, chiefly by the state but to an extent by some university senior academics, of a corporate management structure and style for universities. It is this feature which is nearest to the everyday work of ordinary academics. It is resented by many, who see the models being proposed as a parody of good contemporary corporate management practice, imposing hierarchies and procedures reminiscent of some aspects of 'scientific management' as described by Braverman. A union representative in an English polytechnic voiced a view I heard echoed in a range of institutions in Canada and Australia as well as other places in the United Kingdom:

It's the ethos of the market, the language being used is the management style, completely market led, almost a profit driven type of enterprise and we thought we were academics. The talk is of clients or consumers rather than students. But the management style is discredited, it uses techniques which are pretty naff in terms of modern business practice – the breaking up of academic community into a rigid hierarchical structure. We used to elect Deans!

Others, while recognizing the need for efficiency, swift decision-making and the need to respond to pressures from state and market, do not want to concede the democratic aspects of collegial decision-making. Indeed, they argue that in administering the complexities of academic work the collegial model is still appropriate, effective and better than many of the corporate management procedures being currently inflicted.

Note

Acknowledgements are due to: Edna Bland, Jennifer Green and Pat Newman in the Organizational Studies and Applied Psychology Division office of Aston Business School for wordprocessing a difficult manuscript; John Bowen of Keele University English Department for saving me from some of my worst excesses of style and syntax; Susan Robertson at Edith Cowan University in Perth, Western Australia for arranging a research fellowship; and the Canadian Studies Faculty Research program for a grant both of which materially facilitated my research and to all the hundred or so academics who gave me their time and attention to explore the issues discussed in this chapter.

References

Association of University Teachers (1990) *Goodwill under Stress.* London, AUT.

Braverman, H. (1974) *Labor and Monopoly Capital: the Degradation of Work in the Twentieth Century.* New York, Monthly Review Press.

Carroll, D. and Cross, G. (1989) *University Stress Survey,* research report, School of Psychology, University of Birmingham.

Currie, J. (1991) Award restructuring for academics: the negotiating process, paper to TASA Conference, Perth, Australia, December.

Dawkins, J. (1987) The challenge of higher education in Australia, Ministerial Statement, Canberra, 22 September.

Dawkins, J. (1988) *Higher Education: a Policy Statement* (White Paper). Canberra, July.

Department of Education and Science (1987) *Higher Education: Meeting the Challenge.* London, HMSO.

Department of Education and Science (1991) *Higher Education: a New Framework.* London, HMSO.

Derber, C. (1983) Managing professionals: ideological proletarianization and post-industrial labor, *Theory and Society,* 12(3), 309–41.

Filson, G. (1988) Ontario teachers' deprofessionalization and proletarianization, *Comparative Education Review,* 32(3), 298–317.

Gregor, A.D. (1991) The universities of Canada, in *Commonwealth Universities Year Book.* 1013–26, London, London Association of Commonwealth Universities.

Halsey, A.H. (1992) *The Decline of Donnish Dominion*. Oxford, Oxford University Press.

Harrison, M.B. (1991) Cost-effectiveness and efficiency in universities: a British perspective, paper to Conference of Executive Heads, the Association of Commonwealth Universities, New Delhi, India, 14–18, January.

Harvey, C. (1988) Retrenchment strategies in two Canadian universities: a political analysis. Research Paper 88.08. Montreal, McGill University.

Holdaway, A. and Meekison, J. (1990) Strategic planning at a Canadian university, *Long Range Planning*, 23(4), 104–13.

Jarrat, M. (1985) *Report of the Steering Committee for Efficiency Studies for the Committee of Vice-Chancellors and Principals*. London, HMSO.

Laurens, R. (1990) University management: tensions in a changing environment, *Journal of Tertiary Educational Administration*, 12(1), May.

Miller, H. (1991) The academic labour process, in C. Smith *et al. White Collar Work: the Non-manual Labour Process*. Basingstoke, Macmillan.

Miller, H. and Wheeler, S. (1989) Changing patterns of power in higher education: a case study, paper to Ethnography and Educational Reform Conference, Warwick University, September.

Pedersen, K. (1991) University autonomy (a Canadian perspective), paper to Conference of Executive Heads, the Association of Commonwealth Universities, New Delhi, India, January.

Perkin, H. (1972) University planning in Britain in the 1960s, *Higher Education*, 1(1), 111–19.

Pusey, M. (1991) *Economic Rationalism in Canberra: a Nation Building Society Changes its Mind*. Cambridge, Cambridge University Press.

Robertson, S. and Woock, R.R. (1989) Towards a social analysis of Australian education, paper to the 7th World Congress of Comparative Education, Montreal, June.

Science Council of Canada (1987) *Winning in a World of Economy: Canadian Universities and Economic Revival*. Ottawa, SCC.

Simon, B. (1991) *Education and the Social Order*. London, Lawrence and Wishart.

Smart, D. (1989) The Dawkins reconstruction of higher education in Australia, paper to American Educational Research Association, San Francisco, March.

Smith, C. and Willmott, H. (1991) The new middle class and the labour process, in C. Smith *et al.* (eds) *White Collar Work: the Non-manual Labour Process*. Basingstoke, Macmillan.

Smyth, J. (1991) Theories of the state and recent policy reforms in Australian higher education, *Discourse*, 11(2), 49–69.

Tancred-Sheriff, P. (1985) Craft hierarchy and bureaucracy modes of control of the academic labour process, *Canadian Journal of Sociology*, 10(4), 369–90.

Tapper, T. and Salter, B. (1992) *Oxford, Cambridge and the Changing Idea of the University*. Buckingham, Open University Press and SRHE.

Wilson, T. (1991) The proletarianisation of academic labour, *Industrial Relations Journal*, 22(4), 250–62.

Yeatman, A. (1990) *Bureaucrats, Technocrats, Femocrats: Essays on the Contemporary Australian State*. Sydney, Allen and Unwin.

3

Canadian Universities and the Impact of Austerity on the Academic Workplace

Howard Buchbinder and P. Rajagopal

Introduction

The thrust of social and economic policy over the past half century has been dominated by welfare liberalism, informed by the theories of John Maynard Keynes. The emergence of the welfare state provided the vehicle for the implementation of social and economic policy. Governments began to manage the economy through fiscal and economic policies geared towards the manipulation of aggregate demand. The moral basis for this policy agenda was couched in terms of social justice. The results of the policy (aided and abetted by the Second World War) ameliorated the ravages of the depression and put North American capitalism back together as they encouraged a long period of economic growth which extended through the 1960s (with occasional 'slumps'). The Canadian university system is by and large a product of that growth. The subsequent emergence of economic crisis in the mid-1970s, accompanied by contraction and restraint, contrasted sharply with the period of growth and expansion during the 1960s. The emergence of harder times was accompanied by a shift in the ideology which informed social and economic policy. The 1980s continued the directions which began to develop during the 1970s.

The result is that the financial context of the Canadian university has, for the past decade and more, been bleak. Universities have been chronically underfunded in a period where enrolments have steadily climbed. From 1980 to 1990 there was an enrolment increase of more than 30 per cent across Canada while operating grants during the same period rose by only 3 per cent in real dollars. In 1990 the federal government froze the level of transfer payments to the provinces for higher education and health until 1995 (Feschuck 1992).[1] In November 1991 the Council of Ontario Universities indicated that they would be forced to cut faculty members and staff and limit student enrolment unless they got an increase of 7 per cent from the provincial government (Lewington 1991). In fact, the provincial government announced an increase of 1 per cent. One can cite examples from across Canada. All add up to the same grim picture: a picture of rising enrolments, reduced funding, growing deficits and drastic exercises in budget cutting. Funding policy has proceeded from a wide open arrangement in which more students meant more money, to one in which more students meant lowered value per basic income unit value, and finally to one in which a corridor has been imposed which regulates university admissions by imposing penalties if corridor limits are exceeded. This centrally imposed policy correlates with the development of a centralized managerial process within the universities. This is the status of the system. How are the universities coping with or responding to the situation?

Within the universities the professoriate and the university management join in a common denunciation of government funding policies, yet the professoriate does not appear to play a critical role as management redistributes internal resources in an ever tightening belt of austerity. This managerial response to austerity has a severe impact on the integrity of academic work as conditions deteriorate within the academy: large class sizes, reductions in the range of courses, examinations instead of essays, inadequate library and reading room facilities and insufficient student advising.

Management processes and governance

The governance of the university and the process by which it is managed are reflective of the various funding policies and the options open to universities in an atmosphere of significant underfunding. Thus, the process we are discussing in this chapter can be identified through the shifts and alterations in governance structures and patterns. We look to a particular university by way of example.

The York University Act of 1965 provides the legal basis for the establishment of the university (the Act of 1959 was repealed and replaced by the Act of 1965). It provides for a bicameral system, with the senate being responsible for the academic policy of the university (standards for admission of students, contents and curricula, requirements for graduation, conduct of examinations, conferring of degrees). The board of governors is responsible for government, conduct, management and control of the university and its property, revenues, expenditures, business and affairs, including the power to appoint, promote and remove all members of the teaching and administrative staff, and for all matters except matters specifically assigned to the senate. The president was to supervise and direct the implementation of the educational policy as well as have power to recommend to the board on appointment, promotion and removal of teaching staff, officers and employees of the university.

Until the early 1970s York University enjoyed a developmental momentum nourished by a political economy of growth and expansion. Much of the initiative and power was in the hands of the deans, who were instrumental in building and developing the various faculties. The president presided proudly over this expanding university. All were blessed with a generally increasing bounty of money.[2] Thus the structural impetus for growth resided at faculty levels with support from central administrative bodies.

The first wind of change came in the autumn of 1972. Enrolment was up by 'only' 12 per cent rather than the anticipated 15 per cent. The expected funding increase was short by about 5 per cent. Unaccustomed to such a 'reversal', the administration went into a 'tizzy'. Proposals for laying off 135–145 faculty members were brought to discussion, only for it to be found that the case was not defensible; the proposal was withdrawn after eight weeks of frenzied activity. The administration had tried to be directive; a perceived (later unproven) shortfall had generated a precipitous move towards layoffs. The response was arbitrary and centralized. This sort of approach in a new climate of increasing underfunding left academic staff feeling increasingly vulnerable. The university administration had brought to the senate the proposal, and when the proposal was withdrawn the administration and the professoriate (through their representatives on senate) 'learnt' different lessons. The faculty association responded to the increasing pressure by unionizing; in 1976 the York University Faculty Association (YUFA) was certified as a trade union under the provincial labour relations act. The administration became the employer, negotiating with the employees in a new adversarial context, and eventually became the management of the university.

Unionization altered the climate and practice of university governance in some significant ways. The university governing structures had been bipartite, with the administration/board as one party and the academic senate as the other. Now, with the inclusion of the Faculty Association as a legal entity, there was a shift. Prior to unionization, the faculty association was not a legally constituted body and was not mentioned under the empowering legislative act. The Faculty Association had been recognized by the board as representing the faculty for purposes of discussing salaries, benefits and working conditions. The faculty members were also represented on the senate (in fact, teaching staff were to be a majority on the senate) and thus contributed to the making of academic policy. Unionization changed that balance. It also created a division between academic policy and terms and conditions of employment. A good example of this is evident in the structure and process of tenure and promotion. After unionization, amendments to the criteria and procedures governing tenure and promotion required agreement of the *two* parties to the agreement: university management (i.e. the employer) and the YUFA (i.e. the employees). The senate argued that tenure and promotion was a matter of academic policy, and therefore the senate should have standing. The YUFA argued that tenure and promotion fell under terms and conditions of employment, which is union business. The management tended generally to side with the senate, which helped to exacerbate the divisions between what were basically two different faculty bodies.[3] A second significant change was to an adversarial mode, from what was thought to have been a collegial mode. The rules, procedures and processes of collective bargaining operate within the context of two parties representing adversarial interests. And in this bipartite division the senate has been co-opted into seeing itself as part of the management.

In the next decade, with the universities becoming more and more underfunded, the York University management attempted to cut costs through a spectacular increase in the use of part-time teachers as course directors. This was also accompanied by a steady increase of the number of students. The management response to this situation was to encourage the development of a rational planning process for the university. On the surface this seemed like a reasonable idea. In a June 1985 memo to senior administrators, board members and officers of the senate, the newly appointed York president put it this way:

> I have been struck over the past few months by the extent to which basic policy decisions are either obsolete or entirely absent, or improvised on short notice by unlikely actors (e.g., myself), directed to external rather than internal constituencies, often vulnerable to revision by administrative action, or inaction, or decentralized, Faculty-level interpretation. The corollary of this observation is that it seems possible to get some things done by the assertion of administrative will and hands-on-control – but that is not how York is supposed to run.
>
> (Arthurs 1985)

The Report of the Task Force on Academic Planning at York came out on 18 November 1985. It stated that: 'In spite of the best efforts of our academic administrators to ensure that academic considerations have primacy in the annual budget exercise, the absence of a planning process has led to the perception that budgets have come to drive policy rather than the reverse.' It went on to make the case that a planning process would provide a more rational basis for policy formulation. In spite of this stated objective the academic senate has tended to be a reactive body, rubber-stamping management decisions, even while management was lamenting that it ought to be otherwise.

York University went on to start a planning process. The York Academic Plan (YAP) was intended to be a bottom-up process. Planning proposals originated in departments and units, and were then processed by the faculty council. The flow was upwards, from there to the academic policy and planning committee of the senate (APPC) and thence to the senate as a whole for approval. The senate would approve a plan in about May; it would then become the basis for decisions being made for the following year. In fact, when autumn came the flowing down of plan results was accompanied by a new flow up of the rolling five-year plan update. A veritable cornucopia of plans, plan updates, fact books, justifications, rationales and undergraduate programme reviews germinated. All this was accompanied by a steady increase in appropriate infrastructure to support this impressive array of planning activity. The number of senior tenured faculty members who were withdrawing from the classroom to service and staff this impressive machinery has not been tabulated or reported.[4]

With the development of corporate–university ties the patterns of governance are further altered. Research, emerging from external contracts, interface institutes, centres of excellence and innovation centres is usually negotiated with the university's central administration rather than the particular department which is by-passed. In addition, the development of such specialized bodies within a university transforms the existing arrangements outlined in the legislative act. For example, a provincially funded centre of excellence is established within a particular university but has its own board. It is not really part of the host university's structure although it is staffed by university academics. Thus a contradiction emerges. As the concentration of governance is centralized in managerial structures, academic process and collegial influence is diminished and even marginalized. Yet the centralization which occurs is itself by-passed in some instances. The university becomes more centralized from within but also becomes more exposed and vulnerable to external market forces via some of the structures which develop.

The presence of academic autonomy and collegial decision-making is therefore tied to both internal and external forces. The influence of the political economy (external) and the changes in the structure and dynamics of governance within the university (internal) seem to have caught universities in a predicament: they have responded by drifting, and in the process the university administration, seeing no opposition from the professoriate or its organizations (senate, union), has moved in to fill the vacuum. This appears to have allowed the administration's conclusion that things needed to be done through the assertion of administrative will and hands-on control. The professoriate appears to have colluded in these moves; it has not registered opposition nor has it been an alert contributor to the resolution of the problems.

Directions

There are various directions which appear to be emerging at York University as aspects of the overall process outlined in this chapter. The meaning of these developments is not always clear, and there are not always hard data. Nevertheless, several things are happening, some of which are listed below.

Base budgets and operating costs

At York, a certain amount of enthusiasm was generated in the early years of the presidency of 1985–92. A new building programme was initiated, and it was to provide much needed relief from the overcrowding which had become an ever-present reality. This building programme was made possible by the sale of 22 acres (9 hectares) of university land to a well-known developer.[5] But even as the new buildings were coming into use their operation costs were adding to the deficit. All this was happening while the government was producing a new funding plan based on corridors. It was put into operation during 1991–2. At the same time the economies (of the province as well as the country) were slowing down. By about May 1991 the funding situation for the coming year started to look bleak. The board of governors of the university approved a plan to cut back the base budget of the university by 10 per cent over three years (but did not do it[6]). Thus, the shift to budget-driven policy became a fact of life. The result was a growing climate of austerity. Academic planning was likewise affected. The York University Academic Plan Exercise was now entering its sixth year. The Sixth Academic Plan was a complete top-down revision of the previous one and was rewritten by the president himself. It was approved by the senate and the board in June 1992.

Developments in the dynamics of unionism

The president had been concerned with the steering effect of the Faculty Association salary settlements on the overall budgetary situation and initiated what can be called 'fast-track' negotiations by calling into action a long range planning committee (a joint committee of the YUFA and the administration, which had been inactive for many years). This joint committee was to look at all aspects of incomes and expenditures and presumably come up with a plan for a multi-year compensation package agreement. In actual practice, 'normal' negotiations are taking place; at the same time what effect the joint committee initiative will have remains to be seen.

One dean who has been a management representative in negotiations with the YUFA has declared the administration's intent to scrap major portions of staff retirement benefits in the continuing negotiations. Whatever the outcome of these potential initiatives there is little question that the traditional pattern of union–management negotiations is seen as a block to 'efficiency', and management negotiating strategies will be aimed at changing the face of faculty unionization.

Plans and planning

Another possible action has to do with the restructuring of the faculty of graduate studies. It is being done on the grounds that no legislative action is required, only administrative action. This scenario would do away with the faculty of graduate studies (which provided a federal structure to ensure that cognate staff are all drawn into the graduate programmes) and integrate graduate study programmes within the separate disciplinary departments. As well, there seems to be a move afoot to restructure three undergraduate arts faculties at York University. These are the faculty of arts, Atkinson College and Glendon College. The proposed new structure is generally being 'leaked' through a number of conversational comments by 'high placed sources'.[7]

Provincial government policies

The provincial government announced (on 21 January 1992) funding increases for the university system of 1 per cent for 1992–3 and 2 per cent for each of the following two years. Tuition fees are to be increased by 7 per cent in the first year.[8]

The provincial government has set up task forces to encourage restructuring of the university system and the community college system, and to look at accountability. In a recent policy statement (which included the announcement of these task forces) the Ontario Ministry of Colleges and Universities stated that two-thirds of the jobs that will be created in Ontario in the next ten years will need at least 17 years of education.[9] This has been widely interpreted to mean that among other things there will be a need for more engineers, more physicists and more computer scientists. But as universities receive a declining share of the GNP the shape of the economy points to fewer such high-tech jobs needed to service the emerging needs. In any case, what the shape of the employment needs is, in the light of the Free Trade Agreements between Canada and the USA and the inclusion of Mexico, has not been considered by the universities.

Pronouncements of politicians continue to be at the level of 'we have created the preconditions for prosperity' or 'jobs are leaving the country'. Neither the universities nor the post-secondary sector as a whole have yet joined the debate. Instead they have been in a more defensive position, preparing to react to the impending funding crisis of next year using the tactics shaped for responding to the funding crisis of the current year. At best, much of the activity in the university has been to replace retiring professors with 'stellar' appointments that do not renew former teaching obligations and may be made outside the usual collegial processes.

The institutions of higher education have been reacting in a defensive, *ad hoc* manner to the continuing crisis in university funding. Some of the institutional responses have been to consider the usual options: increasing tuition fees; reducing enrolments; redefining the mission of the university; seeking other sources of revenue. In the past 15 years all these have been considered, with varying degrees of commitment and consistency. Although funding policies encourage and even dictate enrolment reductions, universities continue to increase enrolments. At the same time there appears to be an internal redistribution of enrolments: from undergraduate to graduate, from social sciences and humanities to hard sciences and technology. There is also a reluctance on the part of both administration and the professoriate to examine what universities are doing. It has been pointed out that on a per capita basis Canada has 39 times as many lawyers and 14 times as many accountants as Japan, yet there have been no initiatives to examine the universities and the production of lawyers or accountants (Canadian Press Report 1991). The most recent such report is about the number of MBAs. It has been pointed out that MBA programmes producing no more than 750 graduates a year would fully serve the Canadian market; yet there are now more than 9000 full-time students in MBA programmes in the country. The class graduating at the end of the academic year 1992–3, in June 1993, was expected to approach 5000 (Lewis 1992). The funding formulae of governments are such that many universities grasped the highly valued MBA programmes as a panacea, a short-term cure for financial ills and a means to boost prestige. The social cost is going to be a large number of jobless MBAs.

The increasing use of part-time staff has been one of the ways in which universities have coped with the enrolment increases that have accompanied the underfunding. The large number of PhDs educated in graduate programmes begun in the late 1960s and early 1970s have provided the pool from which the part-time staff are recruited. Many of them are women. They have no hope of being absorbed into the regular faculty ranks; they are a 'lost generation' of academics, a part of the '*maquiladora*' industry spawned by universities and government funding policies. It has been estimated that in the Ontario system the part-time salary total in 1987–8 was about $53 000 000, contrasted with full-time salaries of about $651 000 000. Part-time salaries come to about 7.6 per cent of the total, even though part-timers represented 32.4 per cent of total faculty members and did about a fifth of the total teaching. In that year women comprised 17 per cent of the full-time staff, and 38 per cent of the part-time; for the year 1989–90 these figures were 20.2 and 44.3 per cent respectively (Rajagopal and Farr 1993). Since 1987–8 the situation has worsened. The result is a segmentation of the academic workforce in the university into researchers and teachers.

The increasingly restrictive funding policies outlined in this chapter are part of the deficit-reduction strategies which dominate public policy formulations. Declining tax revenues, increasing deficits, economic stagnation and rising unemployment develop side-by-side with greater demands on the social assistance system and the health care system. In this context funding of universities will continue to fall. In addition, the shift in ideology discussed above leads towards tuition fee policies which are privatizing as the cost of studying is shifted more and more on to the shoulders of the students. Spokespeople for our provincial government continue to extol the virtues and the importance of higher education. However, the context changes to a focus on 'restructuring' the institutions of higher education, with greater emphasis on 'training' opportunities.

Results

The crisis of funding is exacerbated by a climate of deficit reduction which generates restrictive social policies in which universities slip in governmental priorities. Business-centred orientations are encouraged as a response and public knowledge education becomes more market-oriented. This undermines the real purpose of the university; namely, teaching and research in an open environment. Academic autonomy and openness in the production and exchange of knowledge are threatened. What has been public knowledge now becomes private knowledge, and knowledge is treated as private property (Buchbinder 1992). These changes signal an overall transformation in the universities in which intellectual excellence, free inquiry and scientific imagination may be at risk.

The issue of the university as a respondent to external events or rather as a primary agency for change runs through our remarks. This chapter deals with the linkage between the state of the political economy, resulting funding policy options and their impact on the university. The range of institutional change is wide, deep and penetrating. The options for action are influenced by the forms of institutional change. However, the shifts in the state of the political economy have been accompanied by an ideological shift which influences the outcome. Right now the initiatives have been grasped by the higher levels of management and the university workplace is less and less the terrain of academic workers. Students are preoccupied with negotiating the obstacles imposed by escalating tuition fees and deteriorating conditions for learning. As a result, they seem to have opted for a role of 'let us get on with our careers' and so are not joined in the debate in a major way.

We are not able to account for why universities have acted in the way they have with regard to enrolment growth or governmental funding policies. Contractions in funding ought to suggest a corresponding decline in enrolment, not the opposite. It is remarkable that the last three governments in the province of Ontario (Conservative, Liberal and the social democratic New Democratic Party), when faced with economic contraction, have been unified in their response: all have pronounced on prosperity but have acted in response to their concern for the cumulative deficit. The cumulative deficit has continued to escalate and the funding has continued to decline.

We are left with a major question on which to reflect. The marginalization of the university as a whole, resulting from faculty members' loss of control over the organization and process of academic work, has been attributed to the financial and resource allocative functions of top-level university administrators (Newson and Buchbinder 1988). Ironically, however, the faculty members themselves appear to contribute to this process by their reluctance to involve themselves in the formal bodies at the faculty or university levels.

Why has the process described in this chapter proceeded apace without any significant resistance from the professoriate, in fact without so much as a whimper? University professors serve as advisors to governments, consultants to corporations, experts for the media and public policy advocates. Yet when it comes to directing our insights to our own organizations the professoriate seem to lose interest. As a result the initiative has been grasped by the higher levels of management and the university workplace is less and less the terrain of academic workers. The politics of funding reveals a university system in the throes of major readjustments. No sector is exempt from scrutiny, certainly not the professoriate. The orchestrated reorganization of higher education in Canada is proceeding at a time when fiscal austerity is the order of the day.

In this process, discussion of issues to do with social justice, gender, access, participation, equity and the improvement of the quality of life through higher education has been sidelined. It is sad that the professoriate are nowhere in the picture!

Conclusion

There are a series of contradictions which emerge in a consideration of the impacts of funding policy on student enrolment and the impact of revenue distribution on the differential allocation of financial resources in the academic workplace.

The results of funding policy are intriguing to contemplate. As university funding has become tighter the thrust of funding policy has been towards an equation of more students equals less money. Yet we have indicated that, regardless of the policy, enrolment figures continue to escalate. However, they do not appear to escalate uniformly. The response is differential. The enrolment of higher-weighted students (e.g. graduate students, MBA students) is encouraged, while the enrolment of lower-weighted students (e.g. undergraduate students) is discouraged. The internal allocation of resources appears to be shifted from undergraduate students to graduate students. This is reinforced by the funding policy, which assesses graduate students as having a higher value (in terms of the basic income units) than undergraduate students. So the pressure to reduce resources creates a stratification of the student complement, with the layer of graduate students given primacy over undergraduate students as resources are internally redistributed from the lower layer to the upper layer.

This dynamic correlates with the stratification and diversification of the academic workforce within the university. This process occurs along two lines. First:

> Altering the structure of the academic workforce was one administrative response to the fiscal crisis. Through diversification, several categories of academic workers have been created, each having distinct terms and conditions of employment, including salary scales, benefits, career chances, duties and prerogatives in university governance.

The three categories are 'tenure-track', limited contract, and part-time academics.

(Newson and Buchbinder 1988: 25)

The second aspect of this process is the fragmentation of the role of university professor into the teaching, research and service functions. 'Each part can be organized as a distinct, specialized task and assigned a different value.' Thus, as the academic workforce is restructured research becomes the major function of the full-time professoriate and the primary means of achieving high status, with teaching becoming the primary responsibility of part-time and contractually limited staff. Assignment of workloads, awarding of honours and achievement of status are then correlated with the research function. This carries over into the differential value placed on graduate students, where the main focus is research, and undergraduate students, where the teaching classroom predominates. Thus, diversification of the academic workforce is accompanied by the diversification of the student cohort: research-focused graduate students and full-time professors are in a preferred status while teaching-oriented part-timers and classroom-oriented undergraduates are in a secondary status.

We can also identify two other functions of academic work which can inform our understanding: the production and transmission of knowledge. Full-time faculty members are mainly involved with the production of knowledge (research); part-timers are mainly involved with the transmission of knowledge (teaching). Production–transmission, research–teaching, full-time–part-time, graduate–undergraduate are the variations in this model of diversification and stratification. These formulations are important to the consideration of funding policy, enrolment policy and hiring policy in the universities. They also relate to the intramural divisions and struggles that exist within the academic collegium. For example, if the 'production of knowledge' aspect is seen as more important than the 'transmission of knowledge' then the replacement of retiring academic staff will be by 'stellar' appointments who are producers of research and knowledge. Yet the rationale for enforcing a strict policy of mandatory retirement at age 65 is to replace expensive retirees with less costly junior appointments.

Another dimension of this complicated process is the separation between management (academic administration) and the academic collegium. There is a shift from administration to management, and an increasing centralization of management functions. These have occurred in part to increase 'efficiency', and in part as a response to the unionization of faculty members. This unionization has, however, divided the academic workers and centralized the management which deals with them within the context of collective bargaining.

At York University the full-time staff are in a union certified under the Ontario Labour Relations Act. The part-timers are organized into another union, the Canadian Union of Educational Workers. At times the interests of each of these unions conflict with the interests of the other. Part-time employees would love to have full-time jobs but their negotiations are geared towards protecting their presence as part-timers. The hiring of part-timers as course directors is governed by qualifications, very broadly defined, and seniority. The academic programmes are under the control of full-time academics. However, the seniority clauses limit full-timers in their ability to control who teaches the courses.

Students are overwhelmed by the escalating tuition fees, less and less outside employment to help them through university, poorer conditions for learning and bleak prospects even after a university degree. Consequently there is a minimum of political activity; students seem to be more involved in the difficulties of surviving. When one compares the student activism of the 1960s with today one must note that the political activity of the 1960s occurred during a period of growth and expanding possibilities. Perhaps political activity comes more easily in a political economy of growth.

We have dealt with our colleagues rather harshly in this chapter. Within the changing picture of academic work we have charged that the professoriate are nowhere to be seen. They are not active in responding to what must be seen as a crisis in the structure and organization of academic work. The picture we have sketched is one of fragmentation and stratification; perhaps also of alienation. The collegium is divided within itself: full-timers against part-timers; senate against faculty union; research-oriented professors against those with a major commitment to teaching; those following the policy of accessibility (to high quality education) against those with a more restrictive and elitist orientation (while paying lip-service to accessibility by approving 'cheaper' education for the undergraduates).

How can one understand this fragmentation? We can hypothesize that there is a great difficulty in achieving a sense of cohesion under the impact of such centrifugal forces; one can write it off as resulting from the inward-looking stance of academics. We have posed here some of the dynamics which have fragmented academic workers and centralized academic managers. Hard times have led to greater compliance as academics have focused on 'getting by'.

The analysis cannot end with a sole focus on the professoriate as complicit in the transformation of the academic work place. We need to develop our critique within the context of institutional change. Within this context the role of the professoriate will be a focus for examination.

Notes

1. These transfer payments are part of the established programmes financing programme. Cash and tax credits are transferred to the provincial governments although, it should be noted, they are not compelled to spend it for those items.
2. Sometimes one left for summer vacation having planned for, say, a 15 per cent increase in enrolment and worked on a 20 per cent increase in operating funds, only to come back in late August and find that enrolment was up by 20 per cent

and funding by 30 per cent. These were glorious days for being a dean, or a chair, or a member of the academic planning and policy committee.

3. Prior to unionization the university senate was concerned with academic policy, and as an academic body it was to have teaching members as a majority. It also included the administration (e.g. all deans, all vice-presidents and two members of the board) in its membership. In the course of time its composition changed to include a number of academics whose titles were academic but who were holding administrative positions or performing management functions (directors of institutes or organized research centres, assistant and/or associate vice-presidents, provosts, representatives of centres of excellence and so on). The literature is generally unanimous in its view that academic senates are usually controlled by the administration (whether it is also management or not). Thus the designation of the senate as a 'faculty body' can be a bit misleading. Whatever it was before 1975, since about 1980 this has been so at York University.

4. Two observations related to planning are relevant. The first is the view that writing the plan update each autumn is a necessary condition to making any request (for a new appointment, or for a replacement of a retirement, or for the addition of new options in the programme) but is not a sufficient condition (if you have not put in your plan update you won't get anything, but if you have put in your plan update you are not assured of getting anything). The other comment is related to the secondment of professoriate (called to profess a subject) to non-teaching jobs; after the faculty of arts, the faculty of sabbaticals and the faculty of Atkinson College, the *fourth faculty* in the university was the faculty of non-teaching secondments! All their teaching has to be done by somebody else.

5. The developer has had financial problems. The money that was to accrue to the university, which was to be used to pay for part of the building plan, has not materialized. As a result the university has added to its capital deficit, interest on which is carried by the operating part of the budget.

6. In the first year there was to be a cut of 2.7 per cent, but for the second year (i.e. 1992–3) no budget cut has been made. It would appear that, without any formal announcement, the 10 per cent cut over three years has been shelved. A new president took office in September 1992. What this augers remains to be seen.

7. Atkinson College provides degree programmes for part-time students; Glendon College provides bilingual arts programmes; both are separate faculties in York University. The graduate programmes in any discipline were constituted by the cognate faculty in all faculties; the existence of the FGS ensured this shared structure. The changed structure for the FGS was approved only two weeks before the president left office; it had been preceded by another move to bring all arts faculties together, a move which was abandoned for lack of consensus! The move to dismantle the FGS was thus an 'afterthought', and has posed questions of possible fading away of the separate arts faculties, which were part of the proposal made to the provincial government in 1958, on the basis of which the Legislative Acts of 1959 and 1965 are based.

8. In November 1992 the provincial government announced that for 1993–4 it would cap the transfer payments at the 1992–3 level. Thus the funding increase for 1993–4 is zero. It also announced a one-time only 2 per cent restructuring fund for 1993–4. There was no indication from the government regarding the universities' share or how this fund would relate to the restructuring exercise. The government also announced a tuition fee increase of 7 per cent as well as changes to the Ontario Student Assistance Plan. Much of the assistance is to be

shifted towards a relatively greater loans component, although some grants will be retained. A pilot project to examine the feasibility of income-contingent repayment is in the offing.

9. If there are indeed jobs created, whether they will be in service industries or in high-tech knowledge industries in not clear.

References

Arthurs, H.W. (1985) Memo to officers, York University, June.

Buchbinder, H. (1992) The market oriented university and the changing role of knowledge, paper presented at the Conference at the Ontario Institute for Studies in Education, October.

Buchbinder, H. and Rajagopal, P. (1992) Canadian universities and the politics of funding, International Conference on Higher Education, Washington Conference.

Canadian Press Report (1991) Education shakeup urged, *The Globe and Mail*, 24 September.

Feschuck, S. (1992) Ontario universities fear payment freeze, *The Globe and Mail*, 20 January.

Lewington, J. (1991) Universities warn of staff cuts without 7% funding increase, *The Globe and Mail*, 22 November.

Lewis, M. (1992) 'MBA schools just don't know when to quit', Plethora of programs across country adding to an already-crowded field, *The Globe and Mail*, 19 November.

Newson, J. and Buchbinder, H. (1988) *The University Means Business*. Toronto, Garamond Press.

Rajagopal, I. and Farr, W.D. (1993) The part-time faculty in Canada (private communication).

4

Goal Setting, Domestication and Academia: the Beginnings of an Analysis

Mick Campion and William Renner

Introduction

In the muted but contentious debate over goal setting and academic staff appraisal within Australia the focus has frequently been on questions of detail, for example in relation to the industrial award (Lublin 1992). In this chapter we seek to relocate the debate within a broader context by examining parallels with an analysis of changes in another profession.

In 1984 Peter F. Meiksins offered a dissenting view of the history of scientific management. We believe that an analysis of his version of the transformation of the engineering profession at the beginning of the twentieth century provides many pointers which assist efforts to understand the situation that Australian academics find themselves in at the end of the twentieth century.

However, before focusing upon that analysis, we wish to draw upon Frank Musgrove's article entitled 'The domesticated university' in order to outline two very different versions of the university. Both Musgrove (1978) and Meiksins (1984) rely upon notions of domesticity which fail to reveal a grasp of the violence that can be hidden within such environments; however, neither is commending domesticity. What we hope this chapter will display is the potentially negative consequences of an academic community becoming committed to an emasculated professionalism through a half-hearted acceptance of an uncritiqued, imported set of managerial tools from industry. We believe that the frequently ambivalent, contradictory, divided and, at times, muted voice of the academic community on specific issues, such as the current debate about goal setting, provides evidence that the fate of Meiksin's engineers may well await the academic workforce.

The domestication of the university

The core aspect of Musgrove's article is illustrated in the following quotation:

> The shift (in higher education) is from roast to boiled; and this in turn
> reflects the long-term shift in English education from one of the two
> primary models of education to the other: from the military-monastic
> model to the integrated-domestic model. In this second and now domin-
> ant mode it is the curriculum 'package' and the fool-proof 'curriculum
> kit' that symbolise and celebrate the new learning environment: in
> which there is neither risk nor waste.
>
> (Musgrove 1978: 404)

The somewhat surprising metaphor is grounded in Lévi-Strauss's view of
the transformation from nature to nurture, which is seen as occurring in
both cooking and language (Musgrove 1978: 404). The precise origins of
the metaphor, and its accuracy or inaccuracy, need not concern us, for our
interest is in how these concepts resonate with issues of contemporary importance in higher education. To elaborate, Musgrove draws upon Lévi
Strauss as follows:

> Lévi Strauss has looked for the social correlates of the roast and the
> boiled, which are to be found in all cultures; and a universal distinc-
> tion is this – that the boiled is typically for small, intimate, inturned
> social groups; the roast is for banquets which turn outwards on the
> world and bring in the stranger as an honoured guest. The roast is
> exocuisine: socially out-turned, aristocratic and prodigal; the boiled is
> endocuisine: cautious, bourgeois. The difference in educational meth-
> odology is whether we put the young on a spit or in a pot. In the
> domesticated university they're all in a pot – at a carefully regulated
> unvarying temperature.
>
> (Musgrove 1978: 406)

Musgrove goes on to describe the domestic as carefully timetabled, planned,
frugal, protected, cautious and parsimonious rather than wild, extravagant
and untamed. In the former we may recognize features of our own institutions which we value, normally fail to notice or resentfully accept. We may
also want to reflect upon how different educational technologies mediate
between nature and nurture in these different models. However, in
Musgrove's view, 'The great tradition of English education has been about
personal growth and development through access to other significant forms
of thought and feeling: it has been about breaking the stranglehold of the
present on the mind. Domestication intensifies it' (Musgrove 1978: 404).
Musgrove argues that given contemporary orthodoxy we have

> more direct forms of accountability and a consciousness dominated by
> the arithmetic of staff: student ratios; curriculum construction which is
> concerned above all to prevent waste – which emphasises 'covering the

ground' and uses the vocabulary of control engineering; monitoring systems which enfold students to protect their progress and prevent 'wastage' more (apparently) job-related degree courses; and other degree courses which foster a preoccupied and indulgent self-concern. This narcissism (even solipsism) is part of a constellation of powerful contemporary values.

(Musgrove 1978: 407)

The military-monastic or aristocratic model referred to by Musgrove involved placing the students in what Goffman (1961) and other sociologists would call *total institutions*. Within these all-encompassing institutions students are separated from bourgeois culture: a culture which Musgrove views as having enormous potential for ordering, reordering and containing reality. He sees bourgeois culture as having domesticated the savage mind, and argues that while the military-monastic model was

marked by apartness, even foreignness – foreign languages, even dead languages, were at its centre. Domestication has meant the following: greater sensitivity to the needs and interests of local communities; the decline of languages from curricular pre-eminence; the arrival of integrated-hybrid degrees; and perhaps above all the spectacular rise of 'introverted' subjects which feed on the student's own absorbed self-interest: psychology, sociology, modern social and local history, English literature after Jane Austen.

(Musgrove 1978: 404)

Having focused on issues of difference and apartness, distinctions such as that between endocuisine and exocuisine, between the inward-looking, the self-centred and the out-turned and adventurous, he points out a difference in relation to the use of rules. In bourgeois culture, rules are constructed to make things easier. In contrast, in aristocratic cultures, rules are designed to make things more difficult than they would otherwise have been. To be more pointed, his argument is that in the bourgeois culture rules are designed to assist in goal attainment, whereas in the aristocratic rules are designed to prevent it (Musgrove 1978: 406). This is particularly apposite given the contemporary debate about goal setting in the university.

For Musgrove the aristocratic model relied upon a paradigm of the university experience as the process of artistic creation. He contrasts this with the domesticated university, which is analogous to a knowledge industry generating pollution. The domesticated university is a vast apparatus of scholarship which has made books apparently accessible and safe, and hence consumable like any other commodity. However, for Musgrove, the real problem is not the distribution of the superabundance of knowledge; it is restricted access to minuscule stocks of real experience. Musgrove concludes by relating his 'concern about the need to bring back wonder and terror into the university experience' (Musgrove 1978: 412).

We have drawn selectively from, and leaned heavily upon, Musgrove in this section in order to separate and juxtapose these differing models. In our view the models tell us something of the divisions in the contemporary Australian academic community which simmer not too deep below the surface. Where we might differ from Musgrove is that we imagine that many of our colleagues are not located clearly in either camp, but are torn apart, and as a result effectively silenced by commitments which appear to be based on selected, and perhaps contradictory, elements of each of these seemingly mutually exclusive and opposed ideologies.

University life and goal setting

In the face of such large-scale changes as are occurring in higher education, many academics are tentative about the direction tertiary education is currently taking. Having experienced the many major changes to higher education since the 1980s, academics are still unsure of what to expect, and what future changes may continue to shape their working lives. Certainly, there is a tension between an understanding of what universities were once about, and the emergence of new more overtly instrumental concerns. However, we suspect that many academics still quietly revere the Oxbridge academic ideal, with its emphasis on individualized tuition, self-paced work, intellectual freedom and the high status with which academics appeared to be bestowed.

Elitist and aristocratic, the Oxbridge notion of a collegial and cloistered university environment forms a traditional conception of academic life. Intellectual activity is viewed as the right of the leisured class. Those considered part of this elite group appeared to pursue knowledge for its own sake. Academic study thus reflected, perhaps unwittingly, the interests and world view of those aristocrats who were leisured enough (and interested enough) to partake. Practical disciplines (like engineering) were the unknown world of another class, and were given little credence. In the era before mass communications and mass education, access to information and knowledge was very much a closed shop. Scholars were a small and privileged group much like the artisan or craftsperson, with unique access to the accumulated knowledge of generations. The pursuit of knowledge was considered an end in itself and was disengaged from modern (capitalist) concerns of education and training, industrial efficiency and economic progress.

Clearly, academic life has changed considerably since the aristocratic period. In tandem with society's transition to, and perhaps through, industrialism, the role of universities is rapidly being transformed into that of a knowledge industry. The question remains, however: what do these dramatic changes really mean for academics and how should they respond? We believe that an analysis of the engineering profession in the United States at the turn of the century provides some clues for those engineers who were facing an industrial transformation comparable to that of the Australian academic community today. Moreover, the experiences of both groups are similar in that members are threatened by loss of proprietorship, loss of autonomy, loss of status; and in both cases, ideological divisions may have strengthened the prospects of this process ensuing.

The domestication of the engineering profession

Meiksins's (1984) history of the engineering profession begins with the premise that, as middle-class professionals, the engineers could not identify clearly with either capitalist or proletarian. This problem came to the fore when dramatic changes in the labour process forced engineers to become employees in large manufacturing corporations. For many, this involved severance from their traditional role as proprietors of small machine shops and involved their alienation from the means of production. Frederick W. Taylor, founder of the scientific management movement, sought to optimize their effort to secure more autonomy over their work and to carve out a defensible position in the new corporations. Caught in an ambiguous position somewhere between management and wage labour, (the now co-opted) engineers fervently adopted certain of the principles of scientific management espoused by Taylor. It was an ideology which came to accept both the exploitation of wage labour and the right of the capitalist owners to make a profit, while seeking to regain some control for engineers over the production process. Taylor's plan was to exclude not only shopfloor workers from control over operations, but also executive management: 'The shop, and indeed the whole works, should be managed not by the manager, superintendent or foreman, but by the *planning department*. The daily routine of running the entire works should be carried on by the various functional elements of this department' (Taylor, cited by Meiksins 1984: 181). Indeed, Taylorism 'represented a manifesto in favour of control over production by engineers' (Meiksins 1984: 181).

However, Meiksins argues that the engineers did not get all that they wanted. They chose to compromise, as is illustrated in the following quotation:

> The defeat of the Taylorist project was thus important to the domestic-ation of the engineers. At least as significant, however, was the formulation and success of an alternative engineering ideology that posed less of a threat to capitalist domination than did scientific management – the ideology of professionalism. . .The old 'shop culture' engineers who developed the tenets of scientific management were not the only engineers in turn-of-the-century America. As American industry grew larger and more complex, the demand for engineering personnel to occupy the middle layers of corporate employment skyrocketed. The old 'quasi-apprenticeship' system of training engineers proved inadequate to meet

this demand, so a new, school-based system of training engineers sprang up. The engineers who were produced by this system were very different sociologically from the older group. They tended to come from less elite backgrounds, had no experience of the shop culture, and, indeed, knew no world other than the large organisations into which they were being recruited. The 'gentlemanly' shop culture engineers who dominated the ASME (the American Society of Mechanical Engineers) looked down upon these newcomers and fought against their attempt to argue that practical experience was less important than formal training. . .It was among these school based engineers that the new ideology of professionalism took root.

(Meiksins 1984: 199)

Big business financed and established engineering colleges from which they could instruct a new, more compliant generation of engineers. The new 'safer' form of professionalism which was espoused by the engineering schools emphasized teamwork, service and loyalty to the company, and abandoned the potentially radical elements of scientific management. Following graduation, this new breed of engineers were rewarded for their compliance, with formal recognition being given to their profession. Thus engineers who had resisted the transition to corporate employment had been defeated, and the emerging profession had been domesticated to the needs of the rising corporate power holders.

Some uncanny resemblances to the current experiences of the academic profession should by now be apparent; most notably clues as to the consequences of the dissolution of the binary divide for the Australian academic community. Certainly, a professional division still simmers between the traditional and former College of Advanced Education (CAE) sectors of university academics. The traditional universities are often characterized by their elitism and staff autonomy, whereas the newer institutions are often presented as having more heterogeneous student populations and related commitments to equity objectives, while, perhaps paradoxically, their managerial style is frequently more autocratic. The destruction of the binary divide, however, has forced the academic profession to seek a new path between these two extremes. Given the larger size of the latter group, it might seem likely that the balance would settle in favour of a professional ethic based more on the CAE managerial style. However, it must be noted that many institutions within this sector are attempting to emulate the education traditionalists and the associated style of professionalism. Hence, while the future for academic professionalism is still unclear, on the basis of Meiksin's analysis of the engineers, the threat of moving further towards a co-opted professionalism – indeed, a domesticated professionalism – must be considered very real.

As an account of a significant profession spawned out of industrialism, the case of the engineers provides us with a window through which to view some of the current challenges facing the academic profession. Indeed, a variety of parallels and conclusions can be drawn. Like Meiksins's engineer, academics are also living through a period of great structural change. From a situation of proprietorship over their craft, they too are becoming professionals within large and bureaucratic organizations. Just as the skilled services of the engineer were co-opted into the complex and expanding manufacturing industry, so now are academics co-opted into a complex and expanding higher education industry. The presumed transition and expansion of tertiary education into a form of mass provision challenges scholars to reject elitist orientations. Their traditional role as autonomous and free-thinking scientists is rapidly declining in the face of more instrumental concerns. Research is increasingly directed towards 'national priorities', while teaching is moving ever closer to commodification and standardization. The emphasis is changing from personal goals of scholarship and enquiry, to goals of institutional and national efficiency and productivity. This is true both with the subject matter taught and, more recently, with new forms of work organization which structure university life. Like the engineers described by Meiksins, academics today are juxtaposed between two opposed ideologies, between an artisanal tradition and an instrumental industrialism, between aristocratic elitism and the claimed equality and openness of mass provision. Yet each model carries its advantages and disadvantages. It is small wonder that academics are torn between these conflicting ideologies and cannot find sure footing on which to take a stand.

Meiksins's analysis offers an account of how and why the engineers came to align themselves with capital rather than with other members of the workforce, and how in the process the potentially radical elements of scientific management were dropped. Engineers were, for example, likely to exercise authority in the workplace, likely to perceive management as a potential career pathway. They were also likely to hold relatively privileged places in the workforce and consequently to consider that they would benefit from processes that differentiate them from other workers rather than emphasize commonalities. Furthermore, as with other professional groups they were likely to be attracted by an ideology that appears critical of both labour and capital; an ideology that appears untainted because of its 'scientific' nature (Meiksins 1984: 194–7). Once again we imagine that it will not be too difficult to see how this analysis casts light upon the situation of academics.

Meiksins draws upon the work of Larson to pull some of these issues together:

> The social worth of the educated individual, his [*sic*] greater social productivity, and the value of his time are asserted in relative and hierarchical terms: in a fusion of practical ability and moral superiority the expert appears to be freer and more of a person than most others. Himself a choice victim of the subjective illusion, he is also, by his very existence and actions an effective propagator of bourgeois individualism. It is along this crucial dimension that the ideology of profession and

the 'possessive individualism' of expertise work to sustain the dominant ideology.

Thus, stripped of any ability to sustain a claim to professional auto-nomy, the ideology of professionalism poses no threat to the capitalist employer. Indeed it becomes simply a claim to status, totally compat-ible with the dominant ideology of individualism, that serves to wed the individual to capitalist social structure and ideology.

(Larson, cited by Meiksins 1984: 200)

This may be where the analogy ends, for the engineers at the turn of the century developed a strong counter-ideology, i.e. scientific management, in an attempt to regain some authority over their work even if it did not prevail in anything but an emasculated form. If academics are to do likewise they may need to take on board a similar ideology, one that accepts their ambiguous position (between general staff and their employers) and allows them to recover some control over their work. The specialist area of instruc-tional design (based on principles of scientific management) remains a possible contender. It should be remembered, however, that in education, exogenous forces have come to play an ever more powerful role and that the most likely outcome is an emasculated professionalism, co-opted to government objectives.

Scientific management and the university

To protect their vulnerable position in the changing university scene, some sections of academia are, perhaps unwittingly, embracing scientific manage-ment techniques as a way of securing more control over their work. Certain elements of the distance education sector and proponents of 'instructional design' are perhaps the greatest exponents of this ideology. They argue for curriculum to be packaged into foolproof instruction kits, complete with clearly stated study methodologies, objectives and means of assessment. Monitoring, programming and feedback loops are also used to regulate student progress and to ensure that education runs efficiently and easily. The result of this approach may disengage students from full participation in knowledge acquisition. It tends to standardize the learning process and alienates teacher from student, and student from teacher. The commodi-fication of curriculum is a very real example of how a particular instrumental form of goal setting has structured work practices and has dramatically altered the education process in universities. The application of Taylorism to higher education has considerable impact on work. Most notably, it suggests a deeply cut division of labour; specifically, the separation of con-ception from execution. A scientifically managed university could be de-picted as one in which the task of instructional design is undertaken by small elite groups of specialized academic staff, while the labour of teaching is carried out by a pool of dedicated tutor-grade staff. Although adding security to high-level academic employment, Taylorism would seem to offer few benefits for either student learning or democracy in the workplace. Indeed, it would seem that higher education is in the process of being transformed into a factory (as popularly perceived), where work is governed by managerial directives and is hierarchically structured to maximize the division of labour.

Meanwhile, the workplaces of other industries, particularly knowledge-based, high value-added sectors, are experiencing a shift in precisely the opposite direction. Whereas at one time the ideologies of Taylor and Henry Ford were actively embraced, now industries are purging themselves of its remnants, and adopting a so-called *post-Fordist* approach to work. Arguably, this entails greater participation, autonomy and (perhaps) democracy for employees than was the case in the past; which, in turn, permits greater labour and product flexibility, and therefore greater responsiveness to the market. Post-Fordism (or *flexible specialization* as it is sometimes called) is a new approach to work which seeks to minimize hierarchy, in favour of an orientation grounded in multi-skilling, teamwork and labour autonomy. It is important to make clear that post-Fordist techniques of production have emerged out of the private sector's search for ever greater profits. The rise to pre-eminence of companies which have adopted such a strategy does, however, raise questions about the supposed superiority of Fordism and its commitment to standardization, and begs the question that a post-Fordist orientation in higher education may be a plausible and preferable alternative.

Conclusion

Governments and employers want assurances that universities can boost the efficiency and quality of their enterprise. This has led to a debate based primarily on the application of industrial models to university work. Many of these models, however, find their industrial origins in the remote past and are shunned by many contemporary organizations. For example, Taylorism dates back to the turn of the century, goal setting (termed MBO in industry) dates to the 1950s (see Koontz and Weihrich 1988: 87), while *Fordist* ideals of standardized mass production and rigid commodification are becoming antiquated concepts in today's highly diversified marketplace. Indeed, as the prior outline of post-Fordism indicates, some sectors of industry are openly rebelling against conventional industrial ideologies, and are effecting new approaches to work which enable gains in quality and efficiency as well as improved democracy in the workplace. Open-mindedness to current developments in the sociology of work are essential if Australian higher education is to move into the twenty-first century with a chance of playing a significant role within the international community.

To return to the focal issue of goal setting what we are suggesting is that goal setting in relation to academic work is likely to fortify negative aspects of commodification and standardization inherent in Fordist approaches to work organization. Indeed, implemented unmindfully, goal setting will engender greater hierarchy and division than is presently the case. However, it is possible that the parallels with the engineers which have been referred to in this chapter may assist in the promotion of analyses of academic work which reduce the likelihood of this occurring. In this regard it is important that we emphasize, as did Meiksins, that none of this happens automatically; that much depends upon how a profession responds. In other words, there is nothing in the structural location of academics that necessarily leads them one way or another, though there is much to suggest that domestication is the most likely outcome.

References

Goffman, E. (1961) *Asylums: Essays on the Social Situation of Mental Patients and Other Inmates.* New York, Anchor Press, Doubleday.

Koontz, H. and Weihrich, H. (1988) *Management,* 9th edn. New York, McGraw-Hill.

Lublin, J.R. (1992) Staff development, staff assessment and the industrial awards, *Higher Education Research and Development,* 11(1), 73–83.

Meiksins, P.F. (1984) Scientific management and class relations, *Theory and Society,* 13, 177–209.

Musgrove, F. (1978) The domesticated university, *New Universities Quarterly,* Summer, 402–12.

5

Higher Education and the State: the Irony of Fordism in American Universities

Wesley Shumar

Introduction

One recurrent theme in the discourse surrounding universities today is a confusion regarding the locus of power. On one hand, universities are seen as a 'community of scholars' with the faculty members in control of their practices and with scholarship as a goal. In this view of the university, ideas reign and the university is an 'ivory tower' set off from secular life, including commerce. Arthur Sussman (1981: 27) tells the following story in an article on the 1980 Yeshiva decision.

> Dwight Eisenhower early in his brief presidency of Columbia University greeted a group of faculty members expressing his delight at meeting some of the 'employees' of Columbia. The resulting silence, as the story continues, was broken by a senior professor who rose and said, 'With all due respect, sir, we are not the employees of Columbia university. We are Columbia University.'

Clearly Eisenhower and the senior professor had different models in mind for the university. Equally clearly, the professor was not comfortable with Eisenhower's assumptions that he was a mere employee and Columbia a business to be guided by ideals of scientific management. This approach gives administrators critical power, leaving faculty members the role of labourers. As this model becomes more widespread the university increasingly follows a factory model where scholars are labourers in the sweatshop of thought.

In this chapter I present examples of the binary nature of the public image of the university. I suggest that current conceptualizations fail to pay sufficient attention to the recent changes in the image of the university, particularly the increasing domination of university by the state and corporate capitalism. I trace these two images, which intertwine and affect one another, showing the hybrid character of the university. This true character has been neglected by other scholars who have more simplistically drawn on one or the other of these two models. I use court cases and historical research to demonstrate the presence of contradictory models. Moreover, I argue that there has been an increasing domination of the factory model owing to political and economic forces in the broader culture. The government's current fiscal crisis all but ensures that, if present trends continue, market forces will continue to dominate policies and thinking in higher education.

The current tendency to see universities as either 'communities of scholars' or factories keeps researchers and faculty members from seeing more complex changes in the university as it falls more and more into the economic sector. I propose the notion of commoditization as a superior model for understanding these complex forces of which we are a part.

Community versus factory

Ernest Boyer, in *College: the Undergraduate Experience in America*, discusses the importance of community. According to him some current trends in higher education threaten that sense of community. For instance, he feels that the increase in part-time staff threatens the cohesion of the university because part-time staff have less investment in or commitment to the university community (Boyer 1988: 137–9). Boyer is also concerned with unions and governance. He makes the 'ivory tower' point that unions interfere with the traditional community of scholars governing their own (Boyer 1988: 141–2). These concerns are echoed elsewhere. The Sussman quote above neatly captures the conflict over imaginations of the university, but it also evokes the anxiety of faculty members who fear the loss of community and their standing within it. Boyer documents that fear clearly.

While Martin Finkelstein (1984: 221) doesn't see social science faculty members as a community, he does see them as 'a world apart from most other workers'. For Finkelstein, university professors still have the autonomy and independence traditionally imagined for the community of scholars, but others disagree.

In *Killing the Spirit*, Page Smith argues that faculty rule is often tyrannical and academic freedom is often illusory. He further shows that one important theme in the student movement of the 1960s was a reaction against Clark Kerr's (1982) view that the university was becoming more a part of the larger economy.

Many have expressed fears of the loss of academic freedom and the transformation of the university into a knowledge factory. Daniel T. Seymour (1988: 38) responded to those fears in an article in *College Board Review*:

> while some may totally believe that we have sold out our academic institutions to 'managers' the fact remains that most universities, including Harvard, have evolved quite nicely and will probably survive this latest corporate invasion – an invasion that may have begun almost 80 years

ago when, in 1909, a Harvard faculty member wrote: 'The men who control Harvard today are very little else than businessmen, running a large department store which dispenses education to the millions.'

In other words, the reinterpretation of the university as business is natural – i.e. evolved – and nothing to be concerned about; but more importantly, Seymour's implication is that the university has always been either factory or community. Ideologies do tend to produce a reified binary opposition which sets the poles of what can be said, controls the imagination and, most importantly, glosses over more complex dialectical reality. In this case, that reality is one where universities are double-bound in a number of catch 22s of capitalist economy and culture.

The above binary opposition, produced as a text of our culture, was codified into law by the Supreme court in the Yeshiva decision in 1980 (US Reports 1982). Although the court was split, the majority ruled against allowing the faculty members at Yeshiva to form a union because in their view the faculty members were not workers. Justice Powell, writing for the majority, invoked the image of the medieval community of scholars. The dissenting opinions did acknowledge the other view of the university as factory, however.

The legal struggle has continued as staff attempt to gain protection under the law. At the University of Pittsburgh, a group of staff were able to move beyond Yeshiva by going through the state court system and successfully arguing that as they do not have much financial control it would be difficult to call them managerial employees.

Legal battles deepen our commitment to the binary model of community versus factory. We come to live these realities at some level while they disguise workings in the society at other levels. Transformation is going on but it is much more complex than a simple move from community to factory.

Imagination and the university

Using Benedict Anderson's (1983) notion of imagination to understand the university, we can see that the image of 'university' is directly tied to the larger imaginations of 'community' and 'nation' which have changed over time. At present, the university in the United States hangs between two important models, the medieval community of scholars and the knowledge factory. It is important to realize that these models are not ancient but are both products of capitalism. The medieval community of scholars is a model that rose in the early twentieth century during Fordism (Albertsen 1988; Harvey 1989) to serve the needs of a growing industrial economy. The model of the knowledge factory developed more recently and is a product of the crisis of Fordism and the global crisis of capitalism. These two images demonstrate historically how the university's relationship to the larger society has changed.

Anderson argues that all communities are imagined. By imagination, Anderson means the ways people see themselves being connected to each other. He sees nationalism as a particular form of imagination and he attempts to analyse its repercussions. Anderson understands imagination as the ideological view produced by a culture at a point in history which gets inscribed in the practices of people, their lives and institutions. In his work, Anderson gives substance to Althusser's notion of ideology: 'the imaginary relation of those individuals to the real relations in which they live' (Althusser 1971: 165).

In the following sections of this chapter I will discuss the development of these imaginations of the university and how current economic crises are being expressed in the university. I rely on a theoretical model called commoditization to discuss how institutions change in a capitalist society. Further, I will discuss how consciousness and subjectivity are affected by this shift of imagination and the ways in which people and institutions struggle with these models.

Commoditization

I suggest commoditization as a way to understand the dynamic tension between the two models of the university. For our purposes commoditization is a particular response by institutions in capitalist society, especially those Althusser designated 'ideological state apparatuses'. Commoditization is what happens to institutions other than profit-making businesses when they respond to crisis with the instrumental, market-based responses to crisis. These responses tend to change the structure and ideology of the institution that utilizes them, as we will see when we look at the changes to the university in the post-war period and again in the 1960s.[1] Commoditization also involves the infiltration of the profit-making sector into non-profit institutions, in order to exploit them to reduce costs.

Commoditization is a way to move beyond Althusser's notion of the ideological state apparatus. Education is not only a site of contestation (Apple 1982; Barrow 1990) and serves an ideological function as in Althusser's view; but with the collapse of Fordism it became part of the fiscal crisis of the state. The need for educational institutions to prioritize the selling of product to stay financially solvent undermined the ideological function of the educational institution. Both the product of education and the school's image became tarnished as commoditization generated the crisis of legitimacy.

The commoditization of higher education in the United States is a process that developed over time and had a number of important stages. First, the early twentieth century saw a notable increase in the number of businessmen and other industrial leaders on university boards of trustees (Noble 1977; Barrow 1990). Second, the post-Second World War period featured a resounding boom in higher education owing to returning servicemen followed a scant generation later by their children entering college in unprecedented numbers in the 1960s. Third, the 1970s began an inevitable (considering the demographics) period of bust; which was dealt with in ways familiar to the businessmen and marketers who had come to dominate the boards – management of enrolment, rationalization of teaching and the active solicitation of research dollars – but relatively new to university administrative thinking.

Commoditization is part of a larger set of transitions in capitalism. Following Lash and Urry (1987), Albertsen (1988), Harvey (1989) and others, I see the US economy, like other capitalist economies, as moving from a period called Fordism to what many are calling post-Fordism. Fordist production began with the process of monopolization and the development of large-scale production in the early twentieth century. Efficient large-scale production required a system of balances to manage distribution and consumption and to regulate the flow of capital. Under Fordism, the state performs this role of regulating capital.

Post-Fordism, located by Harvey as beginning in 1973, is a period of crisis caused by the collapse of balances created by Fordism. As profits shrank, companies moved to secure them in a number of ways. First, corporations became decentred as they sought less expensive workforces and explored new production processes. These efforts expanded the use of part-time and temporary labour and necessitated moving factories to developing nations where labour was cheaper. This decentred production was made possible by new technologies and has resulted in a truly global marketplace. In this global economy the regulation of capital has become much more complex, and economies are much less stable. National boundaries have ceased to have the economic relevance they once had; regions either prosper or starve depending increasingly on the decisions made by corporate institutions, not governments, as was once true.

Fordism in the university

The dominant image of the institutions of higher education before the turn of the century drew inspiration from the clergy and the idea of an educated entrepreneurial professional. Beginning around the turn of the century, that vision of the university began to be replaced by a corporate vision. This corporate vision was part of a slow set of changes which happened in the United States in general.

Clyde Barrow (1990) documents the development of the relationship between the universities and corporate capitalism. Barrow begins with the transformation of boards of trustees of American colleges and universities around the turn of the century. His model looks at universities by region because he correctly suggests that capitalism developed at different rates and that there were different capitalist groups for each region of the country.

The change of university trustees from non-commercial professions (physicians, clergy and academics) to businessmen marked the beginning of the commoditization of the university system. Barrow (1990: 38) shows that from 1861 to 1929 the percentage of clergymen, doctors, educators, lawyers and judges on the boards of trustees of major private universities and technical institutes in the north-east declined from 60 to 28.7 per cent. Over the same period in the same institutions the percentage of merchants, manufacturing and railroad tycoons, engineers and bankers increased from 25 to 53.4 per cent. This new network of board members expected the university to serve the interests of the industrializing economy, and they brought a much more instrumental approach to the previously hallowed and idealistic halls of academe.

Meanwhile, the turn of the century brought a new complexity to the industrial infrastructure, and with it a new need for technologies of consumption (Ohmann 1987). These technologies of consumption fostered the growth of the social sciences, especially as 'predictive technology for social control' (Haraway 1989: 108). Universities produced the social scientists who could manage workers in the workplace and manage consumption by creating marketing and advertising. In response to these and other developments, the university – like other institutions at the same time and for similar reasons – began to bureaucratize. This bureaucratization led to the development of a new middle class and a far-reaching set of changes in values and orientations in American society (Wiebe 1967: 147–63).

In order to make a profit under new conditions, companies began to decide that it was too risky to take their lumps in a free market and started investing more in advanced technology and large factories. Monopoly was the direction corporate America chose, with large corporations taking over the entire productive process from raw material to finished goods. More and more resources had to be dedicated to the securing of consumption in order to protect these vast investments. Education, the state and the media were all marshalled to provide trained professionals for this new complex economy, to invent new products to keep the economy growing and to make sure goods and services were consumed so that these vast organizations and networks of organizations remained financially solvent. The management of the new corporate capitalism rapidly became a very complex matter in which escalating numbers of dollars were at stake.

While all this was going on in the economy, the university was becoming an important site for corporate development in three ways (Noble 1977). First, the invention of new products and the running of complex factories require skilled technicians, so inventors and technicians had to be trained. Universities expanded existing technical programmes and scrambled to build new ones specializing in the new technologies. Second, university laboratories could provide research and development free from cost-effectiveness concerns, resulting in new products that business could not have afforded to develop. Third, social research in the university developed techniques that rapidly became useful in focusing the marketing of new products. This research came to be vital to the management of the new consumer mass culture. Conveniently, the new social management techniques were useful for managing workers as well, especially in highly routinized, boring, factory jobs. As the new corporations of the twentieth century came to require more skilled labour, scientists, managers, lawyers and advertisers, universities began a period of expansion, partly (but only partly, as I will show) in response to these needs.

All these forces gave corporations a vested interest in the university. At the beginning of the twentieth century organizations like the Carnegie Foundation for the Advancement of Teaching and the General Education Board began to bridge the gap between the corporation and the university president, bringing corporate management to the university even before the benefit was clear (Barrow 1990: 61–6). Corporate interests quickly merged with the elite class which forms the administrations of the major universities, and to a large extent the university's interests came to be perceived as identical with the interests of corporations.

A culture of administrative workers was created, subordinate to presidents and board members. This culture of the modern university was intended to serve the interests of corporate capitalism in the name of knowledge, advancement, reason and a better life, while allowing the university some autonomy from the economic sphere – a fact that, as I have noted, business finds useful. However, even until late in this century many higher education policy-makers and economists have been careful to note that the university is in fact not structured much like a business or a corporation. It is often pointed out that the needs of academic freedom, the tenure system and the very nature of the process of education have together tended to produce a unique institutional structure very different from the corporation. Barrow (1990: 251–9), using Althusser's notion of the ideological state apparatus, has argued that higher education is a site of contestation, where the corporate elite pays lip service to democratic education ideals while extracting as much as possible from university research and technological innovations.[2]

The post-war boom

The trend early in this century saw the universities becoming more important to the needs of the rising corporate capitalism as a source of skilled technicians, research for new products and consumption management techniques; and the post-war period accelerated these changes. After the Second World War there was a tremendous expansion of the corporate/liberal monopoly capitalist model, sometimes called Fordism or Fordism/Keynesianism. This was characterized by rapid and sustained growth of the economy, fuelled by an unprecedented demand for American goods (Bluestone and Harrison 1982). American manufacturers were not only selling goods abroad but rebuilding basic industries and receiving royalties on that investment. And as it turned out, this newly expanded economy dovetailed nicely with the workforce being turned out by the university system.

The growing American economy was populated by a growing and increasingly well-educated workforce. The reasons for this had less to do with democracy or education than social control. Towards the end of the war, Congress realized that there would be a tremendous influx of returning servicemen on the job market and there would be massive unemployment. After the experiences of the 1930s the government was afraid that people would not tolerate the unemployment and there would be riots. So it was fear of revolution that led to the creation of the GI Bill. Congress's intention was to use universities as a holding tank for workers, to allow slower integration into the workforce (Nasaw 1981: 176). It worked well. This new workforce, as it did emerge, fitted in very nicely with the growing call for US goods and the unprecedented growth in the US economy. The economy – and higher education – boomed.

It is interesting that the image of the university as 'ivory tower' became more pervasive at this point, precisely when, thanks to government policy and corporate needs, the university was becoming more inscribed in the economy and the world of the corporation. This was at least in part a reaction to the increasingly obvious truth that university professors weren't high priests of knowledge, but employees of an organization dedicated to stamping out large numbers of college students. As the university became more inscribed into the political and economic realities of the post-war period, the image of the scholarly community was mobilized, perhaps in an effort to forestall the perceived devaluation of university education.

Crisis management in higher education

In the 1960s, the maturing baby-boom generation presented a new set of challenges to business and the state. Again, as after the Second World War, there were an unprecedentedly large number of people to integrate into the job market. Higher education was again used by the state as a place to put the baby-boom generation, but this time the plan was more complex (Nasaw 1981: 182). The 1960s saw the growth of higher education into a much more stratified system, with two-year programmes, technical degrees and many new, but less-prestigious, four-year programmes with a variety of aims and intentions.[3] Kerr (1982) describes this with his term 'multiversity'. Universities, like corporations, became complex structures, with multiple campuses and purposes. There was a clear parallel with the corporations and their development of multinational subsidiaries and specialized branch offices. Administration became the university's 'home office', with the task of rationalizing a large, diverse entity. As colleges and universities became more corporate in their administrative structure, they borrowed techniques as well as priorities from the corporate sector. Gradually, bureaucratic management took hold in the university and problems that were formerly dealt with by a community of scholars became management problems to be dealt with by a professional manager class. This class grew dramatically, not just in numbers but in power. The long-standing belief that the faculty members run the university, rather like a medieval guild (Kerr 1982: 1), has been dying a lingering death, but few involved in any modern university would describe it as primarily a 'community of scholars'.

The cumulative effect of the GI bill and the demographic anomaly of the boomer generation produced a major crisis in higher education. There were perhaps other ways to respond, but most universities adopted the dominant metaphor of the times: growth. Because of the corporate influence now well-entrenched at the university, sky-rocketing enrolment was thought of in instrumental economic terms: a crisis of growth. Higher education writers of the time congratulated themselves that it was 'boom time' in higher education.

The dream of the turn-of-the-century businessmen had come true. Scientific management had come to the university. Educational problems were conceived in instrumental terms and each solution awarded greater power and size to the administrative apparatus. University administrations grew to outnumber the staff, outpace them in pay and hold more power in the institution. This new order was well established long before the phenomenon received any sociological attention. Faculty members still living their guild reality found themselves enmeshed in a university that had little regard for their concerns, either personal or ideological. The university had become a bureaucratically run system tightly networked with corporations and the state, attempting to manage the escalating crises of the capitalist system (Habermas 1975; Foley 1990).

There were two important results of this growth model. First and foremost, it became the model for later crises. Specifically, the inevitable enrolment decrease was seen – and treated – as a fiscal disaster, rather than, say, a normal fluctuation in enrolment creating an opportunity to decrease class sizes and perhaps improve the quality of education. Second, the function of forecasting achieved much more importance than it had had. The Carnegie Foundation established a commission in 1967 to analyse and forecast the various problems of the university because of a perceived need to analyse unrest. It quickly moved to forecasting the decline in enrolments and other problems. Other agencies began forecasting as well, as the university quickly became dependent on its forecasters and planners. This has had repercussions and has served to entrench corporate sensibilities at the university even further.

In 1971, all predictions were for continued boom until 2000. Over the next few years forecasts became ominous. The college-bound population was going to dwindle, and now it was abruptly obvious that schools had expanded too quickly during the 'boom' years and needed to regroup in order to maintain economic growth. I suggest that this, the so-called crisis in higher education spoken of during the 1970s, was a product of imagination – an invented crisis. I am not suggesting that the crisis wasn't real, but rather that the ways in which it was imagined, structured and dealt with were a product of the coming of corporate management to the campus, and of the ways in which the larger economic crises of the 1970s were imagined and dealt with. Demographics produced the effect of lower enrolment and greater political-economic forces helped to form the perception of that effect on the part of higher education planners.

Harvey (1989) places the breakdown of Fordism at around 1973. Bluestone and Harrison (1982) place the demise of industrial America and the beginnings of 'deindustrialization' at about the same time. It is no accident that these social scientists were marking the large economic changes at the same moment that planners in higher education began to make plans for a coming enrolment crisis. Higher education officials nervously watched economic decline in the 1970s and (for the first time in 12 years) declining enrolments, rapidly followed by the slowing down of federal monies as the government began to run out of cash and face rampant inflation. Universities, their corporate leaders in place, began to manage this crisis with the instrumental techniques of the marketplace. Signs of decline were there, and the invention of crisis was a particular way of responding to these signs. Just as higher education had seen the early increase in enrolment as an 'economic boom', it began to predict and prepare for an 'economic crash' *well before the crash actually came.*

Post-Fordism and commoditization

The new legions of higher education professionals produced by the post-war booms organized through the Carnegie Commission and other professional organizations a number of specific policy shifts in response to the expected crisis.

First, education began to be more consciously treated as something that could be sold. If it could be sold, then demand could be created for it. Demand was particularly important because, as pointed out above, the degree was rapidly becoming less valuable in the eyes of the potential 'consumer'.[4] But as marketers know, consumers can always be found, invented or manipulated. This realization meant that the image-producing function of the university became much more important. Public relations, advertising and market research were put to work finding new students. If degree inflation was depressing enrolments, then new target groups, like non-traditional students, had to be identified. New markets in the form of specialized degrees had to be created.

The management of the new functions of the school required scientific rationality given a new name: 'strategic planning' (Uhl 1983; Newman 1985; Clark 1987; Hardy 1987). The creation of image, the coordination of the staff and students in this new environment of educational production, new corporate endeavours like selling bookstore chains and other promotional ventures, and the traditional responsibility of corporate research all require a huge and growing professional class to manage them. Administrations continued to grow in order to manage the new education industry. While teaching and research are nominally the business of universities, if employee growth and salary levels are considered, it is clearly the 'business' sector of higher education which has become the business of the university. Second, when education became a product, faculty members became labourers. Once they were labourers, they could be exploited to produce more product, more efficiently and for less cost. The number of faculties seeking to unionize went up dramatically in the 1970s as they were forced to respond to the increased pressures to proletarianize them.

At this juncture, management experienced a fortunate (for them) consequence of degree inflation. The dramatic increase in PhDs could be strategically imagined as a surplus labour pool, working alongside the permanent labour pool in the form of part-time instructors; a flexible, temporary and inexpensive group of workers. Even before most universities experienced enrolment decline in the late 1970s and early 1980s, the number of unemployed PhDs was large enough to provide a permanent surplus labour pool. While some colleges, especially community colleges, might have gladly used an entirely part-time faculty, most universities and colleges used their permanent staff to maintain the valuable image of prestige, using part-timers to deal with the vagaries of term-to-term enrolments, especially those created by new programmes and degrees.[5]

The third policy shift involves the hiring out of research services by universities. The relationship between corporations and research universities became even closer as more corporations arranged to have their research done without absorbing all the costs.

The upshot of this was that crisis became the norm. Institutions moved into a new era where the continuing need to recruit new students, to put out new advertising images, to create newly desirable product in the form of degree and certificate programmes, ensured that crisis would never end. The university could never be sure about enrolment size or profitability; it had to remain forever poised to take action, to stimulate enrolment, to cut costs, to keep growing. The permanent flexibility this required meant that the staff had to be proletarianized and stratified into temporary part-time workers, permanent teachers and permanent researchers. It also meant that education itself was something no one any longer had time to worry about. For mass-produced education, as for other goods produced in capitalist society, image has become more important than product. More money, time and care was put into the image of the college and its degree than into the quality and substance of the education itself. The National Center for Educational Statistics (1989: 111–12) reports that for all public institutions in the period from 1977 to 1986 administration costs increased by 21 per cent while instruction costs increased by only 6 per cent. For private universities instruction increased by 21 per cent over the same period while administration increased by 39 per cent. While these statistics are not conclusive they show a clear shift in emphasis.[6]

The new success of colleges and universities was modelled on the image of scarcity and surplus: there was a scarcity of students and a surplus of labour. The way these images are used is the particular reinvention of higher education in the late 1970s and early 1980s. It implied that an institution needed permanently to produce images to draw students, and therefore had to have and maintain large and expanding image-making apparatus. If image of product, prestige or public awareness declined, then the scarce student might go elsewhere. Schools could never be sure how well their advertising would work in any given year, so beside the general tendency to teach about half of the classes with part-time labour, colleges needed another group they could hire or fire to deal with the unpredicted ups and downs of consumption.

There have been several important changes in the 1980s that are beyond the scope of this chapter.[7] These changes led *Academe,* a publication of the AAUP, to devote the September 1990 issue to the 'entrepreneurial university'. This issue was a response to the above-mentioned changes in the university, and said that research universities could no longer meet their operating costs, no matter how high the tuition went. In the final stage of commoditization, universities are forced to be businesses and realize that to survive they must make a profit.

Conclusion

Throughout this century capitalism has been using institutions of higher education for its own ends. As corporate capitalism has undergone several crises of its own, business and the state have mobilized universities to create new products and a skilled workforce, to provide a place for unemployed workers and to help with the management of both workers and consumption. The various pressures exerted to achieve these ends have produced enormous changes in higher education in this country. At each juncture, changes were made that led to the transformation of higher education into an industry: from the turn of the century when universities were 'rationalized', through the imagined 'booms' of 1945 and 1960, to the invented crisis in enrolments of the 1970s. By rationalizing the productive sector (formerly known as teachers) and dedicating the lion's share of resources to the management of the university and the marketing of image at the expense of education itself, universities have moved from being like business to being business. Commoditization, the cumulative effect of a series of instrumental, marketplace-driven responses to fiscal and legitimacy crises directly caused by the actions of the state and corporate sector, is the result.

What has been lost is democratic and participatory education, once an institution at the heart of our cultural ideal, free from considerations of corporate bureaucratic efficiency or profit rationale. While many staff and students are in conflict about their position in this sea of change – and like the frog in Aesop's fable, who was cooked before he realized the water was boiling, the people who work in these situations have been slow to perceive them – there seem to be some developing patterns. Students and teachers alike are recognizing the threat to legitimacy and raising questions of what knowledge and for whom. Faculty members are realizing the extent to which they have been proletarianized and mobilizing to deal with these realities. For them, as for the university, it is a matter of survival.

Notes

1. For a more in-depth analysis of commoditization, see Shumar (1991). See also Taussig (1980), Mitchell (1986) and Amariglio and Callari (1989).
2. For a detailed analysis of the contradictory trends in higher education in the early twentieth century, see Noble (1977) and Barrow (1990).
3. The baby-boomers, raised on television and born of relative affluence, expected material well-being but were disappointed. As Bourdieu (1984: 143–4) says in *Distinction*, this is the generation that expected things to get forever better and in fact experienced decline. And to add insult to injury, they also experienced what Bourdieu calls degree inflation. So many people had college degrees they became a glut on the job market. The college degree lost much of its aura when it became so much less rare.
4. See note 3.
5. This process is very much like Harvey's (1989) description of the flexible workforce in corporations. After 1973 corporations begin to use a larger pool of temporary workers, part-time workers and hired consultants to increase the companies' productivity and respond to a less stable market for goods and services. Harvey calls this process 'flexible accumulation'.
6. It might be interesting to point out at this juncture that from ethnographic observation I have noticed an interesting pattern of administrator ideology. One popular joke among administrators at many colleges is 'if we could just get rid of the faculty, this would be a nice place to work'. That ideology, although spoken as a joke, has a very real feel to it. Many staff are in situations with old equipment, decaying buildings and scarce resources, while administrations have a lot more of the material resources.
7. In the early 1980s the federal government made a significant change in policy on federally funded research (Noble 1989; Cowan 1990). Rather than the federal government holding the patent, now the university would hold the patent. This change opened a floodgate of transformation of the university. Corporations, as Barrow and Noble have shown, had been using universities for research since the turn of the century and corporate priorities had greatly influenced the structure and orientation of university research. This new move, however, made it possible for corporations to practise flexible accumulation by closing their own R&D facilities and farming that work out to the universities.

   Corporations gave universities large grants targeted for research equipment, which the university could use to obtain federal matching funds. The corporation then laid down some guidelines. Money from the grant could not be used for maintenance. Maintenance was to come out of the university's operating budget. And any inventions resulting from this research would be patented by the university but leased exclusively to the corporation. Now the corporation had the best of both worlds. The research took place in an environment free from cost-effectiveness constraints on creativity, it was publicly sponsored, corporate cost was kept to a minimum and there was a guaranteed return. It was the breakdown of Fordism and the new image of flexible accumulation that made this new arrangement possible.

The impact on universities has been dramatic. In effect, corporations solved their cost problems by creating a permanent crisis in American universities. Tuition costs have soared. Even very wealthy and prestigious universities now need to use temporary and/or part-time faculty members. Students are channelled into two groups: those who will be sold a prestigious diploma at a high price; and the exceptional few to benefit from capitalism, those destined for the prestige research teams.

References

Albertsen, N. (1988) Postmodernism, post-Fordism, and critical social theory, *Environment and Planning D: Society and Space*, 6, 339–65.

Althusser, L. (1971) Ideology and the ideological state apparatuses, in *Lenin and Philosophy*. New York: Monthly Review Press.

Amariglio, J. and Callari, A. (1989) Marxian value theory and the problem of the subject: the role of commodity fetishism, *Rethinking Marxism*, 2(3), 31–60.

Anderson, B. (1983) *Imagined Communities: Reflections on the Origin and Spread of Nationalism*. London, Verso Editions and NLB.

Apple, M.W. (1982) *Education and Power*. London, Routledge and Kegan Paul.

Aronowitz, S. and Giroux, H.A. (1985) *Education Under Siege*. South Hadley, MA, Bergin and Garvey.

Barrow, C.W. (1990) *Universities and the Capitalist State*. Madison, University of Wisconsin Press.

Bluestone, B. and Harrison, B. (1982) *The Deindustrialization of America*. New York, Basic Books.

Bourdieu, P. (1984) *Distinction: a Social Critique of the Judgment of Taste*. Cambridge, MA, Harvard University Press.

Boyer, E. (1988) *College: the Undergraduate Experience in America*. The Carnegie Foundation for the Advancement of Teaching. New York, Harper and Row.

Clark, B.R. (1987) Planning for excellence: the condition of the professoriate, *Planning for Higher Education*, 16(1), 1–8.

Cowan, R. (1990) Academia un-incorporated, *Z Magazine*, February.

Finkelstein, M.J. (1984) *The American Academic Profession*. Columbus, Ohio State University Press.

Foley, D. (1990) *Learning Capitalist Culture: Deep in the Heart of Tejas*. Philadelphia, University of Pennsylvania Press.

Grassmuck, K. (1990) Big increases in academic-support staffs prompt growing concerns on campuses, *Chronicle of Higher Education*, 28 March.

Habermas, J. (1975) *Legitimation Crisis*. Boston, Beacon Press.

Haraway, D. (1989) *Primate Visions: Gender, Race and Nature in the World of Modern Science*. London, Routledge.

Hardy, C. (1987) Turnaround strategies in universities, *Planning for Higher Education*, 16(1), 9–23.

Harvey, D. (1989) *The Condition of Postmodernity*. Oxford, Basil Blackwell.

Kerr, C. (1982) *The Uses of the University*, 3rd edn. Cambridge, MA, Harvard University Press.

Lash, S. and Urry, J. (1987) *The End of Organized Capitalism.* Madison, University of Wisconsin Press.

Mitchell, W.J.T. (1986) *Iconology: Image, Text, Ideology.* Chicago, University of Chicago Press.

Nasaw, D. (1981) *Schooled to Order.* Oxford, Oxford University Press.

National Center for Educational Statistics (1989) *The Condition of Education 1989: Volume 2, Postsecondary Education.* Washington, DC, US Department of Education, Government Printing Office.

Newman, F. (1985) *Higher Education and the American Resurgence.* A Carnegie Foundation Special Report. Princeton, NJ, Carnegie Foundation for the Advancement of Teaching.

Noble, D. (1977) *America by Design: Science, Technology and the Rise of Corporate Capitalism.* New York, Alfred A. Knopf.

Noble, D. (1989) The multinational multiversity, *Z Magazine*, April.

Ohmann, R. (1987) *Politics of Letters.* Middletown, CT, Wesleyan University Press.

Seymour, D.T. (1988) Higher education as a corporate enterprise, *The College Board Review*, 147, Spring.

Shumar, W. (1991) College for sale: an ethnographic analysis of the commoditization of higher education, Philadelphia, Temple University, unpublished PhD dissertation.

Smith, P. (1990) *Killing the Spirit: Higher Education in America.* New York, Penguin Books.

Sussman, A. (1981) University governance through a rose-colored lens: NLRB v. Yeshiva, in P.B. Kurland and G. Casper (eds) *1980 Supreme Court Review.* Chicago, University of Chicago Press.

Taussig, M.T. (1980) *The Devil and Commodity Fetishism in South America.* Chapel Hill, University of North Carolina Press.

Uhl, N.P. (ed.) (1983) *Using Research for Strategic Planning.* San Francisco, Jossey-Bass.

United States Reports (1982) National Labor Relations Board v. Yeshiva, *United States Reports*, 444 (October term 1979), 672–706.

Wiebe, R.H. (1967) *The Search for Order: 1877–1920.* New York, Hill and Wang.

6

The Culture of Assessment

William G. Tierney and Robert A. Rhoads

Introduction

Over the past decade both the federal and state governments in the United States have argued that higher education should become more 'accountable'. Some might posit that the literature on accountability and assessment has become the primary concern in American higher education. The manner in which critics raise their arguments primarily derives from an ideology based on human capital that defines educational goals as outcomes that can be measured. In essence, the critics have tried to create an input–output model for academe that parallels measures of effectiveness and efficiency in the corporate sector.

Assessment efforts also implicitly or explicitly underscore who is in control and who is not. That is, administrators and outside evaluators (accreditation agencies, federal legislators, state educational offices) have tried to assert more authority about what counts for quality on campuses. To a much lesser degree, faculty members have been engaged as 'experts' who might also participate as arbitrators of quality. Students are largely ignored, as if they have no role in the discussion.

In this chapter we investigate how the discourse of higher education in the United States has shifted from a language of access and equity to a concern for outcomes and assessment. In turn, we consider whose interests have been advanced, and whose have been muffled or forgotten. We argue that the language of the 1960s and 1970s was primarily a debate pertaining to how higher education might respond to the needs of groups previously excluded from academe – women, people of colour and the underclass. In the 1980s and 1990s the discussion has moved in the opposite direction; instead of discussions about increasing access, the debate has largely focused on how to exclude individuals from post-secondary education. Although one might choose any number of activities as evidence for such a proposition – attacks on affirmative action and reduced financial aid policies are but two examples – we focus here on the consequences of what we call a 'culture of assessment'.

We utilize Braverman's insights pertaining to labour process theory to examine this 'culture of assessment', extending his idea in two ways. First, however helpful Braverman was in delineating a class analysis of society, he insufficiently considered other ideological forms of control, such as gender, race and sexual orientation. Second, we extend Braverman's ideas about economic capital by a consideration of cultural capital. Thus, in addition to Braverman we call upon the work of individuals such as Apple, Giroux and McLaren to interpret the culture and ideology of academe; in particular we utilize Pierre Bourdieu's notion of 'cultural capital' as a way to understand the division of labour in the academic enterprise.

Accordingly, the chapter divides into three sections. First, we review the literature on assessment and delineate how the argument has been structured. We concentrate on the nature of the argument and who controls the discussion. We then turn to an analysis of assessment by utilizing the work of Braverman, Apple and Bourdieu, among others. We suggest that the manner in which questions have been raised conveniently overlooks traditional notions of education as an effort concerned with issues of democracy, social justice and empowerment. We argue that a wealth of learning experiences cannot be reduced to measurement outputs, and that assessment ought not to drive the teaching and learning process if we are concerned with transformative education. In doing so, we work from critical notions of society based on a social constructionist perspective. We conclude with a consideration about how we might reorient the discourse away from elitist notions of excellence and towards a concern for issues of democracy. We consider who ought to be involved, how issues might be evaluated and who might decide such matters.

The discourse of assessment

What are the values and beliefs inherent in the assessment movement? The answer comes by way of a description of assessment as it has emerged over the past decade. We organize the discussion around three themes derived from the assessment literature: crisis, change and control.

The academic crisis

The assessment movement initially had two stimuli. Internal to colleges and universities, administrators felt that their institutions needed to adapt to the changing needs of the external environment. Increased competition for students among colleges and universities coupled with declines in federal and state support created a sense of urgency in academe. This urgency was translated into a decision-making style labelled 'adaptive strategy' (Tierney 1989), where students became 'markets' that needed to be 'captured', and education became a 'product' that had to be 'sold' to 'consumers'. The transformation from institutions of teaching and learning to institutions of markets and consumers logically brought about a desire for measurable outputs. Competition in the marketplace necessitated that institutional managers be able to tell the consumer how their product differed from, and was better than, a competitor's. Hence, the internal stimulus for assessment measures and student-oriented outcomes was borne.

Externally, national and state critics tied the economic and social problems that American society faced to the failure of educational institutions. Indeed, a torrent of reports delineated the problems in academe (Newman 1985; National Governor's Association 1986; Boyer 1987). Most studies argued for dramatically improved educational standards as the solution to America's woes. In a national report produced by the Study Group on the Conditions of Excellence in American Higher Education (1984), for example, Americans were informed that the Study Group sought 'ways to renew the trust our students and our Nation place in higher education, especially in the undergraduate years' (p. 1). From the report's perspective, the United States had lost its competitiveness because of the erosion of academic standards. The curriculum had become a 'cafeteria' without any coherent menu, and postsecondary institutions had ceased training individuals for the increased demands of the workplace.

The solution to renewing trust in higher education was the 'pursuit of excellence' – the catch-all phrase of the 1980s. As the Study Group wrote, 'To assure excellence, our colleges, community colleges, and universities should establish and maintain high standards of student and institutional performance. The results (or "outcomes") of the education offered by these institutions must be measured against their clearly and publicly articulated standards of performance' (p. 3). Excellence thus became grounded in measurable student performance.

In *To Reclaim a Legacy*, William Bennett (1984) defined the problems of American higher education as rooted in the humanities, which needed to be reconfigured and re-established as the core of higher learning. Bennett also pointed out that higher education had heretofore escaped the scrutiny of the public eye and that the situation 'should and will change'. He went on to note:

> With more than half of all high school graduates now going on to some form of postsecondary education, the public – parents, employers, alumni, and the students themselves – is beginning to ask, and has the right to ask, whether today's colleges and universities are offering to America's youth an education worthy of our heritage.
>
> (Bennett 1984: ii–iii)

The critics offered up alarming statistics to prove their case about the failure of post-secondary education: undergraduate and graduate examinations (SAT and GRE scores) had continually declined; more college students dropped out rather than completed their degree; narrow vocational specialities were chosen over the more intellectually demanding sciences and humanities. Consequently, as the report by the Association of American Colleges (AAC) concluded, 'There must be ways of demonstrating to state legislatures, students, and the public at large that the colleges know what they are doing (or do not know) and that they are doing it well (or poorly)' (AAC 1985: 33).

The critics believed that the individuals who caused these problems were, logically enough, the people who had been involved. Lack of presidential authority and faculty leadership came in for a good deal of criticism. As Bennett (1984: 2) noted, 'The decline was caused in part by a failure of nerve and faith on the part of many college faculties and administrators, and persists because of a vacuum in educational leadership.' The AAC (1985: 2) report continued: 'Central to the troubles and to the solutions are the professors.'

Yet the real culprit was neither the faculty nor the administration; rather, the problem was the context in which academic institutions found themselves. As Saul Bellow noted in a foreword to Allan Bloom's *Closing of the American Mind*, 'The university has become inundated and saturated with the backflow of society's problems' (Bloom 1987: 18). The 'problems' Bellow referred to were previously under-represented constituencies in academe such as people of colour and women. It is these people, the critics argued, who had caused the curriculum to become watered down and the goals of academe to become trivialized. In short, educational access had been identified as the central cause of the problem. The AAC report elaborated:

> As laudable as it may be as an ideal, the widening of access also has contributed to the confusions that have beset the baccalaureate experience. The tension between democratic values and the effort to maintain standards for an undergraduate education can be creative, but too often numbers and political considerations have prevailed over quality.
>
> (AAC 1985: 5)

The report prepared by the Commission for Educational Quality (1985: 2) agreed:

> The issue of access has dominated higher education since the 1960's. Quality became a secondary concern, in part because the early covenant did not specify standards for the programs to which access should be provided. . .as a way of extending access to all levels of higher education, faculty and administrators lowered standards for courses, student promotion, and graduation.

Academe seemed engulfed in a crisis. The managers of the enterprise – faculty members and administrators – had not done enough to reconfigure and redefine academe in order to avoid fiscal exigency, the public had lost confidence, America's strength as a nation was in jeopardy and institutional excellence had been compromised on behalf of access.

A time for change

With the recognition that American higher education was in a state of crisis the time was ripe for academic change. What was needed, the critics argued, was greater verification that higher education was in fact achieving what it purported to accomplish. Assessment was seen as the answer.

Boyer *et al.* (1987) noted that in the span of one year American higher education had gone from only a handful of states with assessment initiatives to two-thirds of the states that had some form of assessment in their plans. El-Khawas (1987) reported that three-quarters of colleges and universities were discussing assessment, half were developing assessment plans and eight out of ten expected to introduce some form of assessment in the next few years.

The expansion of assessment initiatives was described by Ewell (1990) as the 'changing voice' of the states. He characterized this changing voice by five key precepts: (a) higher education was no longer an isolated enterprise; (b) higher education had to prove its worth to get state investment; (c) higher education institutions, with all their expertise, should be able to direct its own assessment programmes; (d) higher education could not be as complicated as some claim; and (e) if assessment did not move forward institutions would suffer. Ewell went on to note that these imperatives reflected a changing view of higher education and new economic realities in the nation:

> Once viewed primarily as a provided 'public service' whose chief concerns were equitable access and operational efficiency, public higher education is increasingly being viewed as a strategic investment. As such, its major perceived payoff lies in such areas as enhanced economic development and increases in common skills among potential workers and citizens.
>
> (Ewell 1990: 5)

Clearly, from this point of view higher education was seen as the training ground for corporate and economic development. Post-secondary education was neither simply an intellectual enterprise for individual gain nor a socializing experience for democracy; rather, the health of the country demanded academic accountability.

In examining the nature of assessment, Terenzini (1989) suggested three questions as key to understanding assessment initiatives:

1. What is the purpose of assessment?
2. What is the level of assessment?
3. What is to be assessed?

Thus far we have dealt principally with the critics' response to the first question: assessment was a source for validating the learning process and for marketing the institution. In the following paragraphs we deal more extensively with discussions associated with the latter two questions: the level of assessment and what is to be assessed.

Although many might have agreed with the critics about the need for assessment, debates about who and what should be assessed have been major barriers to the success of assessment initiatives. Does one assess academic programmes or students? What 'outcomes' does one try to measure? Clearly, as Jacob *et al.* (1987: 19) have argued, outcomes may be considered a 'wide range of phenomena that can be influenced by the educational experience'. Student outcomes may include knowledge, skills, attitudes, values and/or behaviours. In actuality, however, those outcomes, which have become components of most assessment programmes, are not all the possible phenomena but merely those that could be operationalized and quantitatively measured, principally through psychometric tools. Even Astin's (1985, 1991) talent development approach, which at first glance seemed sensitive to the shortcomings of operationalism and measurement, in the end resorted to an over-dependence on measurement, statistical analysis and comprehensive databases. Individualized notions of talent development that Astin so highly praised became lost in the need to produce aggregate information where quantification took precedence.

Essentially, two overarching frameworks of assessment surfaced. One perspective emphasized assessing student knowledge and abilities. How well did students write? How much maths did they know? How much history did they understand? This form of assessment fell in line with discussions about national standards and competency criteria. Students could be given standardized tests and recognized experts would be able to evaluate the strengths and weaknesses of individuals, programmes and institutions. States and federal agencies were the principal advocates for this format.

The second perspective emphasized a 'value added' notion of higher learning. This kind of assessment was institutionally based and sought to test how much students learned while they attended college. Students might be tested on their writing and maths skills, for example, when they entered college and later retested when they graduated. The significance of the gain in the test scores would then be attributed to the institution's teaching and learning environment. This format tried to take into account the quality of the 'raw materials' that an institution had to deal with, so that a community college would not be unfairly judged against Ivy League institutions.

In actuality, these two forms of assessment are more complementary to one another than different, for they are based on similar assumptions. Both conceptions attempt to measure student learning by way of quantitatively designed student tests. The explicit assumption is that if we are able to demonstrate how much students learn, we could, in turn, determine if institutions and programmes achieve 'quality'. Assessment, as the primary tool of accountability, is thus seen as a source for gaining greater control over higher education institutions and specifically over the teaching and learning process. In this light, the discourse of assessment was not only a discussion about institutional accountability; it was also a discourse of control.

Issues of control

An important aspect of assessment relates to the source of assessment initiatives: from where do these initiatives derive? Where is the locus of control? This question revolves around issues of autonomy and who ultimately decides on the legitimacy of an assessment programme, and in turn on the purpose of an educational institution.

As noted, assessment has come to a certain degree from internal actors such as college administrators, and to a much greater degree from external sources. State legislatures and boards of higher education, in particular, have played central roles in formulating assessment plans for public institutions. Ewell *et al.* (1990: 5) highlighted the perception that assessment was seen by state legislatures as 'a powerful "lever for change" '. Relatedly, Ewell (1990: 21) noted that, 'If the "new accountability" is real, a substantially more proactive state leadership strategy is called for – one that attempts to actively shape institutional agendas to embrace improvements in quality while at the same time providing institutions with sufficient resources and decision latitude to flexibly undertake needed innovation.'

Internally, administrators have taken the lead with regard to implementing assessment plans. In particular, institutional research offices or newly created 'directors of assessment' have developed plans for institutional assessment. Thus, it turns out that the architects of assessment are also the ones who identified the crisis and determined that institutions need to be held more accountable.

A brief review is in order. The discourse of crisis was related to notions that the United States must be number one economically and politically and, if not, then education must be failing. To solve the problems of higher education, increased public scrutiny was seen as the answer. Through assessment, learning outcomes could be quantified and analysed, thus removing the lid from the black box that was seen as the college classroom. In enacting a culture of assessment, legislatures and administrators gained greater control over the academy, the curriculum and the multiple constituencies involved in post-secondary education. We now turn to an interpretation of these efforts.

Assessment: values and beliefs

In the previous section we asked what the values and beliefs inherent in the assessment movement were. We now extend that discussion by considering how these values and beliefs have in turn defined academic knowledge, work and power. We suggest that all three concepts are inextricably related to one another, that they are central components for enacting change in academe and that the movement for assessment has generated particular definitions of each term.

Defining knowledge

What we test and the educational outcomes we desire help to define what we mean by 'knowledge'. The processes in which we engage to reach these decisions also reflect definitions of what counts for knowledge and what does not. When we centralize decision-making about what ought to be assessed and what ought not to be assessed, we create a portrait where some individuals are experts who rightfully define knowledge and other individuals do not have the skills to participate a discussion about defining knowledge. In effect, the assessment movement has tried to circumscribe knowledge in a manner that creates specific curricular and pedagogic arrangements.

To be more clear, knowledge may be defined in three ways: knowledge *that, how* and *to* (Apple and Jungck 1990: 233). Knowledge *that* is the easiest knowledge to assess on standardized tests since it pertains to factual information, such as that Mozart lived in the eighteenth century or that Shakespeare died in 1616. Knowledge *how* pertains to skills, such as knowing how to use the library to find out when Shakespeare died. Knowledge *to*:

> is what critical theorists call 'dispositional knowledge' such as the values and ethics that guide life in community. What it means *to* be a member of a democracy, or *to* work for social justice, or *to* understand one's racial heritage are examples of dispositional knowledge.
>
> (Tierney 1992: 140)

Clearly, knowledge *to* is not the kind of knowledge that is amenable to test-taking or even definition in terms of outcomes. Dispositional knowledge pertains more to the processes one engages in on a daily basis than it does to any fixed end-point on a multiple choice exam. Standardized assessment criteria give priority to factual information that demonstrates thinking skills, but not norms, values or beliefs that ostensibly guide future action.

There are many reasons why advocates of student outcomes do not measure dispositional knowledge. Some argue that values ought to be taught in the home and not in the classroom. Others believe that in order to teach dispositional knowledge one must first master the other forms of knowledge. In this light, there is a hierarchy to learning, and one must first learn facts and then skills, before entering into a discussion about values. Still another practical argument is that knowledge *to* is not easily adapted to a standardized test.

One failure of the assessment movement is in its inability to confront more forcefully the dilemmas these rationales pose. A wealth of literature has pointed out how educational institutions are cultural sites where knowledge gets defined. As McLaren (1991: 237) notes, the culture of schooling 'is fundamentally a struggle over meanings and about meanings. It is a struggle over events, representations and about meanings.' However, the definition of knowledge used by assessment advocates works from the assumption that knowledge is static and preordained. Such a notion has its epistemological roots in the positivist belief that reality exists, as opposed to the social constructionist stance we have adopted here; that is, that reality is constructed through social interaction. The primary failure of the positivist approach is that it is based on a notion of shared moral values that does not bring into question how those values are defined; in effect, students are never taught about how they might become critically engaged with dispositional knowledge. By the primacy the assessment movement gives to testing, students are taught that facts are more important than values, that some facts are more important than others and that some individuals are repositories of these facts and others are not. Further, these definitions of knowledge act in concert with how academic work has been reorganized.

Defining work

Braverman's analyses highlight the centrality of coming to terms with how work is organized. We suggest that it is as crucial to understand how academic labour is being reorganized as it is to understand how other forms of labour change. The importance of understanding how academic labour is reorganized not only highlights how one occupation's social relations have changed, it also underscores how the purposes and goals of the organization have been reorganized. An analysis of the academic workplace, then, points out how the occupation has changed, which in turn has changed the nature of the social relations of the enterprise. Braverman (1974: 72) is helpful here:

> The social division of labor divides society among occupations, each adequate to a branch of production; the detailed division of labor destroys occupations considered in this sense, and renders the work inadequate to carry through any complete production process. In capitalism, the social division of labor is enforced chaotically and anarchically by the market, while the workshop division of labor is imposed by planning and control.

The assessment effort is an example of how academic labour gets reorganized to meet more suitably the needs of the marketplace. On the one hand, we have seen how academic managers adopted corporate language and defined labour in a particular manner. On the other hand, we have seen how the faculty's expertise was superseded, segmented and redefined. Faculty members are no longer the individuals who have control over the 'product' – the students. Instead, assessors exist who will plan what needs to be taught and how well it has been taught.

What we are suggesting is that the assessment movement has defined teaching essentially as a labour process, even though the 'labour' is in part intellectual. Teaching is a labour process different from working on an assembly line, of course, but the processes involved in both tasks fit within the same capitalist framework. From this perspective labour is a process whose forms and activities are defined by the end result, the product.

Assessment has enabled the management and control of the process and product to be run by experts, so that complicated tasks have been broken down into segmented activities. Planning occurs not by the 'workers' – in this case, the faculty members – but by administrators or individuals and groups such as state legislators. The result is that the individuals involved in doing the job have lost sight of the entire process and, in consequence, have lost control over their own labour. In turn, they also have lost a particular skill: the skill of assessment and evaluation.

Historically, the clearest example of this process was seen in the Tayloristic principles of scientific management (Taylor 1987: 66), where authority was centralized and work was compartmentalized. 'The managers assume', noted Braverman (1974: 112), 'the burden of gathering together all of the traditional knowledge which in the past has been possessed by the workmen and then of classifying, tabulating and reducing this knowledge to rules, laws, and formulae.' A further consequence is that this expertise for the entire enterprise becomes the exclusive province of administrators and thus the managers gain control over the entire process.

It is incumbent to observe that the assessment movement in the United States came at a time when more women and people of colour entered the ranks of the faculty than at any other time in the history of higher education. Thus, assessment's challenge to faculty autonomy and control came about when historically disenfranchised groups began – however slowly – to achieve power and voice in the academy. Assessment, then, might be seen as a tool of control where managers exert more authority, and academic labour becomes deskilled and less powerful.

Defining power

The previous sections have intimated how the assessment movement has defined power. Definitions of knowledge privilege some and silence others. Definitions of work give increased authority to managers and less voice to the academic workers. We extend that thinking by way of Bourdieu's concept of 'cultural capital', which refers to the general cultural background, knowledge and skills that get passed on in educational settings (McLaren 1989: 190). We raise this issue here because Braverman's analysis primarily focuses on economic capital. To be sure, the movement for assessment does have economic consequences that are tied to larger capital interests. However, cultural capital points out how education is used to confer particular rights and privileges, which in turn affects economic capital (Bourdieu 1986).

We are suggesting that assessment acts as a filter which seeks to control the 'backflow' of society's problems. As a defining agent of what an individual knows, and what an individual is supposed to know, assessment acts as a unifier. As Bourdieu (1977: 339) notes:

Academic culture is a common code enabling all those possessing that code to attach the same meaning to the same words, the same types of behavior, and the same work. School [becomes] the fundamental factor in achieving cultural consensus.

Thus, education in general, and the assessment movement in particular, reproduces power relationships that already exist in society. The educational system merely mirrors the demands of the state, so that institutions are 'incapable of affirming the specificity of its principles of evaluation' (Bourdieu 1977: 494), because they may conflict with or challenge the norms within society. Instead, the state defines knowledge in a particular way, and educational institutions see to it that such definitions are implemented.

The consequence is that educational institutions are used by society to reproduce society rather than change society. A unitary definition of knowledge, a segmentary division of labour and the reinforcement of traditional lines of authority and power in effect lessen education's role as a change agent. Assessment becomes a controlling force where checks may be placed on who enters academe, who controls academe and who exits from academe with cultural capital.

Redefining assessment

We conclude with a caveat. Our argument here has not been to dismiss assessment as entirely mistaken, or to paint those in the assessment movement as academic villains in an outmoded Marxian play. Assessment does have a role in redefining education, and many of the central characters desire an educational system that is more democratic. The state, for example, has often played a key role in bringing about positive change on campuses in the United States. Colleges and universities adhere to affirmative action and equal opportunity not because of proactive policies, but because the state and federal governments mandated equal employment policies. Access for the disabled and statements of non-discrimination against under-represented groups on college campuses came about not because of enlightened faculty members, but because of federal and state laws. Consequently, to paint the state as intrusive, or the staff as a group who have the interests of the powerless in mind, seems historically mistaken. Similarly, the idea that instructors, programmes and institutions ought to know how well they are serving their students is not wrong; indeed, in a democratic society such an idea is imperative.

However, our concern is with the manner in which assessment has been structured. As we discussed, assessment came about when different individuals either decried the loss of academic standards or sought to think of students as markets to be captured. Assessment has tried to create abstract standards which all individuals need to meet, and these standards revolve around a static conception of knowledge. Rather than a democratic discourse where all of an institution's citizens are involved in developing dispositional knowledge, assessment has tried to create a sharper division between managers and workers and to reinforce norms rather than bring them into question.

A democratic notion of assessment would more concretely engage students and staff in ongoing dialogues about the processes in which they are engaged. The point is not so much to develop minimalist criteria that everyone should meet, but to develop pedagogic encounters where knowledge is self-reflexively argued over and understood. Nancy Hartsock (1983: 90) has astutely observed: 'Theories of power are implicitly theories of community.' One could extend her comment to theories of assessment as well. A critical theory of assessment and community reconfigures power and knowledge. We assess, then, how well we enable students to find their own voices and histories rather than merely learn the rules of community that reinforce unequal relationships.

We need to be clear here. At a basic level one might find it difficult to disagree with the assessment movement. Of course students should be able to read, write and communicate. Of course students should have employable skills. But high standards and a commitment to excellence are not the sole property of those who advocate student outcomes. We are suggesting that unequal power relationships and cultural and economic capital will not be changed simply by advocating high standards. Rather, efforts at assessment need to begin by accepting students as co-learners who have keen insights about the educational process (Tierney 1992). In effect, the focus of a community's education ought to revolve around discussions of dispositional knowledge, and students need to become the architects of assessment, rather than its passive recipients.

Note

This chapter was prepared partially with financial support from the US Department of Education's Office of Educational Research and Improvement (OERI) Grant R117610037. The opinions expressed herein do not reflect the position or policy of OERI, and no official endorsement should be inferred.

References

Apple, M.W. and Jungck, S. (1990) 'You don't have to be a teacher to teach this unit': teaching, technology, and gender in the classroom, *American Educational Research Journal*, 27(2), 227–51.

Association of American Colleges (1985) *Integrity in the College Curriculum: a Report to the Academic Community*. Washington, DC, Association of American Colleges.

Astin, A.W. (1985) *Achieving Educational Excellence*. San Francisco, Jossey-Bass.

Astin, A.W. (1991) *Assessment for Excellence: the Philosophy and Practice of Assessment and Evaluation in Higher Education*. New York, American Council on Education, Macmillan Publishing Company.

Bennett, W.J. (1984) *To Reclaim a Legacy: a Report on the Humanities in Higher Education.* Washington, DC, National Endowment for the Humanities.

Bloom, A. (1987) *The Closing of the American Mind.* New York, Simon and Schuster.

Bourdieu, P. (1977) Systems of education and systems of thought, *International Social Science Journal,* 19(3), 338–58.

Bourdieu, P. (1986) The forms of capital, in J.G. Richardson (ed.) *Handbook of Theory and Research in the Sociology of Education.* New York: Greenwood Press, 241–58.

Boyer, C.M., Ewell, P.T., Finney, J.E. and Mingle, J.R. (1987) Assessment and outcomes measurement, *AAHE Bulletin,* 39(7), 8–12.

Boyer, E. (1987) *College: the Undergraduate Experience in America.* New York, Harper & Row.

Braverman, H. (1974) *Labor and Monopoly Capital.* New York, Monthly Review Press.

Commission for Educational Quality (1985) *Access to Quality Undergraduate Education.* Atlanta, GA, Southern Region Education Board.

El-Khawas, E. (1987) Colleges reclaim the assessment initiative, *Educational Record,* 68(2), 54–8.

Ewell, P.T. (1990) *Assessment and the 'New Accountability': a Challenge for Higher Education's Leadership.* Denver, CO, Education Commission of the States.

Ewell, P., Finney, J. and Lenth, C. (1990) Filling in the mosaic: the emerging pattern of state-based assessment, *AAHE Bulletin,* 42(8), 3–5.

Hartsock, N. (1983) *Money, Sex, and Power: toward a Feminist Historical Materialism.* New York, Longman.

Jacob, M., Astin, A. and Ayala, F. Jr (1987) *College Student Outcomes Assessment: a Talent Development Perspective.* ASHE-ERIC Higher Education Report No. 7. Washington, DC, Association for the Study of Higher Education.

McLaren, P. (1989) *Life in Schools.* New York, Longman.

McLaren, P. (1991) Decentering culture: postmodernism, resistance, and critical pedagogy, in N.B. Wyner (ed.) *Current Perspectives on the Culture of Schools.* Boston, Brookline, 231–57.

National Governor's Association (1986) *Time for Results.* Washington, DC, National Governor's Association.

Newman, F. (1985) *Higher Education and the American Resurgence.* New York, Carnegie Foundation for the Advancement of Teaching.

Study Group on the Conditions of Excellence in American Higher Education (1984) *Involvement in Learning: Realizing the Potential of American Higher Education.* Washington, DC, National Institute of Education.

Taylor, F.W. (1987) The principles of scientific management (originally published 1916), in J.M. Shafritz and J.S. Ott (eds) *Classics of Organization Theory,* 2nd edn. Chicago, Dorsey Press, 66–81.

Terenzini, P.T. (1989) Assessment with open eyes, *Journal of Higher Education,* 60(6), 644–64.

Tierney, W.G. (1989) *Curricular Landscapes, Democratic Vistas: Transformative Leadership in Higher Education.* New York, Praeger.

Tierney, W.G. (1992) *Official Encouragement, Institutional Discouragement: Minorities in Academe – the Native American Experience.* Norwood, NJ, Praeger.

7

Entrepreneurial Science and Intellectual Property in Australian Universities

Sheila Slaughter and Larry Leslie

In the 1980s and early 1990s, industrialized nations had to deal with the growth of transnational corporations and the globalization of labour markets. These worldwide changes often created great difficulties for the economies of industrialized nation states. The political-economic response of English speaking industrialized countries – the USA, UK, Australia and Canada – generally was the initiation of conservative economic policies designed to invigorate domestic private sector industries so they could compete more successfully in global markets (Phillips 1990; Bartlett and Steele 1992). These conservative domestic fiscal policies had implications for the financing of higher education. Generally, higher education financing in these countries tended to move away from student grants, basic research subsidies, and state subsidies to higher education to block grants, student loans, research support designed to serve university-industry partnerships, and state categorical grants to institutions, and even to decreases in overall support for higher education. In turn, these changes in higher education financing influenced the nature of professional labour in universities and colleges in many ways. We will explore aspects of these changes in this chapter, using data from Australian universities.

Before turning to our data, we want to touch briefly on the higher education finance policies and national science policies that set the stage for the drama that professional labour is now playing out. Although the UK initiated more Draconian higher education finance and research and development (R&D) reforms than any other of the English speaking countries, the impetus for reform probably began in the USA in the early 1970s. American elites, in an effort to cope with the social chaos of student unrest and the increasing cost of ever more accessible higher education, began to formulate new higher education finance policies. Associations like the Committee on Economic Development (CED), an organization composed of 200 members, most of whom are CEOs of large corporations or presidents of universities, and the Carnegie Commission on Higher Education argued that states should raise tuition fees to cover approximately half of the actual cost of higher education (Committee for Economic Development 1973). Although the major motive of the CED was probably to reduce subsidies for public higher education in order to promote the competitiveness of private higher education, the overall effect was to increase the amount paid by most students. In terms of legislation, at the margin, financial aid shifted from the institution to the student though a broadening of the Pell grant and, later, the student loan programme. Students chose where to spend their aid, becoming more like consumers in a market-like environment.

Student choice of college did not contribute to reduced costs; in the 1980s, as costs soared, the USA, in a reversal of a 100 year policy with regard to state universities, favoured high over low tuition fees for the majority of students and high student aid for the minority of students who were most needy. In an effort to limit tuition fee increases to a politically acceptable level, institutions substituted more and more federal and private research and donated funds for state funds. In other words, more and more professors were engaged in raising external funds, primarily through participating in competition for federal monies, but increasingly through engaging in a variety of business–industry partnerships or through the generation of intellectual property owned by universities. In just a few years, these funds became necessary to keep universities and colleges solvent.

In the 1990s, as fiscal crises in the states continue, professors have been increasingly pushed to generate a portion of their own funding, whether from federal, state or private sources (Slaughter 1993). In the USA, this thrust has been reinforced by several factors. The growing federal deficit means that the federal government is unlikely to bail US colleges and universities out, in terms of either tuition subsidies or federal research monies. Uncertainty over the direction of federal research funding, given the end of the Cold War, increases competition for available R&D monies. Finally, the general ideological tenor of the USA under the Reagan and Bush administrations, as manifested in National Science Foundation policy, has valorized the private sector and encouraged the creation of a host of university–industry partnerships (Smith 1990; Slaughter 1990). Clinton has more supported than decried the Reagan–Bush strategy.

In sum, higher education finance policy and US R&D policy, at both the state and federal levels, converged during the past decade to reduce shares of revenue coming from state governments. To compensate, universities attempted to generate revenues by other means. Similar conditions, although often reached through quite different policy iterations, are found in the UK, Canada and Australia. Generally, university managers have responded to these conditions by creating an environment that encourages, even demands, that faculty members act as entrepreneurs, raising monies to fund their units and departments.

The purpose of this chapter is to explore the ways in which faculty members are responding to these changes. Are these conditions changing the nature of professional labour? If so, in what ways? Theoretically, the chapter examines the changes from two quite different perspectives. One author's approach is neo-classical economics, the other is neo-Marxist sociology. We have relied on our shared conviction that materialism is necessary, though not sufficient, to understanding the changing nature of professional labour.

Method

This chapter reports aspects of two broad studies on the commercialization of science and the pursuit of intellectual property by faculty members and universities in Australia. The first study looked at faculty entrepreneurism across seven universities, surveying all instances of entrepreneurism, broadly defined as activity that generated external funds, in whatever department it occurred. The second study looked at units in three universities, where professors were attempting to convert specific pieces of research to intellectual property, defined as patents, trademarks or copyright, for the commercial market. The first study gives a broad picture that covers a wide variety of professional labour, ranging from consulting, the most heavily engaged-in activity, on one end of the spectrum to the development of intellectual property, a relatively rare occurrence, at the other end of the spectrum. The second study had an in-depth focus on those relatively rare instances, involving eight units at three universities, in which professors and professional staff were labouring to develop intellectual property on which they and the universities hoped to realize profits. Thus, we provide a fairly comprehensive picture of the generation of external monies, whether from routine activities, such as consulting, or relatively unusual activities, such as inventing products, and the effect reliance on external funds had on professional labour. Both studies were done in Australia during a six month period in 1991.[1]

Study 1: Entrepreneurism across universities

Method

For the component of the study dealing with faculty entrepreneurism, broadly defined, seven universities were visited; two of these were examined intensively through documents and interviews. Although central administrators and directors of the university companies were interviewed in all seven cases (total $n = 111$), most of the findings emanated from the two intensive cases. These two universities, one urban and one rural, ranked near the middle and near the bottom, respectively, among Australian universities in terms of revenues received for basic research. In the universities the inquiry began with interviews of central administrators, who were asked about the effects of faculty entrepreneurism within the university, which departments were most active and how pertinent financial records might be obtained. Budgets of internal operating units then were used to select the sample for intensive investigation; roughly, 1 per cent of budget or $20 000 had to come from entrepreneurial activity for the unit to be included. The budgets and related documents yielded information as to the source of revenues and objects of expenditure for the entrepreneurial funds. Next, the unit head and the unit financial officer (usually a department staff member) were interviewed to help identify the departmental activities that met the operational definition of entrepreneurism: 'Activities undertaken with a view to capitalizing on university research or academic expertise through contracts or grants with business or with government agencies seeking solutions to specific public concerns.' The restrictions were that the associated funds must have entered university accounts and that the funded activities must have been applied or developmental in nature (excluding basic research).

Faculty interviews began with the persons identified as project directors. In these and subsequent interviews, other faculty entrepreneurs and non-entrepreneurs were identified, the groups being sampled in approximately equal proportions. Unit personnel critical of the entrepreneurial activities were sought out, and essentially all such persons were interviewed. However, because the sample was limited to units engaged significantly in entrepreneurism, there were few such critics, although there were many with some reservations. The first part of each interview was a subjective discussion of the impacts of entrepreneurism on the unit and the university. The second part employed a technique used in economics research to impute quantitative values for qualitative variables (e.g. Dunn 1977; McMahon 1982; Haveman and Wolfe 1984). Subjects were asked to rate, on a ± 1 to 10 scale, the extent to which the revenues associated with the entrepreneurial activity contributed to the university's mission. Using this as a reference point, subjects then rated the relative benefits and costs of the qualitative criteria. This permitted a very rough means for assigning dollar values to the qualitative criteria and for the calculation of a benefits/cost ratio.

Results

To the extent that revenue sources affect organizational activities (the 'He who pays the piper calls the tune' principle), entrepreneurism impacts academic life. Of course, the extra revenue generated may impact academic life directly. Entrepreneurism accounted for $16.3 million in 1989 in University A and $12.3 million in 1990 in University B, representing 10 and 12 per cent, respectively, of total university operating revenues, amounts that were 18 and 19 per cent as large as recurrent funding of these universities by the Commonwealth.[2]

Activities tended to be concentrated within particular fields. This is in contrast to impressions given in most of the literature, impressions that entrepreneurism and technology transfer apply more or less uniformly across the entire university. Entrepreneurism, as measured by revenues raised, is common in only about one-half of internal academic units and is concentrated in applied natural sciences, agricultural sciences and engineering. The humanities and social sciences are largely absent from the entrepreneurial environment, as defined, as are the more 'basic' natural sciences, such as chemistry, physics, botany and zoology. There are interesting exceptions. Two of the most successful entrepreneurial departments were a physical education and a criminology unit. Among those units engaged significantly, 22 per cent of their revenues derived from entrepreneurial activities, with shares running to about 50 per cent and more in several departments. By far the largest share of expenditures was for salaries and wages, both as supplements for regular faculty members and for employment of additional staff. The pattern of concentration in applied areas is not surprising, in hindsight, and has been reported in isolated cases in the USA (Levin *et al.* 1987; Fairweather 1988).

Although our interviews with administrators and faculty members routinely began with mention of amounts generated, invariably the interviewee turned the discussion immediately to the indirect benefits, to the positive 'spillovers' to the academic life of the departments. Sometimes almost defensively, the subjects lauded the non-pecuniary benefits to the academic units. 'The money is not the important factor', a deputy vice-chancellor interrupted, 'it's the benefits for teaching, for students, and for increasing the overall vitality of the units.' This theme carried over into the second part of the interviews, in which subjects were asked to assign specific values to both costs and benefits of entrepreneurism.

In aggregate the mean indirect (non-pecuniary) benefits to the units and to the university were put at 1.83 times as important as the direct (pecuniary) benefits. The indirect benefit was significantly higher at University B, which focused more on applied programmes and less on basic research. However, the (indirect) benefit/cost ratio was assessed as being larger in A than B. The primary reason was that costs were seen as substantially greater in B than A, the benefit/cost ratio being 3.7:1 in the latter and 2.9:1 in the former. The message gained was that as entrepreneurial activities increase, so do the potential liabilities. At low levels of entrepreneurism, indirect 'costs' are small and almost all stakeholders perceive benefits in excess of costs, but as entrepreneurial activities increase problems begin to arise. One of the important related conclusions from the study was that benefit sharing across the department is important to departmental morale and colleague support for the entrepreneurial activities.[3]

In cases where such activities were highly concentrated in a small number of project areas, sometimes special units (independently organized research centres and institutes) were organized. Where this occurred, in some cases there was poor integration of the work of the special unit with academic activities of the department. This lack of integration was avoided where leaders of the special units created mechanisms to assure collaboration. When the special unit leader was an active member of the department, the problem tended to be overcome. Where special unit staff were not faculty members, the activities of these units tended to become quite unrelated to those of the departments. In such cases, in spite of the unrelatedness, it could still be argued that the university mission was being served because research, service or both were being enhanced by the special units.

The list of indirect costs and benefits put to the subjects in part two of the interview was taken from the literature containing issues related to technology transfer and faculty entrepreneurism. Some of these items have direct implications for the changing nature of academic work. Among the most noteworthy of these are effects on teaching and basic research.

Contrary to the concerns of Blumenthal *et al.* (1986a), Fairweather (1989) and Crean (1990), the respondents viewed the impacts of faculty entrepreneurism on teaching quite favourably. The mean 'benefit' rating for 'the impact of entrepreneurism on teaching' was 5.8; the mean 'cost' rating for 'time taken from teaching' was −1.8. No doubt this result reflected, in part, the fact that the locus of these activities was in applied fields. 'What I learn from my projects is what I teach my students' was a representative comment from an agronomy associate professor. By contrast, a senior lecturer in a basic science department responded: 'The applied research involved is far too esoteric for the undergraduates I teach.'

A parallel concern in the literature is the time taken from (other) research, particularly basic research (Blumenthal *et al.* 1986a, b; Geiger 1989). Again, members of the units where entrepreneurial activity was substantial perceived the benefits to be considerably in excess of the costs (means 6.5 and −2.8, respectively). Most entrepreneurial activities involve research and the common response is that these projects create or add greatly to the research atmosphere of the unit. These units are not generally involved in basic science. 'Our business *is* applied research and this is the only research money available to us', was a response that typified the views of faculty members in applied sciences and engineering.

In brief, there were several other responses that may positively impact the effects of entrepreneurism on the nature of academic work (mean scores in parentheses). Rated highest were improved relations with external bodies (7.0), such as government agencies and industrial firms, and prestige brought to the unit and the university by the entrepreneurial activity (7.0). The activities were seen as leading to future consulting opportunities (5.7), employment opportunities for graduates (5.7), student recruitment (4.9), services being contributed to the unit by project personnel (4.5), equipment gains (4.5) and student employment (4.2).

In contrast and in descending order, indirect costs included consumption of departmental resources (−3.1), the aforementioned loss of teaching and research time, the value of time required of support personnel (−2.1), the substitution by government of entrepreneurially generated funds for government support (−2.1), increased claims on departmental equipment

(−2.0) and negative effects of confidentiality agreements (−1.4). None of these costs, however, was perceived by the subjects to be as large as any of the benefits.

Four additional findings warrant special mention. First, there can be little doubt that a relatively small amount of money can effect major changes in the ecosystem of an academic department. Pfeffer's (1981) 'rule of 10 per cent' holds that a revenue source of as little as 10 per cent or even less can drive the marginal behaviour of an organization. Most of the revenues of Australian universities come in block grant form from government; most additional money comes from entrepreneurial activities. The block grant money is often taken by staff as a given, and in the units studied a disproportionate share of departmental energy is directed at obtaining the marginal money for which entrepreneurs must compete.

Second, one of the specific outcomes of faculty entrepreneurism having an important direct impact on the quality of academic life in Australia has been the creation of 'personal staff accounts', whereby those who generate outside funds are permitted to transfer revenues for work done to university accounts over which they maintain control. Examples of the uses to which these accounts are put are professional travel, equipment purchases, staff support and manuscript preparation.

Third are the status and autonomy enjoyed by the successful entrepreneur. As put by one vice-chancellor, 'God help us if these "million-dollar-a-year" men realize how marketable they are. They can almost write their own ticket. We would never be able to compete with better financed universities if a bidding war should start.' The successful entrepreneur may have enormous autonomy and stature on campus. She may travel internationally almost at will; she may possess great freedom of action on a daily basis; and she may have unusual influence or informal authority on matters related to campus governance and policy. Vice-chancellors and deputy vice-chancellors sometimes speak almost in awe of these powerful persons.

Finally, we should not leave the topic of entrepreneurism in Australian higher education without mentioning full-fees paying overseas students. Although not included in our study, the revenues represented by these students are becoming increasingly important. As much as 65–70 per cent of these fees is allocated to the academic units that enrol these students. These funds provide academic units with enormous flexibility. One dean observed that annually he has from this source 'almost a million dollars to enhance internal activities. It has changed our activities totally.'

Study 2: Generation of intellectual property

Method

The second study reports on interviews with 29 faculty and professional staff about their efforts to develop intellectual property. These staff were located at three universities, one a well-established middle-rank university, one a relatively new, somewhat experimental, university, and the third a top-ranked science and engineering university. The sample was selected by asking central administrators what units were most deeply involved in developing intellectual property. At the first university, a single unit was identified and all unit faculty and professional staff were then interviewed. At the second university, two units were identified; again, all unit faculty and professional staff were interviewed. At the third university, only the heads of departments or units that had patented or otherwise developed and protected intellectual property were interviewed. The shift in emphasis with regard to who was interviewed was dictated by the need to speak with more faculty members who had patented. Although faculty members at the first two universities were deeply involved in developing intellectual property and anticipated patenting in the near future, they had not yet patented.

Of the 29 faculty and professional staff interviewed, 27 (93.1 per cent) were male and two were female (6.8 per cent). Twenty-five (86.2 per cent) were caucasian, and five (13.7 per cent) were asian. Eight (25.8 per cent) were professors, two with personal chairs. Three were associate professors, five senior lecturers, six lecturers and seven research professionals. The two universities where all faculty and professional staff were interviewed looked somewhat different from the institution where only the heads were interviewed. At the two universities, one professor had a personal chair and three were professors, for a total of four (18.1 per cent), two (9 per cent) were associate professors, four senior lecturers (18 per cent), six (27 per cent) lecturers and seven research professionals (31 per cent). Those involved in the development of intellectual property were spread across ranks, but the majority (58 per cent) were in the lower ranks and untenured.

The faculty and professional staff were members of a variety of academic disciplines. One was a basic scientist; six (19.3 per cent) were social scientists; the great majority (24) were applied scientists (77.4 per cent). The products or services with which the staff were involved ranged from policy documents to vaccines, batteries, and water and waste treatments.

Interviews lasted from one to two hours, although occasionally they took three to four hours. In this chapter, the patterns from answers to two of the many questions asked were reported: (1) Why did you become involved in developing intellectual property? (2) What does this mean for your daily work? Answers were reported by rank, because rank seemed to affect answers strongly.

Results

All the eight professors developing intellectual property had become involved because they needed resources that they were afraid neither the institution nor the federal government, the two main sources of research monies, could provide. A number saw intellectual property as a logical extension of the applied work in which they had always engaged.

In terms of economics, assessment of the situation was fairly uniform.

> When I came here. . .the university was going though a rapid growth phase, and optimism and excitement and enthusiasm, and money were flowing to the university, but that period only lasted short time, and we've had more and more problems with financing. And so gradually a bit of pressure has been developing to look elsewhere for money and that was one of the pressures that started us thinking about commercial sources.

Explanations of funding problems usually centred on the globalization of labour, which made competition in world markets difficult for highly paid Australian workers, which led to recession, which, in turn, led to less government monies for research. Although these faculty members had turned to transferring technology from academy to industry as a way of resolving the funding crisis they faced, they were not optimistic that their work would create 'the clever country', restoring Australia to a prominent place in world markets in the near future. 'In the short term, I don't think relevant scientific research will improve the economy, [although perhaps] in the long term, universities can contribute to a healthy system of commercialization.' In other words, professors' work on intellectual property was seen as a temporary solution to the intractable economic problems faced by universities and government. Theirs was a short-term strategy, but one to which they were intensely committed, given that they could see no other way to realize their research ambitions.

Although professors felt forced into developing intellectual property to deal with their funding problems, a number saw intellectual property as no more than a logical and inevitable extension of the applied work in which they had always engaged:

> we didn't have to look for this before, [but] I've always been aware of commercial possibilities, logically. When there's a disease problem to solve, at end of day, if I understand what's going on, it leads to some way of dealing with the disease, and clearly, to do that, you have to get commercially involved, if you want to with it on a large scale.

> I'm an engineer. To be a fully fledged engineer, you have to apply your work.

Some of the professors maintained that developing intellectual property was not different from any other type of academic labour. 'My work pattern hasn't changed much. It [commercial work] is another project. I don't view it differently than sitting down and writing a paper.' However, when this professor described his work day, it was clear that he spent a very large portion of his time on management of the complex structures he had created to foster intellectual property development (Etzkowitz 1992). When he was not engaged in managing his large technical and professional staff, complete with public relations director, he was consumed by protracted negotiations with his industrial partner over ownership of intellectual property rights, royalty splits and pay outs, production problems and options on future work. Moreover, his involvement was not likely to diminish as the project became routinized, because he sought a seat on the company's board as a way to maintain some control over product quality and marketing.

Indeed, when the eight professors described their activities with regard to intellectual property, almost all gave voice to a litany of problems, very few of which turned on technical or scientific work. Several described long months of work with various officials and organizations in state government that were necessary to set the stage for raising the public portion of the monies for the venture in question. Another described Herculean organizational efforts on his part in setting up the first phase of a Cooperative Research Centre. His work involved establishing industrial, scientific and professional advisory boards, liaison with government and agreements with regard to royalty pools, all before concrete products for production were even agreed upon. Another had to organize the educational infrastructure necessary to create a market for his product in Asian countries.

All these professors spoke of the difficulty in doing the organizational work and developing the business plans necessary to make their products viable. None of the professors had had experience with the commercial sector, at least initially, and none thought that the university commercial companies or university staff offered significant support. All thought that they, as the scientists in charge, were critical to the success of the enterprise, and spent long hours trying to make it go.

In the pursuit of intellectual property, many of the professors became managers of quasi-independent research units that had few ties to the educational mission of the unit. The professors supervised technical and research staffs that ranged from five or six to 46, almost none of whom taught undergraduates or was involved with postgraduate education. These professors became heads of fairly autonomous units, and spent long hours managing them. Although they sometimes spoke of their units as if they were small firms, the professors all depended on state-funded infrastructure, and, in many cases, the state was either a major source of funding or a client. None of the professors was actually engaged in the bench science that contributed to the products developed in their unit, and only one had contributed much more than conceptual knowledge. In general, efforts to develop intellectual property had transformed these professors from scientists doing what they regarded as fundamental research to managers of enterprises engaged in product development that was not closely connected to the educational mission of the university.

Two of the associate professors were very much like the professors, except that they were not so involved in the management of relations with external entities. The other associate professor was deeply critical of the growing emphasis on intellectual property in his unit, did not participate in the development of intellectual property, but felt powerless to do anything to shift the unit to activity that had less emphasis on profit and more on students.

Like the professors and associate professors, the four senior lecturers became involved in intellectual property because it provided a way to do 'interesting' research. Like the professors and the associate professors, they had other reasons for working on intellectual property, often altruistic reasons, such as solving environmental problems.

In terms of the way that pursuit of intellectual property affected their daily work, all four spoke of managerial and entrepreneurial activities that were similar to those of the professors and associate professors. However, the senior lecturers were somewhat closer to the science, and experienced more difficulties than the professors and associate professors. One spoke of unremitting pressure from his sponsor, who more and more closely monitored his work. Two told lengthy tales of efforts on their part to find second and third commercial partners after their initial partner had gone bankrupt or changed ownership and direction while the researchers projects were in mid-stream. Neither of these senior lecturers has been able to secure money to move from the prototype phase to component manufacturing and to organization of demonstration models.

The difficulties that senior lecturers had were not confined to their relations with external agents. In the process of securing a patent, one of the senior lecturers included two students on the application, only to be told by the university company that they were not appropriate. As the senior lecturer said: 'It was unpleasant, touchy – I had no idea of what an inventor was. It took me a long time to understand. It was awkward for me to tell them [the students]. The graduate student was not happy, but he finally accepted the chain of events.' Another senior lecturer, faced with lack of funds, had to lay off his six technical staff, an action about which he felt responsible and guilty.

All four of the senior lecturers felt blocked in their career. One was afraid he would not have the right mix of commercial and fundamental science when he came up for promotion. The other three had already been turned down for promotion to associate professor. All those who had been turned down attributed their lack of success to their heavy commitment to commercial work.

> I was encouraged to apply. I've got so many PhD students, so many international journal articles. But at the interview, they asked only about my intellectual property. My head of schools said I should have turned the discussion at the interview away from the intellectual property. . .the head of schools interpreted [my failure] as a result of my emphasis on intellectual property.

Another was unable to get out articles because his patenting plans precluded publishing. Moreover, the need for secrecy meant that he could not get students, which further impeded his research. Yet another told a similar story: 'Consulting is a dirty word. In Australia we're run by academic purists. I was ranked first in my school [for promotion], but the deputy vice-chancellor turned me down. . .[he said] we're not doing basic [in my unit], we're doing applied.' The promotional stories of the two senior lecturers tell us much. How much of their failure to be promoted was owing to the universities' unhappiness with the lack of return on investment was not clear. Neither of the senior lecturers accused the universities of prejudice on this point. But regardless of whether the university administrators made judgements on quantity of profits rather than quality of academic work, they were in a position to do so.

An alternative interpretation of the senior lecturers' experience was that they were unsuccessful in gaining promotion because they had not done a sufficient amount of high quality work. Even if this were the case, the senior lecturers' work with intellectual property still indicated some of the difficulties and problems that confronted academics attempting to bridge the gap between university and commercial worlds. The senior lecturers' work also indicates the changing nature of academic labour, especially the disparate demands with which professors have to cope.

The lecturers, on the bottom rungs of their career ladders, were involved in commercial work because they had no other choice if they were to gain support for their research. Three of the lecturers were from an applied science unit, and three from a social science unit. Although they had different experiences with commercial work, they saw it as shaping their daily academic labour, particularly with regard to their ongoing efforts to develop a workable career strategy.

In the science unit, the lecturers generally experienced labour on intellectual property as a speed-up of academic work. They thought they had to do both fundamental and commercial work to succeed, and even then, they were not sure that they were interpreting their seniors' messages correctly.

> You get your promotion more easily if you do commercial. . .most people have that feeling. They have to bring in money. . .I tend to work in priority areas. When they have a priority area, then most of the people tailor their research to that area. . .[but] I got told you wouldn't get a promotion if you got commercial money but not ARC money.

Although all the lecturers experienced their research and career environment as changing rapidly, they responded in different ways. A professor told one lecturer that if he wanted to be promoted he had to get big chunks of money, and offered the lecturer commercial money, which the lecturer refused, and about which he was deeply concerned. Another lecturer developed a strategy to guide his selection of commercial products: 'I have to see a benefit more than actual dollars for me to take the work. My sort of general guideline is that if I can see a scientific paper that I can publish out of this, then I'll do it.' Another lecturer, new to the Australian system, described his gradually dawning understanding that the commercial money he received was in return for product development:

> There's a different perception of what people want out of it [research money]. I thought it was just money to do my own thing. . .on this problem. . .then the commercial people told me that they wanted a product that they could use. It took me a while to finally figure that out. It's not publications that they want – they wanted a product. We discussed what they wanted. It came gradually; they were not rude. It evolved. I came from a very theoretical background, so that it was hard for me to accept at first.

Although this lecturer was willing to do commercial work to sustain his career, he was very clear that it was not his first choice.

> I prefer theoretical. There are no hassles. It's like math. Reality is always much more complicated. You have to know for sure that whatever you develop produces a result. In theoretical, I don't have to do that. To demonstrate that my [product] works is much more difficult.

The social science unit had problems that were different from the physical sciences. Their mandate was to promote the development of technology, generally, and intellectual property, particularly. The state had supplied the unit with seed money, in return for which the lecturers were to become self-sustaining with regard to grants, contracts and intellectual property. They had not. Instead, they supported themselves by developing an academic programme, using the institutional funding formula to justify their positions. They were uncertain as to whether the state would provide them with more monies, and uncertain as to whether the university would make a permanent commitment to their unit.

The situation was made more problematic in that the state had given them their initial monies and was potentially their largest client.

> They [the state] would like us to do it without payment under the argument that they've already given us half a million dollars. We may do it [the project], in terms of establishing our viability, our profile and our credibility as a unit that has something to offer. . .in terms of policy issues to government. We're again in the bind about what we are tied to in exchange for the government giving us seed capital.

The social scientists also expressed what they perceived as a double bind. They were able to get contracts with external state agencies and industry because they were independent, but they could not keep getting contracts unless they pleased their clients, in effect endorsing the client position and weakening their chances for future contracts, because they had undermined their independent stance.

> So the government comes to academic institutions to be able to say, here we have an independent, reliable, objective organization with scientific rigour and some degree of depth analysis. But then. . .they bully you into saying what they want. . .They want you to be independent, but they want you to say what they want to say.

Like the physical scientists, the social scientists were unhappy with commercial norms, but were committed to engaging in the development of intellectual property to sustain their careers. In many ways, they all expressed anxiety about being in a double bind. The lecturers were investing in research and academic careers, and were willing to do commercial work if that was necessary, but thought that commercial work created nearly insurmountable obstacles to academic success.

The researchers were quite similar to the lecturers. They regarded themselves as positioned on the bottom rungs of the academic career ladder, and expressed uncertainty as to whether they would be able to climb it. Their greatest fear was that conditions had changed so greatly that they would never reach the tenure track. As one research fellow said:

> Stability of career path – I don't perceive such a thing in Australia at the moment, because all that seems to be available is short term contracts, commonly three years, sometimes five. . .so we have a dichotomy between haves and have-nots. The haves have been it for at least five years [longer than I have].

There were two exceptions to the uncertainty expressed by researchers. One research fellow saw himself as uncommitted to the academy, as more likely to end up in government, and was not terribly concerned about a professorial career. The other was a research professional who ran a successful, almost free-standing, research institute that had successfully developed intellectual property. He thought his position in the university was secure because he generated royalties for the university, and thought he would be most likely to contribute more in the future.

Conclusions

The two studies found similarities and differences in their exploration of entrepreneurism and the development of intellectual property in Australian universities. The similarities are several. In both studies activity was concentrated in the applied sciences, often in units that hired fairly large numbers of technical and research staff to pursue entrepreneurial or product development activities. The technical and research staff usually had little relation to the educational mission of the university. All the professors and most of the associate professors regarded entrepreneurial activity and the development of intellectual property very positively, especially valuing the improved relations with external bodies, heightened prestige of their units and closer linkage to the economy (consulting opportunities, student employment opportunities), and added monetary benefits. Given that the faculty members were primarily applied scientists, they saw their entrepreneurial work as an extension of the research in which they were traditionally engaged, or, in the case of intellectual property, as a logical, although often substantively different, extension of that work. In both studies, at the professorial levels, benefits far outweighed costs.

There were dissimilarities between the two studies as well. At one level, the differences can probably be explained in terms of differences in terms of theory, sample and method. Neo-classical economic theory directed the first study towards questions dealing with costs and benefits for a broad range of entrepreneurial activities and across fairly large numbers of entrepreneurial faculty members who saw the benefits of entrepreneurism as far outweighing the costs. Neo-Marxian sociology, rooted in the critical literature on professionalization, directed the second study towards differences in power among academics within the institution, and found that those lower in the academic hierarchy were very uncertain and sometimes unhappy with and critical of the development of intellectual property. In the first study the ranking of costs and benefits on a 1 to 10 scale focused attention on quantitative judgements, while in the second study questions about daily academic work during the course of lengthy, in-depth interviews probably encouraged faculty members to give voice to their uncertainty and fears.

However, there are other than theoretical and methodological explanations for the differences between the two studies. The primary commercial activities in the first study were contract work and consulting, fairly routine activities. Consulting had long been part of academic culture, and has been incorporated into the traditional missions of teaching, research and service. Contract work is a long-standing practice, although this work has accelerated greatly in recent years. The central activity in the second study was development of intellectual property, in which academics had to bring a product from idea to commercial prototype and sometimes to batch production. For most academics, this was non-routine activity. Traditionally, the division of labour with regard to invention and innovation has been that academics do the science that gives shape to the product, and industry patents and brings the product to production. In other words, the academics engaged in developing intellectual property were doing something substantively different, not something different in degree. Their academic work had changed much more than that of those in the first study. The obvious questions raised by these studies are as follows. How far can routine entrepreneurial activity be extended before becoming the central routine of academic units? How much can academics invest in the development of intellectual property without becoming heads of small firms more committed to external bodies and markets than to the educational mission of the institution? At what point is there serious division within units over entrepreneurial activity and development of intellectual property, exacerbating distinctions between the privileged and non-privileged? At what point does that division occur in the wider university, between departments and colleges? Will entrepreneurial activity and the development of intellectual property by faculty members substantially reduce or solve the problems addressed at the beginning of this chapter? Will entrepreneurial activity and the pursuit of intellectual property on the part of universities solve system-wide finance problems, or will they simply substitute for government monies, thus failing to ease the financial constraints that institutions are currently experiencing? Will such activity enable Australia, Canada, the UK and the USA to compete more successfully in global markets, or will it turn professors towards safe national market niches? If intellectual property involves professors with multinational firms, which is usually the case in Australia, how much profit will be repatriated?

Notes

1. We would like to thank the Fulbright Commission for the senior research awards that financed our work in Australia.
2. The figures for University A are somewhat misleading. It generated $6.8 million from a single centre having a very marginal relationship to the university mission. More comparable figures for A were $9.5 million and 6 per cent of total institutional revenues.
3. Only three of 59 respondents held that the costs of entrepreneurism exceeded the benefits. None of these three was involved in entrepreneurism and none perceived themselves as receiving any benefits.

References

Bartlett, D.L. and Steele, J.B. (1992) *America: What Went Wrong?* Kansas City, Andrews and McMeel.
Blumenthal, D., Epstein, S. and Maxwell, J. (1986a) 'Commercializing university research: lessons from the experience of the Wisconsin Alumni Research Foundation, *New England Journal of Medicine*, 314(25), 1621–6.
Blumenthal, D., Gluck, M., Louis, K.S., Stato, M.A. and Wise, D. (1986b) University–industry research relationships in biotechnology: implications for the university, *Science*, 232(4756), 1361–6.
Committee for Economic Development (1973) *The Management and Financing of Colleges.* New York, CED.
Crean, S. (1990) Science policy, Conference Papers, the Australian Tertiary Institutions Consulting Companies Association, Canberra, June.
Dunn, L.F. (1977) Quantifying non-pecuniary returns, *Journal of Human Resources*, 12, 347–59.
Etzkowitz, H. (1992) Individual investigators and their research groups, *Minerva*, 30, 28–50.
Fairweather, J.S. (1988) *Entrepreneurship and Higher Education.* Washington, DC, Association for the Study of Higher Education.
Fairweather, J.S. (1989) Academic research and instruction: the industrial connection, *Journal of Higher Education*, 60(4), 388–407.
Geiger, R.L. (1989) The ambiguous link: private industry and university research, in William E. Becker and Darrell Lewis, (eds), *Higher Education and Economic Development*.

Haveman, R.H. and Wolfe, B.L. (1984) Schooling and economic well-being: the role of nonmarket effects, *Journal of Human Resources*, 19(3), 377–407.

Levin, R., Klevovick, A. and Nelson, R. (1987) Appropriating the returns to industrial R and D, *Brookings Papers on Economic Activity*, no. 3, Washington, DC, Brookings Institute.

McMahon, W.W. (1982) Externalities in education, Faculty Working Paper No. 877, Urbana-Champaign, University of Illinois.

Pfeffer, J. (1981) *Power in Organizations*. Marshfield, MA, Pitman Publishing.

Phillips, K. (1990) *The Politics of Rich and Poor: Wealth and the American Electorate in the Reagan Aftermath*. New York, Random House.

Slaughter, S. (1990) *The Higher Learning and High Technology: Dynamics of Higher Education Policy Formation*. Albany, NY, SUNY Press.

Slaughter, S. (1993) Retrenchment in the 1980s: the politics of prestige and gender, *Journal of Higher Education*, 64(3): 250–82.

Smith, B.L.R. (1990) *American Science Policy Since World War II*. Washington, DC, The Brookings Institution.

8

The University of Life plc[1]: the 'Industrialization' of Higher Education?

Richard Winter

Introduction

The increasing subjection of public institutions to the reductive rigours of monetarist economics has gradually, over the past 15 years or so, produced a crisis of confidence in certain quarters. No longer does it seem generally plausible to prescribe the forms and values required for public welfare on the basis of institutionalized expert authority, i.e. that of civil servants, politicians, professionals in general or (in particular) educators. Instead, cultural authority is now projected on to 'the market' and a bereft humanity seems to be condemned for the time being to organize *all* its affairs within the general parameters of capitalism, whose apparent claim is that matters of value and priority must be adjudicated simply by the forces of supply and demand. In other words, since there can be no welfare without profitability, the former can be subsumed under the latter: the good may be equated with the profitable. Faced with this ideological challenge, higher education staff, who have traditionally raised their own serious claim to cultural authority, are called upon to formulate a response which is both critical and constructive, neither retreating into a merely rhetorical expression of lost ideals nor colluding with a social system whose disorders are plain to see. The problem is, as always, one of articulating an explorative, critical, yet practical understanding of the various forces and processes involved.

It is to this end that the argument of this chapter is addressed. The contemporary university is inevitably bound up with the political and economic forces of capitalism, which threaten to submit the integrity of educational and academic values to the forms and priorities of market-oriented production. Fortunately, however, these threats are mitigated by the contradictions within the managerial ideology which tries to implement them. Hence, although we are indeed faced by *attempts* to impose an industrial, profit-oriented logic on to higher education, this situation is not without real educational opportunities, both to shed some of the oppressive practices enshrined in higher education's traditional forms and to begin to realize some innovative and progressive possibilities. In other words, contradictions do not only generate 'problems' (injustices, evasions and suffering), they also generate spaces within which power can be contested and reforms can be won. Let us begin, therefore, by looking at the *ambiguities* underlying current pressures for change in the UK higher education system.

Pressures for change: education *and* economic development

A significant aspect of current higher education initiatives in the UK is that they emanate not from the government Department for Education but from the Employment Department (Employment Department 1990; Duckenfield and Stirner 1992). This, of course, may serve to confirm the worst suspicions of academics, that education is now officially equated with labour force training, having noted that the government's 1985 consultative document *The Development of Higher Education into the 1990s* begins 'The economic performance of the UK since 1945 has been disappointing' (DES 1985: para. 1.2), and immediately continues 'The societies of our competitors are producing. . .more qualified scientists, engineers, technologists, and technicians than the UK' (para 1.3).

Although some HE staff may feel antagonised when the Employment Department introduces accounts of its higher education initiatives by announcing, frankly, its concern 'to support economic growth by promoting a competitive, efficient, and flexible labour market' (Employment Department 1990: 5; Duckenfield and Stirner 1992: 3), the relationship between educational values and economic development is not a simple opposition. The list of headings under which the Employment Department presents its funded projects includes not only 'employer relevance' and 'high level skills supply' but also such acceptable educational concepts as 'increased learner responsibility' and 'continuing professional development' (Employment Department 1990: 88 ff.). It also challenges the restrictive elitism of HE institutions through headings such as 'wider accessibility' (i.e. 'access for non-traditional students'), 'alternative admissions mechanisms' and 'accreditation of prior experiential learning' (*ibid.*).

The latter themes provide an obvious managerial issue, which is frequently presented as higher education's most urgent current problem: how can restricted, elitist HE be extended to become open access HE available to the mass of the citizenry without a loss in 'quality' (see Ball 1990)? But beneath this issue lies another, one which managerial rhetoric takes for granted and at the same time ignores. It is neatly symbolized by Ball's reference to 'UK plc' (1990: 3–4), which subsumes the entire nation state within the conceptual field of commerce. The issue here is the relationship between a theory of decision-making based entirely on market forces, competitive profitability, etc. (as in 'UK plc') and decision-making supposedly based on the direct analysis and judgement of human need, which has traditionally been the province (or at least the claim) of the various professions, including educationists. This is the real challenge currently facing higher education, a challenge which many current initiatives both conceal and render more acute (e.g. the nature of 'personal skills': Employment Department 1990). The first step, then, is to explore the nature of this ideological challenge: how should we articulate the relationship between higher education institutions and those embodying commerce and industry?

Higher education institutions: their nature and function?

We can begin with J.H. Newman's classic and still influential statement, originally published between 1852 and 1873. For Newman, the quality of knowledge appropriate to university education is that it should be both general and 'liberal'. The generality of knowledge is provided by the *unity* of different disciplines within an overarching *theological* framework (Newman 1982: Discourses II, III, IV, IX) and by the community life of the institution, which is explicitly preferred to a prescriptively varied *curriculum* examined by the university but acquired through experiences and efforts elsewhere. This principled disjuncture between practical life and university education is embodied in Newman's concept of liberal education, in which 'liberal' means 'liberated' from the exigencies of manual, commercial or professional work. In other words, 'knowledge is capable of being its own end', and Newman therefore attempts to separate knowledge even from 'virtue', in stark contrast to the complex analysis by Newman's authority and inspiration, Aristotle, concerning the intimate relationship between knowledge, wisdom, and virtue (Aristotle 1976: 212–16). But Newman cannot, in the end, sustain this distinction, as is shown by his later description of the qualities of 'the gentleman' as 'the ethical character which the cultivated *intellect* will form' (Newman 1982: 159–60; my italic). Newman's problem is that his exposition of the nature of knowledge is implicitly subservient to his apologetics for theology-as-the-revelation-of-absolute-truth. His argument that academic freedom must mean independence from practical responsibilities in the moral and economic world is not intelligible in a secular culture, nor even within a broader theology where 'good works' are as important, spiritually, as faith. As Newman himself concedes, 'If. . .a practical end must be assigned to a University. . .it is that of training good members of society. Its art is the art of social life, and its end is fitness for the world' (*ibid*.: 134) But this unhelpfully avoids the very issues which are at stake ('good', 'fitness?').

The contradictions within Newman's vision of university autonomy explain in part the vulnerability of higher education to criticisms such as those of Bourdieu. In *Homo Academicus* (1988) Bourdieu extends his general critique of educational institutions (Bourdieu 1977) to a specific indictment of the university, whose effect is to reproduce and to 'consecrate' oppressive social inequalities behind a 'mask of neutrality' (Bourdieu 1988: 204) by converting contingent social class differences in cultural and economic advantage into the legitimated terminology of intellectual qualities and deficits (*ibid.*: 194ff). In other words, the effect of the university 'community' upon its junior members is not, as Newman hoped, the expansion of mind through free critical discourse, but 'symbolic violence' (Bourdieu 1977: 4), i.e. the 'arbitrary' imposition of meanings which legitimate the exercise of authority 'by concealing the power relations which are the basis of its force' and thereby render it more effective (*ibid.*: 4–5). ('Meanings' here would include, for example, academic grades and their supposed significance in terms of talent and merit.) In this way, Bourdieu exposes the incompleteness (to say the least) of Newman's conception of the university as an institution insulated against worldly motives of politics and economics, devoted simply and exclusively to the pusuit of knowledge for its own sake through the free and critical exchange of ideas. (See also, in this context, Thompson 1970.)

However, Bourdieu's formulation of academic authority as 'arbitrary' is a key to the unsatisfactoriness of his approach. Neither Bourdieu's deterministic vision of cultural oppression nor Newman's vision of genteel autonomy can encompass the ideological subtleties of the UK government's higher education initiatives, whose complex ambiguities have already been noted above. What is needed, therefore, is a theory of the relationship between the changing processes of higher education and the general economic, political and organizational forces which are shaping these developments and thereby challenging conceptions of the professional role of higher education staff. The following analysis is intended as a sketch of some of the resources from which such a theory might be developed.

Changes in higher education and the industrialization of the labour process

Let us begin with an interpretation of the broad historical context, namely Mandel's argument that the fundamental historical pressure of a capitalist economy is a general drive to extend the logic of the market into more and more areas of social activity (Mandel 1978: 47), which, therefore, is now affecting universities, along with schools, hospitals, ambulance services, prisons, the civil service, etc. Mandel's argument is as follows. At any point in time (since the Middle Ages at least) areas of economic activity have been structured in one of two ways: (a) as the investment of capital (seeking dividends) in order to manufacture goods for a market (seeking profits);

(b) as the primary organization of available resources in order to produce goods through craft labour in direct reponse to cultural definitions of social need. The superior dynamism of the former (due to the possibility of dividends and profits, leading to the rapid accumulation of capital for further developmental investment) means that it has tended to supersede the latter: gradually, but (it would seem) inexorably, craft work has yielded to highly capitalized production (Mandel 1978: 46–8). The increasing pace of technological innovation (*ibid.*: Chapter 8) is dictated by the fact that it is the creativity of workers, not machines themselves, that creates profits (because machinery must be bought at a price which has already made a profit for the seller). Consequently, the higher the component of capital expenditure in the costs of production (i.e. with advancing technology) the lower is the *rate* of profit per unit of cost. Hence we see the continual seeking of new domains in which capital can be invested, advanced technology applied and profits created, i.e. in such areas as research and development (*ibid.*: 249), the provision of services (transport, power utilities, accounting, stock control) and thus, finally, for the purposes of our analysis here, education. 'Far from representing a "post-industrial" society, late capitalism thus constitutes *generalized universal industrialization* for the first time in history' (*ibid.*: 387).

From the perspective of Mandel's argument, therefore, higher education may be seen as a sector currently dominated by craft processes and now due for 'industrialization'. The new initiatives and rationales already referred to are thus not simply the imposition of a political dogma, as a set of arbitrary, barbarous and implausible metaphors, but an expression of the inherent developmental logic of capitalism. The next question is, therefore, if this is the nature of the underlying historical forces at work, what does this imply in terms of the actual experience of university staff? What is entailed in a move from craft work to 'industrialized' production in the context of higher education?

Harry Braverman's account of the changing labour process in manufacturing contexts offers various chilling suggestions (Braverman 1974). Braverman looks back to a period of craft labour in which 'the worker was presumed to be the master [*sic*] of a body of traditional knowledge, and methods and procedures were left to his or her discretion' (*ibid.*: 109, 443), and argues that the process of industrialization has entailed a sustained and successful attempt by management (inspired by Frederick Taylor's theories and exhortations) to impose rigid control over the production process by sub-dividing the complex ensemble of craft work into simple stages, none of which allows the worker to comprehend or to take responsibility for the overall process. Decisions about the production process are taken centrally by management, through their control of the complex equipment which in turn dictates the 'methods and procedures' required. From the point of view of the worker, therefore, work becomes fragmentary, and its meaning is displaced from an awareness of its contribution to human needs on to its function within a determined production process over which the worker has no control. This displacement of the meaning of the labour process corresponds to the displacement of the meaning of the product of labour, from its value in meeting human needs ('use value') to its ability to command a profitable price on the market ('exchange value'). In other words, the labour process and the product of labour become mere 'commodities', whose value is defined solely by their capacity to generate profits. This in turn means that the worker is subjected to unmitigated control by management, since management is in charge of decisions affecting the profitability of the enterprise, i.e. concerning the disposition of resources.

Let us see how far Braverman's analysis can be applied to higher education, i.e. to teaching and research. One of the most important current educational initiatives, strongly endorsed by the UK government, is 'competence-based vocational education', in which curricula (in vocational areas) are cast in the form of competence statements that guide students in presenting work-derived evidence to be assessed mainly by staff employed in the students' workplace. These competences (which function rather like curriculum objectives) are established by consortia consisting mainly of employers ('industrial lead bodies'). Attempts are currently being made to apply this curriculum model to professional education within universities, especially in the field of management (see MCI 1991). It appears to entail a reduction in the role of the teacher to that of a supportive tutor: the setting of objectives and the design and sequencing of learning has been on the one hand appropriated by the industrial lead body and on the other hand delegated to the students, and responsibility for assessing students' work is redistributed from HE staff to (a) workplace assessors and (b) university quality control procedures.

Similarly, university courses are increasingly being recast into integrated systems of 'modular' units, allowing students to construct their own 'customized' courses by selecting their own combination of modules. This means that HE staff no longer have responsibility for designing a sequence of learning experiences which might profoundly affect student identities; instead they merely make available a circumscribed fragment of expertise within a computerized system of options. Gone is the general authority of the individual 'educator' (parent-figure or cultural crusader); instead HE staff are purveyors of commodities within a knowledge 'supermarket', which may or may not be selected by the student-as-customer. Responsibility for the overall coherence and progression of students' education is assumed not by the staff who teach individual modules but by the academic managers who design the modular system and by the academic counsellors who guide student choice of modules.

Parallel expressions of the loss of formerly comprehensive responsibilities occur in the context of research. Sandra Harding proposes the rejection of 'industrialized' forms of social inquiry (capital intensive, hierarchically managed) in favour of a return to an earlier model of the scientist as a 'craft worker', who is responsible for the whole process of inquiry, from the selection of problems and methods to the interpretation of results, and thus requires a 'unity of hand, brain and heart' which is the antithesis of the modern labour process (Harding 1986: 248). (See also Julius Roth's (1965) strictures on 'hired hand research'.)

Is this link between the alienation of the assembly line worker and the alienation of the contemporary university lecturer/researcher merely a plausible emotive analogy, or does it also have a theoretical basis? Let us now consider, in more detail, the sense in which the 'products' of education and those of manufacturing industry are comparable, i.e. the nature of the 'commodity' form.

Commodities, knowledge and qualifications

Many would wish to restrict the analogy between the labour process in manufacture and the labour process in education by maintaining a theoretical distinction between 'productive' and 'non-productive' labour. The original basis for this distinction, however, is between labour which *produces* commodities (thereby adding value to raw material) and labour involved merely in the *circulation* of commodities (e.g. transport) (Mandel 1978: 401). But Mandel then generalizes the notion of 'unproductiveness' from the sector of circulation to services in general, and continues: 'The logic of late capitalism is therefore necessarily to convert idle capital into service capital and simultaneously to replace service capital with productive capital, in other words, services with commodities: transport services with private cars, theatre and film services with private television sets, tomorrow television services and educational instruction with video cassettes' (*ibid.*: 406).

However, the theoretical significance of this latter step is not clear: services begin to be incorporated into the relationships of an industrialized market economy when the provision of what is *needed* is converted into the provision of what can be profitably marketed, without necessarily requiring that the consumption of services take the form of purchasing an object. Production and consumption are complementary halves of the same circle of supply and demand (Samuelson 1980: 41); and 'services' are one form of all those 'goods' that can be produced and supplied, demanded and consumed. Thus, in a university context, although there is indeed pressure upon staff to create products that can be *sold* (videos, computer software, patentable technology), it is also recognized that profits can be made through *franchising* other types of product (course units, quality assurance procedures) and by *hiring out* facilities (human and material) for research and 'consultancy'. In the same way, some enterprises *sell* cars and TVs while others hire or lease them. In other words, following Burrell (1990: 292), it can be argued that surplus value can be created and realized wherever a market exists, and that commodities may be 'material or non-material'.

The essence of a commodity, then, is not that it actually is a 'thing', but that its *value* is determined by its capacity for being marketed for profit, rather than by its usefulness in contributing to 'genuine' human need. Its form therefore must be such that its profitability may be calculated, and for this reason it must be considered *as if* it were a 'thing' (with calculable properties). This thing-like quality disguises the fact that these properties are merely contructs necessitated by the social relationships embodied in the structure of the market, within which alone the commodity has value and meaning. The commodity form is thus a *displacement* of meaning: the market acts as a self-justifying decision-making mechanism, prioritizing social activities according to a systematically limited reality, in which the meaning and value of artefacts, actions and people are reconstructed in terms of the restrictive logic of profit generation.

According to this 'market logic', the relationship between teacher, student and curriculum is reconstructed as a relationship between producer, consumer and commodity. This might be seen in two ways. First, knowledge is packaged into pedagogical units ('modules') which correspond to numerical units of academic credit, based on average learning time. Second, academic qualifications constitute a currency with exchange value in relation to employment. The argument would then be as follows. Higher education staff and institutions will promote those pedagogical units and qualifications which have marketable value and students may be expected to attempt to acquire academic credit and profitable credentials at an advantageous 'price' (i.e. for relatively little effort). Clearly, such an analysis is not convincing as a *description* of current educational realities; rather, it delineates the form of an ideological *pressure*, with which HE staff will need to come to terms, a set of *metaphors* whose new-found plausibility may be used to legitimate (in the name of supposedly universal and inescapable market forces) the subjection of educational processes to specific political interests.

However, it is important to recognize that this type of analysis (economic imperatives leading to the commodification of culture) can easily lapse into yet another form of determinism, whose pretensions are always undermined by its lack of reflexivity: if culture in general has succumbed to commodification, then this very piece of writing itself must have the status of a commodity; and if so, what credence can be given to it? I must emphasize, therefore, that the increasing influence of the ideology of market relationships does not mean that human experience is about to be wholly encapsulated in commodity form, as Baudrillard and Wernick, for example, would have us believe (Baudrillard 1988; Wernick 1991). More precisely, an increase in the tendency towards the commodity formulation of knowledge, research and academic qualifications must not lead us (in an excess of melodramtic and self-important pessimism) to deny the possibilities for critical understanding and innovative practice (see Willmott 1990: 358). Indeed, the argument in the next section is that the managers of market-oriented educational institutions will not wish *simply* to restrict the scope of staff responsibility in order to achieve the commodification of the educational process; that (on the contrary) managers appear to have their own reasons for defining workers as possessing the capacity for critical, innovative autonomy.

The contradictions of 'management'

Higher education as the craft work of individual academic staff has always operated under some sort of institutional regulation and sanction, originally that of the Church and latterly that of the university bureaucracy, itself regulated by the state. What is new is the subjection of teaching, curriculum design and research to detailed management processes imitated from those of market-oriented manufacturing enterprises. How far will these new management processes interfere with that freedom of creation, interpretation and criticism which academic staff would wish to claim (following Newman, perhaps) as traditionally characteristic of their work, but which they now see as being under threat (see Thompson 1970)?

Braverman's pessimism concerning management's inexorable domination of the labour process has been criticized as oversimplified (Littler 1990; Wardell 1990). Instead it is suggested that industrialized labour processes are structured by managerial *attempts* at controlling the methods and procedures of work which are only partially successful (Thompson 1990: 100), generating antagonisms which are nevertheless limited by management's need to maintain consent and creativity on the part of workers (*ibid.*: 101). This is the contradiction at the heart of the management role, reflecting, of course, the continuing contradictions at the heart of capitalism (Mandel 1978: 472), which necessitate 'the huge machinery of ideological manipulation' designed to 'integrate the worker into late capitalist society as a consumer, social partner, or citizen' (*ibid.*: 485). However, ideology is not an integrated, rationalized structure of illusions, but a series of fragments, reflections of the contradictions it seeks (with only partial success) to disguise (see Winter 1989). Management theory, therefore, in presenting its insistently harmonious view of the aims and processes of commercial enterprises cannot help accidentally revealing the contradictions it wishes to ignore and thus cannot address.

Hence arise the manifold inconsistencies of Peter Drucker's perpetually reprinted classic text on management (Drucker 1974, reprinted 1991). For example, we are told that 'the ultimate test of management is performance', and that performance must be measured against objectives, but that no one knows how to measure or even conceptualize objectives: even profitability is only measured with 'a rubber yardstick'. Similarly, he emphasizes that managers must live with *uncertainty* but that their decision-making must above all be 'systematic'. In other words, management is formulated both as the necessity for control and as an understanding of the impossibility of control. Hence, there is an emphasis that every job has to focus on the company's objectives and thus on the need for 'clear decision authority', and, at the same time, that workers are colleagues, not inferiors, who 'make genuine decisions' and 'take on the burden of responsibility', so that 'rank and file jobs are potentially managerial, or would be more productive if made so'. (Except that we don't know how to 'define, let alone measure productivity'.)

The analytical power of management theory is thus undermined by its own ideology. On the one hand it promotes a self-justificatory portrayal of the senior executive as the organizational 'brain', activating the enterprise by imposing objectives for all staff on the basis of management's exclusive understanding of the organization's relationship with its economic and political environment (Garratt 1987: 74–81)(which would seem to justify Braverman's nightmare of a triumphant Taylorian hierarchy). On the other hand there is total quality management (TQM), inspired by the work of Kaoru Ishikawa, which emphasizes that *every* worker can (and must) take responsibility for the overall purpose of the organization and for the continued improvement of the quality of its work – *their* work. The TQM model was explicitly developed as a rejection of Taylorian theories, which Ishikawa (like Braverman) saw as responsible for the alienation of workers from the objectives and results of their work (Hutchins 1988: 148–9).

However, the TQM focus on management's responsibility to establish 'commitment' on the part of the whole workforce (Hakes 1991: 66–8) is itself, as one would expect, highly contradictory. The commitment to 'never ending improvement' which provides the motivation for staff involvement in their 'quality circles' is based on supposed efforts to make their 'organization the best in its field' (Hutchins 1988: 23) within a competitive market whose main rationale for efficiency is that failure will be widespread. Hence, workers' sense of 'responsibility' is constructed (through organizational procedures) as a state of mind which management aims to manipulate: 'People have an innate loyalty to their group and to their company, even when their needs are not satisfied and even when they are unsuccessful' (*ibid.*: 132). (The expectation of an absolute loyalty to a specific organization must bring profound professional dilemmas for higher education workers, who will rather subscribe to an *academic responsibility* towards the wider critical community of their discipline.)

TQM's confidence in its vision of no faults, no delays and the harmonization of all organizational interests rests on a failure to address the contradictions between manipulation and responsibility, between customer sovereignty and pre-empting markets by anticipating and creating demand, between 'quality' as 'conformance to requirements' and the continual raising of targets (Hakes 1991). There are therefore grounds for hope: the inherent contradictions of the management role formulated by the model and, in particular, its commitment to the criticism of decisions by those to whom they have been delegated will ensure that industrialized educational institutions will, like their predecessors, afford conceptual and political space in which to formulate alternative practices to those anticipated in managerial rhetoric.

Conclusion: educational possibilities

Let us recapitulate the argument so far. The initiatives currently being urged upon higher education may be explained in terms of the ideological forces of fundamental historical developments. It is not helpful, therefore, to react with nostalgia, contrasting the malign logic of the market (mediated through the power of a profit-oriented management) with a supposed 'golden age' when the craft of the academic was simply the direct expression of moral value, educational need and the search for truth: traditional university culture has its own ambivalent involvement with oppressive social and political power (Bourdieu 1977, 1988). It is also important to note that there is a real sense in which a market decision-making structure can liberate citizens from subjection to elitist cultural authority by enfranchising them as consumers with 'money votes'. But it is equally clear that a market orientation (for educational processes as for anything else) involves not simply a rational functional relevance but a systematic distortion of meaning, an evasion of questions of value, need and ultimate purpose. To acquiesce completely in the commodification of knowledge would thus be, at the very least, a cultural disaster. It might also threaten the continued existence of humanity, since the purposes of market-oriented organizations are limited to the tiny period over which accountants can claim to be able to calculate profitability, while their ecological effects are immense and hardly calculable at all. Management theory is too pragmatic, too self-serving, to acknowledge its contradictions, its inadequacies. Hence, for higher education institutions (as for other organizations) it is essential (for justice, for understanding, even for planetary survival) that managerial perspectives be challenged; and it is the accidental merit of modern management theory that its unacknowledged inconsistencies offer scope for such challenges. In the light of these considerations, then, let us consider how higher education institutions might formulate a critical response to a market-oriented ideology, through the redefinition of some key concepts.

Theory

'Theory' is linked etymologically with the idea of the spectator, and we have seen how Newman, for example, tried to formulate HE as insulated from worldly practices. As universities are drawn by market forces into a structured relationship with economics and politics, theory will no longer be a refuge from the world, and will have to protect itself against commodification by identifying its 'use value'. The separation of theory and practice will then not only be a matter for repeated lament, but will have to be addressed, not only in theory but in practice (Winter 1991). Theory may thus finally cease being merely abstraction (and thus as readily transmuted into commodity form as money itself: Sohn-Rethel 1978) and become (essentially, not merely as an option) intellectual critique, political challenge and a moment in the development of practice.

Scholarship

The scope of decision-making within market-oriented organizations is inherently limited: (i) by the priority given to the objectives of the organization, (ii) by the priority given to profitability, and (iii) by the exclusive focus on the current accounting period. Scholarship's concern with the preservation, collection and mastery of bodies of knowledge will thus be needed to expand the intellectual resources which can be brought to bear to inform (and hence to challenge) the limitations of market decision-making. It will offer the possibility of assembling a tradition and a multifarious range of understandings, from which alternatives can be derived and authorized. It will thus make available a variety of resources for disputing the legitimacy of managerial ideology.

Intellectuals

One aspect of the legitimating ideology of late capitalism is a general belief in 'technical rationality', which claims that fundamental antagonisms (i.e. other than those of 'opinion') have been abolished through rational organizational procedures and the application of innovative technology, thereby rendering obsolete any value systems beyond the calculation of instrumental means and functions (Mandel 1978: 501–2). We can assume that this ideology will come to exercise increasing influence in the debates over educational knowledge, and will need to be contested. Thus, in formulating principles and objectives for the curricula offered by HE institutions, the conceptions of 'the intellectual' to be found in the work of Gramsci (1971) and Gouldner (1979) will be an essential complement to the purely technical specifications which will be promoted by employers. Gramsci's work focuses on the general critical and integrative understandings which are potentially available to all citizens because they can be created upon those 'general conceptions of the world' which are already 'implicitly contained. . .in their practical activity' (Gramsci 1971: 344). Whereas Gramsci is explicitly outlining an educational programme for the future, Gouldner describes a certain aspect of (middle class) culture as though it were already achieved (which is doubtful). But his analysis of the 'culture of critical discourse', with its emphasis on reflexivity, self-monitoring, metacommunication and problematic justification (Gouldner 1979: 28–9) is none the less relevant for planners of HE curricula and assessment criteria. In other words, the ambition of HE staff should be that those who emerge with qualifications from our courses should not only be 'employees', possessing technically relevant knowledge, but should also be (in ways derivable from the ideas of Gramsci and Gouldner) 'intellectuals', and thus equipped to exploit to the full the opportunities for autonomy which the organizations in which they work are likely (following TQM principles) to make available.

The educative workplace

Reference has already been made to the increasing introduction of educational curricula based on evidence gathered and assessed in the workplace, led in the UK by the National Council for Vocational Qualifications (NCVQ). In many ways the current format for this work, based on prespecified 'competences', follows the organizational rationality of 'management by objectives' (Drucker 1974: 38); but it also rests explicitly on a learner-centred educational theory (Jessup 1991: Chapter 1), and this permits reinterpretations of the competence format aimed at reintroducing educational principles, such as critical reflection upon values, into the purely market-oriented version (Winter 1992). The work of the NCVQ evokes the possibility of the 'educative workplace' as an institutional form for the decentralization of knowledge creation, one of the progressive aspects of the 'postmodernist' epistemology (Winter 1991) which, together with the 'technical rationality' previously noted, constitutes the complex ideological underpinning of late capitalism (Jameson 1984). This will pose an interesting challenge to the current institutional structure of higher education. However, where work is structured by the processes and relationships of capitalism there are contradictions inherent in the very phrase 'educative workplace', and these are already beginning to appear. The construction industry is complaining about the narrowness of the competence-based curriculum, suggesting that managements do, in some ways, take seriously the need to increase the scope of workers' responsibilities (Callender 1992); and evidence from the initial phases of our own workplace-focused honours degree in social work suggests that staff find the pressures of the workplace so intense that finding genuine 'space' for reflection is a major problem (Winter and Maisch 1992: 11, 16–17, 29).

In conclusion, higher education institutions are already (and unavoidably) caught up in the contradictions of capitalist development. But for higher education staff this ought not to signify the doleful ending of a sacred tradition; rather, it should constitute the current challenge to our understanding of our role in a historical process which it would be futile to ignore, and which (like earlier phases of the process) offers not only threats but also opportunities.

Note

1. plc: public limited company. A company whose shares are quoted, bought and sold on the commercial stock market, like Unilever and Ford, but unlike a small family business, a charity or a public service institution.

References

Aristotle (1976) *Ethics.* Harmondsworth, Penguin.

Ball, C. (1990) *More Means Different.* London, Royal Society of Arts.

Baudrillard, J. (1988) The system of objects, in *Selected Writings.* Cambridge, Polity Press.

Bourdieu, P. (1977) *Reproduction in Education, Society, and Culture.* London, Sage Publications.

Bourdieu, P. (1988) *Homo Academicus.* Cambridge, Polity Press.

Braverman, H. (1974) *Labor and Monopoly Capital.* New York, Monthly Review Press.

Burrell, G. (1990) Fragmented labours, in D. Knights and H. Willmott (eds) *Labour Process Theory.* Basingstoke, Macmillan.

Callender, C. (1992) *Will NVQs Work?* London, Institute of Manpower Studies.

Department of Education and Science (1985) *The Development of Higher Education into the 1990s.* London, HMSO.

Drucker, P. (1974) *Management.* Oxford, Butterworth/Heinemann.

Duckenfield, M. and Stirner, P. (1992) *Learning through Work.* Sheffield, Employment Department.

Employment Department (1990) *The Skills Link.* Sheffield, Employment Department.

Garratt, B. (1987) *The Learning Organization.* London, Fontana.

Gouldner, A. (1979) *The Future of Intellectuals.* London, Macmillan.

Gramsci, A. (1971) *Selections from the Prison Notebooks.* London, Lawrence and Wishart.

Hakes, C. (1991) *Total Quality Management.* London, Chapman & Hall.

Harding, S. (1986) *The Science Question in Feminism.* Milton Keynes, Open University Press.

Hutchins, D. (1988) *Just in Time.* Aldershot, Gower.

Jameson, F. (1984) Postmodernism, or the cultural logic of late capitalism, *New Left Review,* no. 146.

Jessup, G. (1991) *Outcomes.* London, Falmer Press.

Littler, C. (1990) The labour process debate, a theoretical review, in D. Knights and H. Willmott (eds) *Labour Process Theory.* Basingstoke, Macmillan.

Mandel, E. (1978) *Late Capitalism.* London, Verso.

MCI (1991) *Occupational Standards for Management.* London, Management Charter Initiative.

Newman, J.H. (1982) *The Idea of a University.* South Bend, IN, University of Notre Dame Press.

Roth, J. (1965) Hired hand research, *The American Sociologist,* 1, 190–6.

Samuelson, P. (1980) *Economics,* 11th edn. Tokyo, McGraw-Hill.

Sohn-Rethel A. (1978) *Intellectual and Manual Labour.* London, Macmillan.

Thompson, E.P. (1970) *Warwick University Ltd.* Harmondsworth, Penguin.

Thompson, P. (1990) Crawling from the wreckage: the labour process and the politics of production, in D. Knights and H. Willmott (eds) *Labour Process Theory.* Basingstoke, Macmillan.

Wardell, M. (1990) Labour and labour process, in D. Knights and H. Willmott (eds) *Labour Process Theory.* Basingstoke, Macmillan.

Wernick, A. (1991) *Promotional Culture.* London, Sage Publications.

Willmott, H. (1990) Subjectivity and the dialectics of praxis, in D. Knights and H. Willmott (eds) *Labour Process Theory.* Basingstoke, Macmillan.

Winter, R. (1989) Some notes on ideology and critique, in *Learning from Experience.* Lewes, Falmer Press.

Winter, R. (1991) Postmodern sociology as a democratic educational practice – some suggestions, *British Journal of Sociology of Education*, 12(4), 467–82.

Winter, R. (1992) 'Quality management' or 'the educative workplace': alternative versions of competence-based education, *Journal of Further and Higher Education*, 16(3).

Winter, R. and Maisch, M. (1992) *Accrediting Professional Competences, the Final Report of the ASSET Programme.* Chelmsford, Anglia Polytechnic University.

9

Deck Chairs on the *Titanic*: Award Restructuring for Academics in the Age of Economic Rationalism

Jan Currie and Roger Woock

Like other OECD countries, Australia experienced tightening governmental control of higher education and financial constraints which led to the restructuring of institutions. With its 'clever country' policy, the 1992 Labor government attempted to use higher educational institutions to make the country more competitive internationally.

The movement from an elite to a mass system of education occurred most markedly in the decade from 1980 to 1990 and is demonstrated by the tremendous growth in student numbers. In 1950 there were 31 000 students, by 1985 there were 370 000 students and by 1991 there were 534 538 students. In the period 1983–91 student numbers increased by 53.3 per cent (AVCC 1992). During a similar period (1983–90) funding per student declined by 12 per cent (Zetlin 1992). This has resulted in heavier workloads and a lack of resources, leading to a deterioration in the physical plant of universities and in the quality of education provided to students.

In Braverman's (1974) terms, management (whether that is seen as the government or as the senior executive of universities) is extracting more labour from its academics. It is demanding that academics become more productive. At the same time, management is distancing itself from academics and the term corporate managerialism has been applied to senior executives in universities. A most recent development is the federal government's plan to apply 'quality assessment' to Australian universities. 'Management practices' will be an area of performance to be assessed (Maslen 1992). Academics' teaching and research production will also be assessed. Braverman's notion of applying methods of science is likely to be used to develop performance indicators. These, in turn, may be used to compare or rank institutions on their ability to manage resources efficiently and to teach courses effectively. The use of performance indicators and this notion of scientific management will be contested by academics, who will read this as a further reduction in their autonomy over their own work practices.

The story told in this chapter about award restructuring for academics is subject to different interpretations, particularly in terms of success or failure for academic unions. One thing is clear: whatever losses or victories can be identified, the process of extracting more labour from academic workers continues, although at a different level and in a more focused way.

Entrepreneurial push

Thatcher's reforms for higher education in the UK were spelled out in a White Paper, *Higher Education: Meeting the Challenge* (1987), which has to some extent been a model for reform in Australia. Higher education was to 'have closer links with industry and commerce and promote enterprise', which includes 'more selectively funded research, targeted with attention to prospects for commercial exploitation'.

Similar changes in the orientation and distribution of research funding have occurred in Australia. These have resulted in greater direct government control over research funding (Marshall 1990) and a desire to use research to improve the economy. The principles of selectivity and concentration underlie the government's 1989 Statement on Higher Education Research. There is an emphasis on 'mission-oriented' research, which is directed toward solving problems rather than research which is curiosity based. There has been the introduction of matching grants to facilitate corporate–university research linkages (Liyanage and Mitchell 1992). A recent report (Block 1991) recommends that by the end of 1996 each higher education institution should be required to find an equivalent to 5 per cent of its total Commonwealth funding for research from industry. In addition, at least 10 per cent of Australian Research Council expenditure and 10 per cent of National Health and Medical Research Council expenditure should be set aside for projects that have demonstrated commercial commitment by industry. In sum, the shift to collaborative research schemes focuses on more strategic and industry-driven research and compels academics to adopt a greater commercial orientation to academic research.

Corporate managerialism

One consequence of these changes has been a shift in the discourse of higher education institutions towards that of corporate managerialism in Australia (Ball 1990; Lingard 1991). Lingard argues that corporate managerialism grew from the ideology of economic rationalism. 'Under its rubric, public sector bureaucracies are restructured as a way to achieve greater outputs for given inputs. What is required is a leaner, tighter, more precisely defined management structure, and more precisely articulated policy goals, as well as the devolution to the service agencies at the work face' (Lingard 1991: 86).

This is happening in higher education institutions as universities are turned into corporations that are establishing devolution of responsibility (one line budgets) and at the same time gaining greater centralised control. The Dawkins White Paper (1988) demonstrated the change in terminology that became part of the higher education scene in Australia. Chapter 10, on 'institutional management and staffing', asserted that effective institutional *management* was the key to achieving Commonwealth objectives and it expected government bodies to delegate responsibility for implementing this policy to *chief executive officers*. Governing bodies were to be equated to corporate boards in the private sector. Dawkins also felt that there should be a significant rationalization of the often complicated mode of government by committee within institutions (Dawkins 1988: 103).

Ball, in analysing management as moral technology along Foucauldian lines, examines the effect it has on workers. He notes that 'the costs involved for workers in achieving greater efficiency (intensification, loss of autonomy, closer monitoring and appraisal, non-participation in decision-making, lack of personal development through work) are rarely considered' (Ball 1990: 154). He also suggests that the gap between workers and management appears to be widening steadily and inevitably, while at the same time the paraphernalia of controls upon them is growing ever more sophisticated and oppressive.

To demonstrate Ball's thesis about the changes involved in creating greater productivity or efficiency, here are a few examples of what has occurred in the past five years in Australian universities. Although not all of Dawkins's suggestions from the 1988 White Paper have been imposed upon universities, a number of changes can be identified that have led to an increase in the amount of control upon academics' work in Australia. Universities now have to negotiate their profiles and develop performance indicators or targets which determine their level of funding. Academics are now to undergo staff appraisal based on 'objective criteria', and with the introduction of redundancy and dismissal procedures based on unsatisfactory performance could be retrenched, demoted or fired. Universities are developing strategic plans and now have human resource departments instead of personnel departments to make more efficient use of their 'human capital'. There is an increased emphasis on selection of senior academics using management criteria. Senior management is developing a higher profile of managers for research development, fund raising and public relations to create a 'market niche' for its institutions.

Adversarial model

There is a clear shift from a collegial model of decision-making within universities to a more confrontational model. Although academics have been slow to unionize, in recent years there has been growing frustration among academics that has led to industrial action. This has occurred not only in Australia but also in other English-speaking countries. McCulloch (1992) describes the trend toward academic unionism in Canada, the United States and Australia. For example, the USA experienced a huge upsurge in unionization among academic staff from the mid-1960s to the early 1980s that coincided with the onset of stagnation in higher education. From the mid-1970s the Canadian Association of Universities substantially increased its involvement in collective bargaining. In the 1980s Australian academics became unionized and more militant in defence of their collective interests.

Nielsen and Polishook, who are academics and officers of the American Federation of Teachers, asserted that 'faculty unionism was not an effort to create a bilateral adversarial system of governance, but rather a *response* to the historical transition from "college" to "corporation" in which the administration became "management" and professors were reduced to "employees" ' (Derber 1988: 118). Shaw (1985: 12) described this change in the United States as 'an institutional drift from faculty to centralized control where administrators have adopted management strategies which reduce costs by increasing administrative control.' He commented that centralized control undercuts the autonomy, collegiality and shared governance that is central to the myth of academe.

Movement from professionals to unionized employees

Academics have been one of the last groups in the workforce to become unionized. In 1952 university staff associations joined to form the Federal Council of University Staff Associations, which became the Federation of Australian University Staff Associations (FAUSA) in 1964. The Federation of Staff Associations of Colleges of Advanced Education was formed in August 1968 and later became the Federation of College Academics (FCA) and the Union of Australian College Academics (UACA) in 1983. These associations were only loosely formed to achieve limited goals. There was no suggestion that these associations should act as 'unions' to press for better working conditions and contemplate industrial action to increase wages; however, as O'Brien (1992) has argued, the period from the 1950s to the 1980s was a time when relations in the higher education sector shifted from 'post-feudal community to the achievement of modernity' when the nascent form of an industrial relations model could be detected.

FAUSA first applied for registration as a federal union in 1979. This was denied and a challenge to this decision was lost in the High Court in 1982. The two principal unions covering academics, the Federated Australian University Staff Associations (FAUSA) and the Union of Australian College Academics (UACA), were registered as unions in 1986 and 1987 (respectively) and it was then that they began to negotiate a national award with the employers, who, in the meantime, had formed the Australian Higher Education Industrial Association (AHEIA).

The pressure to become more organized as unions coincided with a dramatic increase in the number of staff and students in tertiary institutions during the 1970s and 1980s. Between 1987 and 1991, there was a corresponding decline in working conditions that especially affected university academics as the government reduced the student per capita funding and introduced a series of 'clawbacks' in research funding. At the same time there was a dramatic decline in real wages. Marginson (1990: 3) analysed the decline of academic salaries between 1967 to 1990 and reported that:

> Since 1975–76 the total annual salary received by a Senior Lecturer has declined by 18.9 per cent in real terms. In the last financial year (1988–89), before any award restructuring increases had been received, Australian academics received less wages in real terms than they did in 1967–1968.

Award restructuring for universities

In the 1980s, the government began to demand greater accountability from universities, first through its statutory body, the Commonwealth Tertiary Education Commission (CTEC), and then directly through the Minister's department after the CTEC was abolished. Two inquiries into higher education (*Review of Efficiency and Effectiveness in Higher Education* by the CTEC in 1986 and *Setting the Course* by the House or Representatives in 1988) reviewed the effectiveness of institutional practices and made recommendations for some changes, but nothing as revolutionary as the changes recommended by the Minister, John Dawkins, through the White Paper (1988).

In many instances, award restructuring highlighted the imperfections that existed in Australian universities over this past century. According to one of FAUSA's industrial officers, the notion of a truly democratic collegial decision-making process was more myth than real. The collegial system, as it was instituted in the older, more 'traditional', universities, was dominated by an academic board that was composed of professors. Junior staff were rarely involved in decision-making at the institutional level. They may have been involved in making decisions at the departmental level regarding their own teaching and work patterns, but overall, this kind of organization structure could not be described as either flat or democratic.

Through award restructuring, it was acknowledged that all employees should have the opportunity to progress to the highest nominated skill level and that the 'availability of vacancies' structure should be abolished. It is not clear at this stage whether institutions will allow an unfettered internal promotion system to operate since the Australian Industrial Relations Commission (AIRC) also specified that promotion should operate on a needs basis which may allow institutions to introduce quotas on the number of academics promoted from one level of the scale to the next. There was also a change to minimum rates awards which was decided by the AIRC on 26

October 1989 at the beginning of the award restructuring process for academics and did not entail extensive negotiations with the unions. According to one of the AHEIA's industrial officers, in the eyes of the vice-chancellors this was the single most important benefit achieved. Even though market loadings had already crept into the system with Dawkins's approval and clinical loadings existed for medical and dental staff, the introduction of minimum rates awards allowed individual institutions to develop their own policies on over-award payments. Before 1989, during the period when there was a national salary structure, only limited flexibility existed.

Another aspect of the system that demonstrated its 'quaintness' was its managerial structure and the lack of specified procedures for settling disputes or processing appeals. Decision-making within universities tended to be based on 'gentlemanly' agreements among the professors and vice-chancellors. With the Dawkins revolution came changes to the management structures within universities. Vice-chancellors were quick to deplore the emergence of an adversarial model with the chief executive officer as part of a distinct management group confronting academics as a separate group (Pennington 1991a). Professor Pennington of Melbourne remarked that 'the language of academia is now infected with the slogans of industrial relations, polarised between "bosses" and "workers".' He felt that this change 'represents the greatest single threat to collegial governance in Australian universities since their foundation in the 1850s' (Pennington 1991a: 8).

The negotiation process

The following discussion of award restructuring details the perspectives of academics and their employers as portrayed in the negotiations between the unions and the AHEIA.[1] It is based on a series of 'negotiated' interviews with seven officials from both unions, two AHEIA industrial officers and one of the vice-chancellors involved in the negotiations during 1990–1 (see Table 9.1).

It was clear at the beginning of the negotiations that the academic unions wanted national standards and better conditions in a number of areas: increased salaries, portability of tenure and study leave, criteria for promotion and probation, a uniform probation period, increased casual rates and reduced percentage of casual staff and tenure for academics on short-term contracts. They were opposed to the introduction of performance appraisals and performance bars within the salary structure and wanted to maintain a paid rates award. They differed from the AHEIA on when payment for PhDs should begin. The unions' position was to see the PhD as an entry into teaching at Lecturer B (first rung) level, whereas the AHEIA felt the PhD should come in at the fifth point on the Lecturer A scale (a lower entry point than had been considered traditionally in the past, although there would be considerable variation across institutions and over time with regard to payment for this qualification).

Table 9.1 Perspectives on award restructuring from the unions' and the AHEIA's points of view

Unions' perspective	AHEIA's perspective
Want national standards on: • criteria for promotion • probation period.	Diversity of methods for probation and promotion, no national standards.
Want portability of tenure and study leave.	Preserve institutional autonomy.
Maintain paid rates award.	Maintain flexibility.
Broad criteria for promotion.	Introduce minimum rates award.
Want higher salaries (15–20% rises).	Broad criteria for promotion.
Point to point translation scale (6 months).	Want higher salaries (15–20% rise).
Improve staff development.	More delayed translation scale (2 years).
Career paths.	Improve staff development.
Limit casualization:	Maintain status quo.
• tighter regulation of numbers and conditions	Preserve right to have casual staff:
• abolish repeat rates (a lesser rate when tutors repeated tutorials) and overall increase in hourly rates.	• a certain proportion of casuals is essential • want differentiation of rates • no limit to number, which is important to some institutions, some sections.
Maintain current probation criteria.	Probation that really bites.
Oppose formal staff appraisal systems (UACA).	Staff assessment linked to increments and performance barriers linked to appraisals.
Oppose in principle but allow individual institutions to negotiate trip wire models (FAUSA).	Minimum payment for PhDs fifth point in Lecturer A scale.
Minimum payment for PhDs at bottom of Lecturer B scale.	

The AHEIA was against any national standards on academic staffing practices, such as recruitment methods, promotion and probation criteria. Regarding these, it wanted to preserve institutional autonomy. In general it wanted the maximum amount of flexibility within the system. It did not want to have any further regulation of casual staff. It believed that each institution could decide on the numbers because a certain proportion of casual staff was essential and might potentially be more important in certain sections of the university than in other sections. It wanted performance barriers linked to staff appraisal and a probation system that would 'really bite' (comment by an AHEIA industrial officer).

After several months of negotiations the AHEIA agreed with the unions on the salary increases. They both decided to argue for increases between 12 and 20 per cent although there was disagreement in the end on the translation arrangements. Rather than a point to point translation of the salary scales, the vice-chancellors argued for and won a two year phase-in for academic salaries with no increments during the two year period. (Many academics saw this as a clear case in which the vice-chancellors sided with the government in an attempt to save the government money.) The AHEIA's position on the translation arrangement was one of the major reasons academics later went on strike.

From discussions with union officials, it emerged that they felt that the AHEIA benefited from the 'second tier' wage round by the government's intervention and they did not want this to recur in the award restructuring negotiations. As a result, a strategy the unions adopted was to lobby particular advisors within the government on contentious issues. Despite having the government on their side on some issues, the unions had to argue quite strongly in the Commission against the government on the salary scales. On this matter, the AHEIA joined with the unions to argue against the government's position.

The AHEIA did not have the support of the government for all its objectives and became particularly angered by the role that the Minister's advisor played in the negotiations. One of the principals commented:

> The covert involvement of DEET and the Minister's advisor, especially, was very unsatisfactory. Commonwealth changed its position at the last moment before the Commission and went against the case for staff appraisal. It was difficult to gain consistent statements from the Commonwealth. . .DEET officers had little knowledge of academic institutions and the advisor to the Minister was drawn from former officers of the union and maintained close links with them.

In the end the government played a political role in trying to limit the salary scales and extend the period of time for their translations. However, it dropped the performance bars as they exist in New Zealand universities, within Level C, after lobbying from the unions and the AHEIA, for both considered the proposal to be unworkable.

Prolonged negotiations

There were several factors that led to prolonged negotiations. This dispute was not just over salaries. There were complex issues dealt with in award restructuring which made it difficult to negotiate all the factors simultaneously. Between August and May 1990 the two parties negotiated on many aspects of award restructuring and by the latter date were able to report to the Commission that they had reached some common ground and could also identify the major differences in their positions. During this time, it was difficult to reach agreement and it was only through compulsory meetings in the Commission that the two parties were assisted in moving toward some agreement. A comment by one union officer demonstrates the difficulties they faced:

AHEIA saw award restructuring as a vehicle for allowing greater management prerogatives, greater flexibility of the workforce. Any idea of
benefit to academics was very limited. Even things that could lead to a
more efficient workforce, e.g. prescribing staff development in the
award, they fought tooth and nail. They fought vigorously against providing career paths for all academics. They felt the positions of tutors
and senior tutors should be seen as an apprenticeship type model.

From May to November 1990 both parties continued negotiating but it
was not until the industrial action approached that they began to find
solutions on some key areas. There is no doubt, in the opinion of one of
the unions' officers, that the threat of industrial action made the AHEIA
agree on some issues, such as the position classification standards, the
payment for PhDs and a career structure for all academics; all these would
have to be seen as a movement toward the union position. This union
official commented that 'the employers caved in on many issues when
industrial action was threatening.' Soon after the industrial action it was
agreed that several items could not be negotiated and would have to go to
arbitration.

Both the main players were undergoing changes in their roles as well as
experiencing 'intra-organizational' conflicts that made it difficult for them
to present a united front. The vice-chancellors were moving from a fairly
autocratic management style to a more corporate management style and
were under new economic pressures from the government to compete for
funds. There were divisions among the vice-chancellors on some of the
issues but the main impetus for the negotiations came from the President
of the AHEIA. One union official commented on the AHEIA's vacillating
positions:

> AHEIA did not have an agenda and had little industrial experience.
> They kept changing their position. The AHEIA Industrial Officers had
> to continually refer to AHEIA principals to get instructions. There was
> the feeling that the ghost of David Pennington [President of the AHEIA
> and Vice-Chancellor of University of Melbourne] was hovering over
> the negotiation table.

The AHEIA negotiators took the lead from David Pennington. However,
there were times when the lack of unanimity among the vice-chancellors
surfaced. Towards the end of the negotiations, a small number of vice-
chancellors broke ranks with the AHEIA and several made public statements supporting the academics' position, especially on performance
appraisal for incremental advance. Pennington, in an article in *The Australian*, pointed to the lack of a united front on award restructuring. 'This
situation has led to incidents where individual Vice Chancellors have declared support for union claims in the midst of industrial action against
policies to which they themselves had earlier agreed upon in meetings of
the AHEIA' (Pennington 1991b).

There was difficulty in finding solutions because of the different perceptions of the process held by the two parties. The AHEIA felt it had to present a package to the government that would consist of some trade-off for higher salaries. It felt the government would not agree to large salary increases without some commitment to performance appraisal by universities. However, union officials felt the AHEIA did not even have a reasonable conception of what was necessary in award restructuring.

AHEIA felt that they could waltz into the Industrial Relations Commission with a deregulated market, a flexible system and the Commission would grant salary rises. They had no idea of what was demanded in terms of the award restructuring principles.

AHEIA officials held a different view:

The delays were caused by the unions preparing for industrial action. We were ready to negotiate soon after the May agreements. The agenda had been laid out in front of the Commission and we had all agreed on the parameters of the negotiations. The union did not keep to the timetable.

It seemed fairly obvious that neither side was able to change the attitude of the other in the early stages of the negotiations. The AHEIA and the unions were not willing to compromise on any of the crucial issues. As a result of this deadlock in negotiations, the unions felt that they were being forced into industrial action because of the recalcitrant attitude of the employers (FAUSA President's Report 1991). On the other hand, the AHEIA believed that the unions were stalling the negotiations to create the climate for industrial action at exam time, hoping this would lead to a favourable breakthrough.

Both sides suggested that other factors impinging on the award restructuring process probably caused some of the delays. The effects of the Dawkins White Paper, especially the amalgamation of institutions that resulted in the Unified National System, overlapped directly with some of the objectives of award restructuring. One of the reasons for the overlapping of these objectives was because the efficiency principle informed both of these restructuring agendas. Academics and vice-chancellors were caught up in the political struggles of either being for or against these 'forced' amalgamations. The whole situation was intensified by the fact that union amalgamations were also occurring at the same time, which created friction between union officials and caused a drain on the energies of officials working on both these issues simultaneously.

The impact of industrial action

Pennington, one of the AHEIA's principals, wrote an article about the unions and the academic dispute in the Melbourne University Gazette. He suggested two reasons why the unions took industrial action: 'One was that the union leadership was convinced that industrial action was necessary to convince the Government of the need for more money. The other was that many unionists were opposed to linking salaries to the individual perform-ance of staff' (Pennington 1990). Pennington decried the use of industrial action, the cost to universities and the long-term effect of polarizing deci-sion-making. 'Matters which were once agreed through collegial processes have been thrown into the arena of industrial confrontation, taking them outside the scope of university decision-making' (Pennington 1990). A union officer expressed another view:

> The industrial action made the antagonism between academics and VCs more visible. The hostility could have been there already anyway. The causes for the antagonism were already present in the system. The existence of unions per se does not lead to an antagonistic relationship.

It was obvious that some staff at the University of Melbourne did not believe that the collegial decision-making process was working to their advantage. Pennington had to deal with sporadic industrial action at his institution for a year, which included the non-cooperation of some union members in the staff appraisal process. The length of the bans on marks in several states also suggests that the rank and file members were more mili-tant and were more willing to engage in protracted industrial action than some of the union officials might have expected. The new militancy of many university academics, particularly in New South Wales, could have resulted from the combined effect of Dawkins's restructuring of universi-ties, which led to a serious decline in the working conditions of academics, the frustration with the delays seen to be caused by the AHEIA and the loss in living standards over the past 15 years which Sydney academics may have felt more acutely.

During the negotiating process and the ensuing industrial action, aca-demics who were union members had to alter their perception of their union. Many academics still thought of the union as a professional associa-tion and had difficulty with the idea that they should take industrial action and act in solidarity. As a result, the militancy portrayed by union members was not uniform across the country. There were some resignations from the unions because of the industrial action. Overall, though, most academics realized that stronger union actions were necessary to improve working conditions.

Conclusion

Historically, academics have had neither strong union organization nor industrial muscle. Nevertheless, by showing that they were prepared to take industrial action and that there existed considerable solidarity among the rank and file membership, they were able to move the negotiations towards a solution. Of course, it is unlikely that they would have gained as much as they did without the backing of the ACTU and the Minister's office. The backing of the ACTU enabled the academic unions to come into the mainstream of industrial relations and they gained the confidence of the Commission. The backing of the Minister's office on the non-salary items was crucial in moving the AHEIA towards a settlement. Finally, industrial action could be argued to have played a crucial role enabling academics to gain a better overall award restructuring package. The final salary scales were closer to those proposed by the unions in their revised claim than those initially suggested by the Commonwealth and the employers. The size of the increases, relative to many other industries, indicates the importance of all these factors working together.

Even though the federal government has implemented a number of changes by restructuring higher education, individual institutions still maintain considerable autonomy. For this reason alone, the long-term effects of award restructuring can truly only be assessed at the institutional level.

One of the first steps that has been taken to implement award restructuring is the establishment of consultative groups which are operating alongside the regular decision-making structures of the university. One of the implications of an industrial relations model is that more power is in the hands of the union, a collective organization, rather than in the hands of individual academics. However, most vice-chancellors have fiercely resisted this kind of model. They have been arguing to preserve their notion of collegiality. Their notion of collegiality is clearly an individualist one which is subject to 'old boy networks' and, with the salary flexibility now available, the offer of increased remuneration for 'outstanding' performance.

Some academics are resisting the move towards a more industrial relations model for they prefer to work in a deregulated environment where no conditions are codified. Their ideal is a community based on trust and professional integrity, not one that is codified and that demands all staff have access to similar provisions. In a sense, like the vice-chancellors, these academics, it could be argued, are living in the past, for the notion of a professional association has already given way to a more industrial organization. Those academic staff associations which have tended to operate somewhat like 'inner clubs' will now have to develop stronger collective organizations in the workplace.

Academic unions have, it is hoped, gained a greater realization of their strengths and weaknesses in the process of negotiation and taking industrial action. Many academics lamented that they had little industrial muscle because, if they went on strike, nobody would notice. However, the very threat of strike seemed to have some effect and the fact that they had some power over management by withholding marks meant that the strength they did have could be targeted at a particular time of the year and have maximum effect, especially given the understanding of the situation and support expressed by the National Union of Students. There may have been some doubt among the union leadership whether the rank and file would have enough resolve to implement the industrial action so that the militancy of academics may have surprised the union leadership as much as it did the vice-chancellors. There is little doubt that this action has meant that a new stage in industrial relations between academics and management has begun to take root.

While award restructuring may lead to some improvements in benefits for academics, it must be noted that it has not remedied injustices that academics have suffered over the last decade. The groups that have been most exploited within higher education, casuals working part-time and those on limited contracts (untenured, temporary, but renewable), have had only minor adjustments to their working conditions. Two major concerns with the current situation are the position classification standards and staff appraisal. These current processes are left to the interpretation and implementation of individual universities.

There is no doubt that working conditions of full-time academics have deteriorated in the past five years in Australia. Stephen Ball's (1990) point that one of the effects of achieving greater efficiency is the intensification of work certainly applies to academics. Workloads in terms of teaching and administration have increased to such an extent that research activities have been reduced, at just the time when increased scholarly output is being demanded for tenure or promotion. It is increasingly evident that 'time' for research is something which academics will have to buy through external grants and consultancies. There has also been a movement to control resources centrally while devolving administrative responsibility which has led to more administrative work for academics with no compensation in terms of time or additional appointments.

As a result of these developments the unions need to negotiate national benchmarks on teaching and administrative workloads. Perhaps the whole negotiating process described in this chapter is best seen as a bridge to a new era in university life in Australia. The almost accomplished fact of enterprise bargaining will produce an era of sharp, local, adversarial and confrontational relationships; a very different one from that envisioned by either staff associations or vice-chancellors eight years ago.

Notes

This research was funded by the Australian Research Council's Small Grants Scheme. Revisions of this chapter have benefited from the comments of Cora Baldock, Russell Blackford, Ray Fells, Joan Hardy, Simon Marginson, Herb Thompson and Julie Tracy. This study could not have been completed without the time given by the individuals interviewed in the UACA, FAUSA and AHEIA and their valuable perspectives on award restructuring.

1. The Australian Teachers Union (ATU) also took part in the negotiations. It had a significant but minor role and officials were not interviewed for this project.

References

Australian Vice Chancellors' Committee (1992) *Australian Universities in a Changing World.* Canberra: AVCC.

Ball, S.J. (1990) Management as moral technology: a Luddite analysis, in S.J. Ball (ed.) *Foucault and Education: Disciplines and Knowledge.* London, Routledge, 153–66.

Block, R. (1991) Bringing the market to bear on research, Report of the Task Force on the Commercialisation of Research (November), Canberra, AGPS.

Braverman, H. (1974) *Labor and Monopoly Capital.* New York, Monthly Review Press.

Commonwealth Tertiary Education Commission (1986) Review of efficiency and effectiveness in higher education, Report of the Committee of Enquiry chaired by H.R. Hudson (September), Canberra, AGPS.

Dawkins, J.S. (1988) *Higher Education: the Challenge Ahead* (Government White Paper on Higher Education). Canberra, AGPS.

Derber, M. (1988) Management organization for collective bargaining in the public sector, in G. Aaron, J.M. Najita and J.L. Stern (eds) *Public Sector Bargaining,* 2nd edn. Washington, DC, Bureau of National Affairs.

Department of Education and Science (1987) *Higher Education: Meeting the Challenge,* Cm 114. London, HMSO.

FAUSA's President's Report (1991) Presented by Ralph Hall at the Annual General Meeting, Melbourne, October.

House of Representatives Standing Committee on Employment, Education and Training (1988) Setting the course, Report on the efficiency and effectiveness of institutional practices in the higher education sector chaired by J. Brumby (May), Canberra, AGPS.

Lingard, B. (1991) Policy-making for Australian schooling: the new corporate federalism, *Journal of Education Policy,* 6(1), 85–90.

Liyanage, S. and Mitchell, H. (1992) Changing patterns of research direction in higher education institutions: evidence from the Australian higher education system, unpublished paper, Wollongong, Centre for Research Policy, University of Wollongong.

McCulloch, G. (1992) In defence of Australian unionism, unpublished paper, 19 May, Melbourne, Union of Australian College Academics and Federated Council of Academics.

Marginson, S. (1990) Academic salaries in Australia, 1967 to 1990, *Australian Universities' Review,* 27 June, 1–10.

Marshall, N. (1990) End of an era: the collapse of the 'buffer' approach in the governance of Australian tertiary education, *Higher Education,* 19(2), 147–67.

Maslen, G. (1992) Extra university grants to be tied to assessment of quality, *The Age,* 9 November, 3.

O'Brien, J. (1992) The emergence of the collective organisation of Australian academic staff 1949–1983, paper delivered at the Annual Conference of the Association of Industrial Relations Academics of Australia and New Zealand, 29 January to 1 February.

Pennington, D. (1990) Collegiality and quality: unions and the academic dispute, *Melbourne University Gazette,* April, 13–14.

Pennington, D. (1991a) State and academia: accountability and autonomy, Speech to Conference of Executive Heads, New Delhi, 15 January.

Pennington, D. (1991b) Masters of our own destiny, *The Australian* (*Higher Education Supplement*), 2 October.

Shaw, G.C. (1985) Debunking the myth of academe, *Thought and Action*, 1(2), 10–15.

Zetlin, D. (1992) Australia's postsecondary education changes revolutionary, *CAUT Bulletin*, 6 June.

10

Beyond the Multiversity: Fiscal Crisis and the Changing Structure of Academic Labour

Clyde W. Barrow

The 1990–2 recession marked the beginning of a severe fiscal crisis in American higher education. Operating budgets at 86 per cent of US higher institutions either remained flat or declined, in real dollars, during 1990 and 1991.[1] In 1992, state governments made total appropriations to higher education that, in the aggregate, were less than the previous year's total appropriations for the first time in more than three decades (Jaschik 1991). Both public and private institutions responded initially with a variety of temporary cost-containment measures, such as employee furloughs, hiring freezes and deferred raises.[2] These initial measures assumed, incorrectly, that the budget difficulties in higher education were a short-term problem related primarily to a normal downturn in the business cycle.

However, this initial assessment has changed rapidly, so that 71 per cent of college and university administrators now view adequate finances as the main challenge facing higher institutions for at least the next five years.[3] Thus, in a remarkably brief time, higher education administrators and state government officials have shifted from a policy of recession-induced cutbacks to the formulation of strategic plans that aim to enhance the long-term academic efficiency of American higher institutions.[4] These strategic plans are moving beyond the multiversity concept to a 'flexiversity' model of higher education that emphasizes market specialization and faculty flexibility, as opposed to programme diversification and faculty specialization (New England Board of Higher Education 1992). The transition from a multiversity to a flexiversity model of higher education is already changing the structure of academic labour and the current changes suggest that the flexiversity of the 1990s will emphasize selective excellence, flexible specialization and workforce dualization in organizing the academic labour process.

A decade of fiscal crisis

Fiscal crisis has frequently been the midwife of institutional reform in American higher education. Indeed, throughout the twentieth century, major institutional reforms have typically been initiated by academic efficiency movements, rather than by any concern for achieving educational objectives (Scott 1983; Barrow 1992). A fiscal crisis is a long-term tendency for expenditures to increase more rapidly than revenues (O'Connor 1973: 9). Widespread reductions in state support, constraints on further tuition increases and deferred capital maintenance expenses have already combined to plunge American higher institutions into fiscal crisis. Moreover, any recovery from that underlying crisis will be offset by the increased costs of rising enrolments in the mid-1990s and the pressure will again be exacerbated as faculty retirements accelerate into the next century. Thus, the theory of fiscal crisis suggests that annual operating deficits will grow larger each year, especially since external constraints on revenue growth will deprive educational planners of a viable revenue option. As a result, educational planners are left primarily with the option of closing structural gaps in operating budgets through institutional restructurings designed to reduce the long-term growth in real costs and expenditures.

Revenues

The operating budgets of American higher institutions are derived primarily from a combination of state support and student tuition. The public institutions depend heavily on state appropriations and, importantly, they enrol 78 per cent of all students attending a higher institution in the United States. State support for higher education is not likely to rebound significantly after the recession because states, as a whole, are facing structural gaps in their own budgets. Despite unprecedented budget cuts in 1991 and 1992, and tax increases of $25 billion during the same period, 30 states approached the end of fiscal year 1992 with unresolved budget deficits. Many states were still struggling with budget deficits as they entered fiscal year 1993 (Eckl *et al.* 1992). As a result, the most recent *Fiscal Survey of the States* (1992), conducted annually by the National Governor's Association, concludes that throughout the nation state officials have begun implementing 'a permanent reduction of state governments that will force attention on...[the] restructuring of major state services such as education, welfare and health.'

There are two reasons to expect that the pressures to restructure public higher education will be particularly strong. First, despite real growth in state appropriations to higher education during the 1980s, a subtle deprioritization of public higher education was already under way in the states. States slowly reduced the percentage of their budgets allocated to higher education, partly in order to fund competing priorities and programmes (Bowen and

Schuster 1986: 95). In 1980, states allocated 8.3 per cent of tax dollars to higher education, but by 1989 the percentage had fallen to 7.2 per cent. The established trend was merely exacerbated by the recession as higher education appropriations fell to 6.9 per cent of state tax revenues in 1991 (Halstead 1991: 148).

Second, fiscal analyses prepared by the National Conference of State Legislatures now emphasize that for the foreseeable future any increases in state revenues will be consumed entirely by inflation and by the higher cost of entitlement programmes such as K-12 education, aid to families with dependent children and Medicaid (Eckl *et al.* 1992: 1, 13, 17). Thus, even if additional tax increases are forthcoming, and even if state revenue projections are unduly pessimistic, higher education will be competing over the coming years with other state services for limited funds and it is not likely, when judged against other claimants, that higher education will be viewed as a major social priority (California Postsecondary Education Commission 1990: 38–9; O'Brien 1990: 4–5). Thus, it is unlikely that higher education will be able to improve its relative budget status and, therefore, higher institutions will be expected to operate, in real terms, off the lower financial base established during the recession.

At the same time, both public and private institutions are encountering severe constraints on their ability to raise student tuition and fees. From a long-term perspective, it is important to note that tuition and fee increases during the 1980s outstripped both the Consumer Price Index (CPI) and the growth in real income. In the decade from 1979–80 to 1989–90, mandatory charges increased at public higher institutions by 109 per cent and at private institutions by 145 per cent. By comparison, the CPI only increased by 64 per cent during the same period (US Department of Education 1991: 161, 298–9). Furthermore, during the same period, most Americans experienced an average 6 per cent decline in real incomes owing to the long-term restructuring of the American economy (Mishel and Bernstein 1992). The disequilibrium between real incomes and mandatory charges was again merely exacerbated by the recession, as public institutions, especially, adopted large tuition increases to offset state budget cuts.

However, this strategy is counterproductive beyond a limited point. Previous research by economists has predicted that as institutions raise prices, the demand for higher education will decline at most income levels (Jackson and Weathersby 1975). Thus, excessive tuition fee increases will result in declining enrolments, which creates a need for more tuition fee increases, and so on, in a downward spiral. Consequently, after a decade in which mandatory charges increased by an average of 8–13 per cent annually, the current rate of increase has slowed to the inflation level as most institutions announced 1992–3 tuition fee increases of only 2–6 per cent (College Board 1992). Furthermore, because the number of high school graduates and, therefore, the potential demand for higher education will continue to decline through the 1993–4 academic year, competition for a declining supply of students will act as a further break on tuition and other fee increases at least until the second half of the decade (US Department of Education 1990: 77).

Expenditures

Despite revenue constraints in the 1990s, there are at least three structural trends that will increase the real operating costs of higher institutions: (a) non-deferrable capital maintenance requirements; (b) a baby boom echo that will increase enrolments beginning in the mid-1990s; and (c) faculty shortages created by a rapidly ageing workforce towards the end of the 1990s. Hence, over the course of the current decade, a series of expenditure waves will engulf higher institutions each time they successfully stabilize their finances.

First, in the midst of recession, United States higher institutions have found that deferred capital maintenance and replacement schedules cannot be deferred any longer. A comparative study of space utilization standards prepared for the California Postsecondary Education Commission (CPSEC) finds that 'a need to renovate or replace many facilities built in the 1950s and 1960s is now emerging' throughout the United States (MGT Consultants 1990: 7). A Coopers and Lybrand analysis prepared for the Association of Physical Plant Administrators estimates that $70 billion is needed to fund the existing backlog in capital renewal and replacement needs on American campuses. More than $20 billion of this amount is needed immediately to address priority repairs and renovations that, if left undone, will place facilities at risk (Rush and Johnson 1989).

Second, even if higher institutions meet their capital renewal and deferred maintenance backlogs in a timely manner, it will only be in time to accommodate the emerging baby boom echo. The US Department of Education (1991: 77) projects that the current decline in the number of high school graduates will start to reverse in the 1994–5 academic year. The Western Interstate Commission for Higher Education (WICHE) projects that in the decade from 1991–2 to 2001–2 the number of high school graduates will increase by more than 10 per cent in over half the states (26), and it seems evident that most of this increase will be compressed into the second half of the 1990s (Western Interstate Commission for Higher Education 1988).[5] The situation will vary in intensity from state to state, but rising enrolments will generate two additional demands on operating budgets: first, for more instructors; second, for expanded physical plant.

California is no doubt the most extreme case, because the number of high school graduates is projected to grow by 49 per cent during the 1990s.[6] However, for this reason, California's dilemma highlights the problem being faced by higher education officials in most states. To fund enrolment growth alone, it is estimated that California's post-secondary education budget would have to grow by 2.3 per cent annually, *in real terms*, from 1990 to 2005 (O'Brien 1990: 4–5). Yet, as elsewhere during the 1990–2 recession, there was a real decline of 6.2 per cent in state appropriations for higher education in California, and a further nominal reduction of 15 per cent was implemented during fiscal year 1993.[7]

Similarly, it is estimated that with California's current space utilization guidelines, $514 million in bond sales would be required each year from 1991 to 2005 in order to generate the capital outlays necessary to accommodate enrolment expansion (O'Brien 1990: 4). Therefore, higher education would have to more than double its current share of the state's total annual bonding. Yet, as with operating budgets, the California Postsecondary Education Commission casts doubt on whether higher education can more than double its share of California's total bonding capacity over the next 15 years, particularly when such claims are juxtaposed against other future infrastructure needs of the state for schools, prisons, highways and other projects (CPSEC 1990: 37).

Finally, a third source of fiscal pressure on American higher institutions will result from a shifting balance in the academic labour market. Loozier and Dooris (1987) predict that by 2003 retirement rates will increase by 25–40 per cent over present rates of retirement. Similarly, McGuire and Price (1989) estimate that the annual faculty replacement rate in 2003 will be 37 per cent higher than in 1989. Finally, the most extensive and widely cited study of the academic labour market, by Bowen and Sosa (1989), concludes that some tightening in the academic labour market may begin as early as 1992–7, although the most dramatic faculty shortages will occur in the period from 1997 to 2002. Thus, allowing for different samples and different assumptions about faculty survival rates, Bowen and Schuster (1986) argue that surveys of the academic labour market clearly point to an emerging faculty shortage in the decade from 1995 to 2005 as faculty members start retiring in ever larger proportions. Importantly, as economist Ronald Ehrenberg (1991: 11) observes: 'to the extent that these projections are accurate, academic institutions will be forced by competitive pressures to increase faculty salaries in an effort to attract and retain faculty.'[8]

Changes in the academic labour process

The chief difficulty in achieving academic efficiencies is that 'personnel typically constitute 85 per cent of any academic institution's instructional budget, with the faculty payroll the largest single component' (CPSEC 1990: 1; see also Bowen 1980: 30–4). In principle, institutions could manage the cost of academic labour with supply-side interventions to increase the number of PhDs or with demand-side interventions related to faculty compensation and working conditions. However, supply-side strategies will be ineffective in the short to intermediate term, mainly because of the time-lag in producing new PhDs (CPSEC 1990: 2–5). Thus, for most institutions, demand-side interventions will be the only option available.

However, if the projections of anticipated faculty shortages are accurate, it is unlikely that administrators will be able to drive down the real compensation of regular faculty members without exacerbating the expected shortages. The dilemma will be especially acute in the coming decade because education administrators curtailed the hiring of assistant professors in the early 1970s. Thus, one result of the skewed age distribution that will lead to accelerating staff retirements is that there will also be very few assistant and associate professors to move up and fill the vacuum left by the massed retirements of senior faculty members (Hoffman 1986). The only way for a university to replenish the ranks of its senior staff will be to entice them away from another institution, thus escalating the competition for senior staff (Ehrenburg *et al.* 1991).

However, according to labour economist Daniel S. Hamermesh, the empirical evidence is overwhelming that the demand for staff responds negatively to increasing salaries. Consequently, Hamermesh (1992: 9) predicts that 'the desirable outcome [for faculty]. . .will be offset in part as institutions of higher education react to pressures on salaries by cutting the number of faculty they wish to hire.' In this vein, the California Postsecondary Education Commission (1990) has already concluded that, given the dearth of alternative options, higher education officials will have 'to improve the management and/or productivity of the faculty itself, in order to mitigate the need for new faculty.' The flexiversity structure of academic labour is designed to achieve these objectives in three ways. First, the strategy of selective excellence allows institutions to reduce their effective demand for academic labour. Second, flexible specialization enables institutions to achieve cost efficiencies by maximizing the productivity of available labour. Finally, the introduction of workforce dualization has allowed institutions to maintain a skill mix with lower aggregate costs.

Selective excellence

The most common theme in recent strategic plans and restructuring proposals is the idea that individual institutions must sharpen their educational focus by concentrating on specialized areas of institutional strength and areas of high student demand. As a result, more and more institutions are abandoning the goal of offering majors and graduate programmes across the entire universe of academic fields in favour of *selective excellence* (Grassmuck 1990: 1).[9] Comparatively weak academic programmes and areas of low student demand are being reduced to a service role, or completely eliminated, so that resources can be reallocated to offset rising institutional costs and so that personnel can be reallocated to maintain programme quality in a fewer number of academic fields (Academy for Educational Development 1979; Office of the Commissioner of Higher Education 1986, 1987). Hence, as a strategy for dealing with fiscal crisis, selective excellence entails a policy of 'narrow but deep cuts', as opposed to across-the-board reductions. Consequently, selective excellence requires the elimination or phase out of entire majors and departments (Ristine 1992b). An internal survey conducted by the Association of American Universities found that nearly 60 per cent of its US members are, in fact, consolidating, eliminating or reducing academic departments.[10]

Importantly, the effort to restructure American universities on the principle of selective excellence is likely to meet with only minimal internal resistance from faculty staff. First, as faculty retirements accelerate, it will be possible to restructure academic programming by reallocating *vacant* faculty lines. Strategic planners and university administrators are increasingly aware that the anticipated surge in retirements presents a once-in-a-century opportunity completely to recast academic programmes. For example, the California Postsecondary Education Commission (1990: 7) expects that 'as senior faculty members retire, there will be an opportunity for new appointments to be made in areas of current enrollment demand, which will result in a net reallocation of positions away from some fields and toward others.' Similarly, a Massachusetts commission on higher education observes that 'the substantial projected turnover of state college faculty during the 1990s will provide an unprecedented opportunity to refocus campus missions and programs and build new program strength.'[11] Hence, as administrators become less hampered by the institutional rigidities created by a heavily tenured faculty, faculty lines will be reallocated more easily to areas of selective strength and high student demand.

Second, in many cases, the strategy of selective excellence is being implemented in cooperation with faculty staff, partly in order to safeguard future salary increases and partly to protect their own programmes from the alternative of across-the-board reductions. Proposals for programme eliminations at Cornell, Johns Hopkins, Yale, Princeton and Washington Universities have all been linked to the goal of providing faculty with future salary increases (see note 10). It is difficult to imagine that many faculties will give up pay rises, or allow their own programmes to be weakened, for the sake of programmes or colleagues that they consider to be below par anyway.

Significantly, it is also becoming evident that programmes with a high degree of multidisciplinary support within an institution are the programmes that are most likely to be targeted for selective excellence. This is because a relatively small departmental nucleus can better offer programming of high quality when it can draw on the personnel and resources of cognate departments. Similarly, those programmes or departments that are not targeted for selective excellence will fare better if they develop a network of interdepartmental connections that wires its members into an institution's targeted areas of selective excellence. Furthermore, as administrators target and concentrate institutional resources, faculty staff will be induced to create intra-campus networks, either to build an area of selected excellence or as a way of gaining access to scarce targeted resources. Conversely, departments and individuals that fail to develop high levels of programmatic interface and interdisciplinary connectivity will simply 'wither on the vine' until they are phased out or terminated.

Therefore, paradoxically, the move towards greater institutional specialization will facilitate and encourage greater interdisciplinary activities among
faculty. The primary peer group for more and more scholars will not be
disciplinary or departmental, but interdisciplinary focus groups that col-
laborate in research and teaching. Indeed, the Arizona Board of Regents'
Task Force on Excellence, Efficiency, and Competitiveness found in its
survey of university faculty staff that 'a substantial interdisciplinary thrust'
was already considered 'a valuable asset' in recruiting (Davis 1988: 1386,
1392; Caldwell 1988: 963–5). Consequently, the Arizona task force recommends a policy of breaking down barriers between departments and even
between campuses in order to facilitate more interdisciplinary cooperation.

The two most dramatic recommendations of this sort have been proposed by Robert L. Carothers, the president of the University of Rhode
Island (URI), and by the Massachusetts Commission on the Future of the
State College and Community College Systems. Carothers (1992) hopes to
reverse URI's 'downward spiral' by abolishing existing departments and
reconfiguring the entire university around eight research centres.[12] Research
centres would be constructed around teams of faculty staff from a variety of
disciplines who share common interests and strengths in areas such as
marine studies, families and children, or human culture. The precise number
and focus of the research centres is to emerge ostensibly from deliberations
among staff and deans aimed at identifying the institutions' core strengths.
In a further departure, undergraduate students would each be enrolled in
a research centre, instead of a department, and by his or her senior year
every student would be a full member of a research centre. In this manner,
Carothers hopes to re-emphasize the University's research mission, carve
out targeted areas of selective excellence and offer an innovative type of
undergraduate education that erases the boundary between teaching and
research.

Similarly, in Massachusetts, a legislative commission has recommended
that the state focus its scarce resources cost-effectively by redesigning each
of its nine public colleges around distinctive 'focus areas' to be assigned on
the basis of current enrolment patterns and regional labour market demand. The commission suggests that a more efficient allocation of resources
could be achieved if each college was to adopt a profession-based focus
area, such as health, communications or applied science and technology.
Thus, each college would offer 'a limited core program of majors', while
programmes that do not complement a campus's unique mission would be
'phased out and program resources reallocated within the campus' (see
note 11).

Most of the degrees awarded by each college would be in fields clustered
around a particular focus area. For example, if a college had health as its
focus area, the major departments and most degrees awarded would be in
fields such as nursing and medical laboratory science. While majors could
be obtained in other selective fields, their staff would be specialized in some
aspect of the college's focus area. Hence, staff in education might specialize

in health education, political scientists in health care policy, or business staff in hospital and health care administration. In this model, traditional departments would be maintained, but the faculty's centre of gravity in each college would shift from departments towards a common interdisciplinary focus area. Although far from being fully implemented, these two proposals certainly represent the final destination for universities and four-year colleges that seek to pursue a strategy of selective excellence.[13]

Flexible specialization

A strategy of selective excellence will work best, and achieve the highest cost-efficiency, where it is linked to *flexible specialization* in the labour process. Flexible specialization consists of organizing a workforce so that highly skilled analytic and technical personnel can be shifted readily from one task to another as required by production demands. In general, the most highly skilled and specialized workers in the new post-industrial enterprises are those who deal in symbolic and conceptual processes and whose work integrates computer-assisted production directly into the labour process.[14] College and university staff are post-industrial workers almost by definition, although the multiversity labour process has not been characterized by the kind of flexible specialization that is generally associated with the post-industrial workforce.

First, the post-industrial worker has more *versatility* than the traditional professor who is restricted by disciplinary boundaries and by firm distinctions between labour and management. On the other hand, flexible specialization involves the ability to apply one's specialized skills to a wide range of problems and production processes. Second, and consequently, post-industrial workers have more *mobility* than traditional professors, because their versatility allows them to move more readily between industries, institutions, sectors and hierarchical levels of the workforce. Up to the present, professors have been organized more like traditional craft workers whose skills are closely identified with a guild (i.e. discipline) which they guard jealously against potential interlopers and 'amateurs'. Third, the traditional idea that a doctorate confers lifetime membership in an academic guild is contrary to the post-industrial ethos of *continuous education*. Flexible specialists must continually upgrade their skills and knowledge to meet the challenge of ever new technologies and expanding information in order to avoid their own obsolescence (Newson and Buchbinder 1988: 71). Finally, because of their versatility, mobility and continuous education, flexible specialists frequently pursue 'non-linear' careers, unlike traditional professors who measure career progress as a straight-line series of vertical steps within a single discipline from graduate school to full professor. The flexible specialist may pursue many 'careers' of varying duration that involve the application of knowledge and skills to particular problems or tasks.

The structural pressures of fiscal crisis are now creating powerful incentives for administrators and education officials to initiate a post-industrial transformation of the academic labour process. As already noted, the strategy of selective excellence is likely to work best where areas of targeted excellence have multidisciplinary support from many sectors of the institution. However, if service departments are to be reduced in number and size but still contribute directly to an institution's focus area(s), it will be viewed as increasingly inefficient for a flexiversity to have its flexible specialists teaching lower-division survey courses, particularly in service departments. Nevertheless, at most colleges and universities, staff currently justify their full-time status by teaching lower-division survey courses that do not require any great specialization and that, while they are necessary to a general education, may not be directly relevant to an institution's specialized areas of selective excellence. This structuring of staff work loads is retained mainly because of inflexible departmental and institutional boundaries, even though many faculty members are already capable of teaching upper-division cognate courses in other fields.

For example, there is no reason why someone who is broadly trained in political theory could not also teach the standard courses in the history of ideas, political philosophy and introduction to sociological theory (or vice versa). Yet, because of inflexible disciplinary boundaries, a well-staffed college or university is likely to hire four specialists to teach duplicate or overlapping courses in political science, history, philosophy and sociology, and to give students credit for essentially the same course under different disciplinary names. It will be more efficient, and probably make more sense educationally, to hire one or two people (instead of four) to teach cognate upper-division and graduate courses exclusively across two to four different 'departments'.[15] This kind of flexibility will be facilitated to a greater degree if research, teaching and faculty appointments are attached to research centres and focus areas instead of traditional departments.

Such arrangements would allow institutions simultaneously to maximize their use of the most flexible and expensive components of the academic workforce, raise salaries to meet staff shortages and manage overall personnel costs through net workforce reductions. Interdisciplinary linkages will allow institutions to reduce the number of core staff members in the programmes targeted for excellence and to have the smaller number of remaining service departments contribute directly to the core mission of the institution. Staff are likely to be more receptive to such arrangements once administrators recognize the potential savings and start offering enhanced inducements to those who are willing to accept interdisciplinary and joint appointments. In principle, an institution could pay one individual 50 per cent more than current salary and still save in salary costs by dispensing with a second individual who would otherwise teach similar courses in a different department.

However, a major contradiction in the strategy of selective excellence is that a campus may offer outstanding programming at its particular level in some fields, but offer little or no programming in other fields that are considered essential to a general education. Thus, the strategy of selective excellence is also likely to accelerate the development of intra-system cooperation in the public sector, inter-institutional collaboratives in the private sector and joint public–private ventures of various types. Although the major public universities are nominally unitary systems with a single governing board and multiple campuses, in practice, most state universities function as a loose confederation of separate and autonomous institutions. The fiscal crisis in higher education is already leading many university officials to search for ways of unifying their separate campuses into genuinely integrated systems. There are several possibilities for system integration that are realistic with a more versatile faculty and with relatively simple technological innovations.

The same economic logic that makes interdisciplinary appointments efficient (and mutually beneficial to institutions and staff) applies to the relationship between campuses within a system. Each campus in a university system will usually duplicate a large number of highly trained and specialized staff who are teaching the same upper-division or graduate courses on different campuses. The costs of this staffing structure are further multiplied by the fact that these individuals will again be teaching lower-division, non-specialized classes to justify their full-time status. In states of relatively small geographic dimensions, such a structure makes little sense for systems confronting the exigencies of fiscal crisis. It makes more sense, economically, to create a group of multi-campus 'system staff' who are employed by the university system, or jointly by two or more campuses.[16] In this manner, flexible specialists can be deployed and rotated to different campuses, and even to different departments or programmes, to avoid the duplication of high cost personnel.

Expanded variations of this arrangement are already possible with the current array of computer and video technologies. As Daniel S. Cheever Jr, the former president of Wheelock College, complained recently, while 'colleges have made enormous investments in technology. . .this investment has not yet transformed the fundamental way – and cost – of how courses are taught. . .the basic economic model is not so different from the 1960s or the 1950s despite this investment in technology' (Cheever 1992). New Jersey higher education officials have already concluded, therefore, that 'part of the solution [to resource shortages] will lie in heavier reliance on the emerging technologies in higher education', because 'advances in telecommunications and computer-aided instruction will permit increased sharing of resources and will allow instruction to take place in various settings' (Office of the Chancellor of Higher Education 1987: 11–12). In fact, interactive video technology, cable television, satellite transmission and electronic mail have all made real-time remote communications possible without regard to institutional or geographic boundaries. It is no longer necessary to be physically present in a classroom in order to attend *and participate* in a class (Ehrmann 1992).

As a result, university systems now have the opportunity to maximize (and genuinely to systematize) course enrolments through remote inter-active video and other distance learning technologies. Courses that are under-enrolled at one campus could be opened to 'remote enrolments' that allow students at other campuses to attend via interactive video (Chatman and Jung 1991). There is also no reason why staff members cannot hold 'e-mail office hours' to answer questions from students at remote locations.[17]

During the trough of Massachusetts state fiscal crisis, a sweeping proposal of this type was put forward by Randolph Bromery (1991), the former chancellor of higher education in Massachusetts. Bromery proposed that the state's higher institutions be organized into five regional clusters. A University of Massachusetts campus would anchor each cluster, while each cluster would include that region's state and private liberal arts colleges, as well as the local community colleges. One of the many hoped-for savings from the regional clusters was that institutions would be able 'to share courses through satellite transmission and the use of television, videos, and computers' (Flint 1990). Although the proposal was dead on arrival, many of its individual components are now being considered by the University of Massachusetts system and are already being implemented by the Five-College Consortium in western Massachusetts and by a nine college public consortium in Vermont. In the city of Boston, several small, but closely situated, colleges are moving to erode institutional boundaries by creating the so-called Fenway University: a collaborative arrangement in which four independent and specialized private colleges will attempt to function as a single 'university' (Cronin and Thier 1992). The New Jersey Chancellor of Higher Education (1987) has referred to such efforts as a 'new collaborative model' whose twin pillars are 'a more flexible departmental structure' and the development of 'new relationships between institutions of higher education and other organizations' (see also Martin and Samels 1993).

Thus, as higher institutions adopt policies of selective excellence and flexible specialization, top staff will become less attached to a single institution, will undertake flexible assignments across disciplines and between institutions, and to an ever greater degree will rely on the productivity of new educational technologies. The entire process should become self-reinforcing, because as more staff become more mobile, and as staff shortages develop toward the end of the 1990s, the most flexible staff will be able to command higher salaries and institutional prestige. Indeed, some strategic planners are already recommending that reward systems be modified 'to encourage faculty to be flexible and to seek out new skill areas and new responsibilities' through 'financial incentives, enhanced job protection, or added prestige' (Lee 1983). Thus, new financial inducements and altered reward structures will become a powerful lure to staff, aside from greater personal satisfaction, to embrace the interdisciplinary movement and to accept flexible assignments.[18]

Workforce dualization

The main planning objective of flexible specialization is to utilize an inter-disciplinary staff nucleus more efficiently by having them teach a variety of upper-division cognate courses within an institution and by teaching low-demand upper-division or graduate courses at more than one institution. Thus, the flexible specialist will be less and less involved with lower-division survey or general education courses. One result of this trend is that flexiversities will probably extend and permanently institutionalize a dual academic labour market.

A dual labour market is 'a systematic and invidious stratification of employment opportunities into two sectors characterized by different working conditions, policies for promotion, and wage structures' (Roemer and Schnitz 1982). In the emerging dual labour market of post-industrial economies, a core workforce of flexible specialists enjoys stable and well-paid professional employment, while a peripheral workforce of temporary and part-time employees suffers uncertain employment and low pay, with little or no opportunity for advancement and little possibility of entering the core workforce (Baron and Bennet 1971; Piore 1971). The organizational advantages of a peripheral workforce are that it provides an institution's management with a low-cost and highly flexible pool of labour that can be increased or decreased rapidly and whose skill mix can be easily adjusted to meet uncertain or changing market demand.

Market conditions and fiscal imperatives combined in the mid-1970s to facilitate the emergence of a dual labour market in American higher education. Conditions favourable to the emergence of a dual labour market were in place by 1972 when more than five times as many PhDs were being produced as could be absorbed into higher education teaching positions (Roemer and Schnitz 1982). The massive imbalance between academic labour supply and institutional demand meant that a larger and larger percentage of new academic personnel were willing to accept temporary and part-time employment. At the same time, as individuals hired during the 1960s academic boom received tenure, there was a slowdown in turnover and attrition among senior faculty. Moreover, by the mid-1970s, college and university administrators were being asked to implement budget reductions owing to the 1975 recession and, simultaneously, had to address changing student interests. The combination of high tenure rates, low turnover and declining resources created rigid and unresponsive institutions. One of the most important mechanisms for regaining institutional flexibility was to 'unlock' inflexible human resources by creating a dual labour market. This policy was promoted in a well-publicized study by the Carnegie Commission on Higher Education (1972), which recommended the use of non-tenured track appointments and part-time appointments as a hedge against the possibility of future budget cutbacks and anticipated declines in student enrolment.

It is now well known that higher education administrators were quite successful in creating a dual academic labour market by the late 1970s. Research universities and many four-year colleges have promoted a dualized labour market mainly in the form of a provisional faculty that consists of PhDs who hold full-time non-tenured track positions. The American Association of University Professors conducted its first study of provisional staff in 1978 and concluded that there had been 'a substantial increase' in the use of provisional staff by that time (Thomson and Sandalow 1978). Roemer and Schnitz (1982) estimated that by the late 1970s 30 per cent of all new full-time appointments were in non-tenured track positions.

Non-tenured track full-time positions are provisional in nature, since they usually terminate after one to three years and are nearly always conditional on minimum course enrolments and institutional revenues. Provisional staff frequently receive a lower salary than regular staff, carry a heavier teaching load and usually teach multiple sections of the same course. Their assignment to introductory and survey courses means that few provisional staff have an opportunity to teach in their area of specialized expertise. This means that the specialized skills of provisional staff are likely to erode over a period of time and, thus, they are frozen into the lower tier of a dual labour market. Yet, because of the size, number and level of courses taught by provisional staff, they now do a considerable amount of many departments' lower-division undergraduate teaching (Roemer and Schnitz 1982; Bowen and Schuster 1986; Finkelstein 1986).

At community colleges, and increasingly at many four-year colleges, the dualization of academic labour markets has taken the form of increased reliance on part-time staff. The number of part-time staff doubled during the 1970s and accounted for 32 per cent of all college and university staff by the end of the decade. The increase was especially dramatic at two-year colleges, where the number of part-time staff quintupled to account for 51 per cent by the end of the 1970s.[19] These proportions levelled off during the 1980s with part-timers now accounting for 25 per cent of the staff at four-year institutions and 54 per cent at two-year institutions (NCES 1991).

Importantly, although dual labour markets can emerge only during periods of considerable imbalance in the supply and demand for labour, studies suggest that once they are established market conditions do not seem to affect the persistence of dual labour markets. Consequently, the staff shortages anticipated for the late 1990s are not likely to have any significant effect on the dual labour market in higher education. Instead, once established, dual markets remain segmented and come to operate as two separate markets drawing on two separate pools of labour. Specifically, in higher education, Leslie *et al.* (1982: 28–32) have found that 'institutional logic', rather than the supply of academic labour, now controls administrative decisions to increase or reduce the number of part-time staff in higher institutions.

Institutions are most likely to increase the number of part-time and provisional staff when administrative decisions are controlled by either a logic of adaptation or a logic of retrenchment (Leslie *et al.* 1982: 28–32). Adapting institutions are those with a staff that is heavily tenured in fields with low or shrinking student demand and with few flexible resources for moving into new fields of research and teaching. Adapting institutions also tend to occupy weak competitive positions so that product pricing becomes an important component in their ability to attract and retain students. Retrenching institutions have intense budget problems that can be characterized as a fiscal crisis.

The vast majority of American higher institutions will be facing one or both problems during the 1990s. Consequently, the dominant institutional logic controlling administrative decision-making will be one that seeks to reduce personnel costs and to achieve greater institutional flexibility (Mortimer *et al.* 1985). It is unlikely that trustees and administrators baptized in the fiscal fires of the 1990s will readily recommit resources to inflexible personnel costs in the near future.[20] Hence, as the salaries of core staff escalate owing to the anticipated shortages, and new expenditure waves strike during the coming decade, the dominant institutional logic will be to maintain or expand dualization at the workforce periphery in order to offset fiscal pressures at the core.

Conclusion

A continuing fiscal crisis will make selective excellence, flexible specialization and workforce dualization the dominant themes of higher education reform in the coming decade. The overarching objective will be to create a more flexible academic workforce that can teach and conduct research in an institutional setting that is lean and mean. It should be emphasized that such objectives are not necessarily in conflict with educational goals. The actual configuration of the flexiversity, and its impact on teaching and research, will depend on the extent to which staff interject themselves into the reconstruction process and use reform as an opportunity for educational innovation.

Notes

1. This figure is based on budget data in Changes in campus operating budgets, 1989–90 to 1990–91, *The Almanac of Higher Education, 1992*, 71, measured against an increase in the United States Consumer Price Index of 9.7 per cent during the same two-year period (see US Department of Labor 1991: 40).
2. The most comprehensive compendium of these developments is the state by state accounts of higher education in *The Almanac of Higher Education, 1991*. Chicago, University of Chicago Press, 1991, and *The Almanac of Higher Education, 1992*. Chicago, University of Chicago Press, 1992.
3. Administrators' views of challenges facing institutions in the next five years, *The Almanac of Higher Education, 1992*, 72.
4. The economic definition of academic efficiency is 'using the minimum necessary resources for *intended* (as opposed to actual) results' (see Halstead 1989: 41).

5. The compression factor is because the number of high school graduates will actually decrease in 1993–4.
6. *The Almanac of Higher Education, 1992*, p. 15.
7. Figures on 1990–2 state appropriations from *The Almanac of Higher Education, 1992*, p. 96, and adjustments for inflation based on *CPI: Detailed Reports*, December 1990 and December 1991. The 1993 budget figures are from Strobel (1992: 1).
8. Despite the short-term impact of the 1990–2 recession on staff hiring, Bowen and Rudenstine (1992: 2–3) note that 'since the main underlying trends in the age distribution of the present faculty and in the size of the college-age population are unchanged, we see no reason to modify our sense that serious staffing problems should be anticipated by the late 1990s.'
9. Similarly, after struggling unsuccessfully since 1990 with a $40 million deficit, administrators at Northeastern University, the nation's largest private university, have concluded that 'unless we make a strong commitment to selective excellence, we will founder in universal mediocrity' (see Marcus 1992). Likewise, Caldwell (1988: 964) concludes that 'resources will become more difficult to obtain', and therefore 'continued interest in excellence and competitiveness will require that resources be focused in few areas.'
10. As reported in 'Cornell faculty panel urges cuts in jobs so pay can go up', *The Chronicle of Higher Education*, 6 December 1989, A25.
11. A Report of the Commission on the Future of the State College and Community College System, *Responding to Change: New Directions for Public Colleges in Massachusetts*, March 1992, 10.
12. According to Carothers, the main impetus for the proposal is funding: 'URI has lost the capacity to support all its programs and to maintain its buildings and grounds' (see McVicar 1992).
13. Two of the nine Massachusetts colleges already specialize in the arts and maritime professions, respectively. The one predominantly liberal arts state college has embraced the commission proposal and is now moving to safeguard its focus area (see Roche 1992). Similarly, a fourth college is now moving to capture a niche in biomedical professions (see Russell 1992).
14. On the post-industrial labour process, see Hirschorn (1981), Piore and Sabel (1984) and Reich (1992).
15. The objective criteria for identifying an interdisciplinary core staff could include holding a master's degree in a field other than one's department, graduate 'minors', paper presentations at conferences outside of one's disciplinary affiliation, or simply a publications list that includes journal articles in fields other than one's PhD.
16. For example, the University of Massachusetts System is already considering a proposal that would create a group of 'university professors' who would be attached to the system president's office, rather than to the individual campuses.
17. CPSEC (1990: 43) sounds a cautionary note in the finding that 'new educational technologies are still some 10 or 15 years away from being implemented in higher education on a wide scale for the purpose of providing a free-standing alternative to traditional means of delivering educational services.' See also CPSEC (1989).
18. There is evidence in the professional associations that staff are already moving towards interdisciplinary flexible specializations. For example, in the American

Political Science Association, the number of specialized 'organized sections' has grown from six in 1984 to 26 in 1992. In 1984, none of the organized sections was interdisciplinary, but by 1992 seven (27 per cent) of the organized sections were devoted to focus areas such as politics and literature, politics and history, political economy, women and politics, politics and the life sciences, science and technology politics, and religion and politics.

19. 'The status of part-time faculty', *Academe: Bulletin of the AAUP*, 67(1) (1981), 29.
20. For instance, The University of Massachusetts Board of Trustees registered a complaint in its latest strategic planning document that 'locked resources' (80 per cent in salaries and benefits) have left the institution with 'little or no flexible funding' even as it faces a period of 'prolonged fiscal uncertainty and stress' (see Policy Working Group 1992: 25). Similarly, in defending the termination of programmes and tenured staff in the California State University System, Chancellor Barry Munitz has cited the need for 'increased management flexibility' as the system slides into fiscal crisis (Ristine 1992a).

References

Academy for Educational Development (1979) *Developing a Process Model for Institutional and State-level Review and Evaluation of Academic Programs.* Washington, DC, Ohio Board of Regents.

Baron, H. and Bennet, H. (1971) The dynamics of the dual labour market, in D.C. Gordon (ed.) *Problems in Political Economy: an Urban Perspective.* Lexington, MA, D.C. Heath, 94–101.

Barrow, C.W. (1992) *Universities and the Capitalist State: Corporate Liberalism and the Reconstruction of American Higher Education, 1894–1928.* Madison, University of Wisconsin Press.

Bowen, H.R. (1980) *The Costs of Higher Education.* San Francisco, Jossey-Bass.

Bowen, H.R. and Schuster, J.H. (1986) *American Professors: a National Resource Imperiled.* New York, Oxford University Press.

Bowen, W.G. and Rudenstine, N. (1992) *In Pursuit of the PhD.* Princeton, NJ, Princeton University Press.

Bowen, W.G. and Sosa, J.A. (1989) *Prospects for Faculty in the Arts and Sciences: a Study of Factors Affecting Demand and Supply, 1987 to 2012.* Princeton, NJ, Princeton University Press.

Bromery, R. (1991) *System and Partnership: a Regional Initiative in Massachusetts Public Higher Education (a Report to the Board of Regents).* Washington, DC, Government Printing Office.

Caldwell, R.L. (1988) Future changes: implications for Arizona's universities, *The Final Report and Working Papers of the Arizona Board of Regents Task Force on Excellence, Efficiency, and Competitiveness*, volume 2, pp. 1386–92.

California Postsecondary Education Commission (1989) *Technology and the Future of Education: Directions for Progress.* Sacramento, CA, CPSEC Commission Report 89–27, September.

California Postsecondary Education Commission (1990) *Higher Education at the Crossroads: Planning for the Twenty-first Century.* Sacramento, CA, CPSEC, Report 90–1, January.

Carnegie Commission on Higher Education (1972) *The More Effective Use of Resources.* New York, McGraw-Hill.

Carothers, R.L. (1992) Earthquake in Kingston, *URI Alumnus*, Spring, 20–2.

Chatman, S. and Jung, L. (1991) Concern about forecasts of national faculty short-ages and the importance of local studies, paper delivered at the Annual Forum of the Association for Institutional Research, 26–29 May.

Cheever, D.S. Jr (1992) Higher (and higher) ed, *Boston Sunday Globe*, 26 April, 75.

College Board, College Scholarship Service (1992) *1991–92 College Costs: Average Fixed Charges and Student Expenses*. New York, College Board.

Cronin, J.M. and Thier, S.O. (1992) Partnerships help contain higher ed costs, *Boston Sunday Globe*, 5 July, 73.

Davis, G.H. (1988) Recruitment and retention of faculty, 'an imperiled national rescource', The Final Report and Working Papers of the Arizona Board of Regents' Task Force on Excellence, Efficiency and Competitiveness. Volume 1, pp. 1386–92.

Eckl, C.L., Hutchinson, A.M. and Snell, R.K. (1992) *State Budget and Tax Actions, 1992: Preliminary Report*. Denver, CO, National Conference of State Legislatures.

Ehrenberg, R.G. (1991) The annual report on the economic status of the profession, 1990–91, *Academe: Bulletin of the American Association of University Professors*, March/April, 11.

Ehrenberg, R., Kasper, H. and Rees, D. (1991) Faculty turnover at American colleges and universities: analyses of AAUP data, *Economics of Education Review*, 10(2), 99–110.

Ehrmann, S.C. (1992) Challenging the ideal of campus-bound education, *Educom Review*, 27(2), 24–7.

Finkelstein, M. (1986) Life on the 'effectively terminal' tenure track, *Academe: Bulletin of the AAUP*, 72(1), 32–6.

Flint, A. (1990) Sharing proposed for state colleges: reorganization would form clusters, *Boston Globe*, 10 September, 1.

Grassmuck, K. (1990) Columbia University uses philosophy of 'selective excellence' to make painful cuts in programs, administration, *Chronicle of Higher Education*, 25 April, 1.

Halstead, K. (1989) *State Profiles: Financing Public Higher Education, 1978 to 1989*. Washington, DC, Research Associates.

Halstead, K.D. (1991) *State Profiles: Financing Public Higher Education, 1978 to 1991*. Washington, DC, Research Associates.

Hamermesh, D.S. (1992) The annual report on the economic status of the profession, 1991–92, *Academe: Bulletin of the American Association of University Professors*, March/April, 9.

Hirschorn, L. (1981) The post industrial labour process, *New Political Science*, 2(3), 5–47.

Hoffman, E.P. (1986) A review of two studies of elasticity in academe, *Economics of Education Review*, 5(2), 220–1.

Jackson, G.A. and Weathersby, G.B. (1975) Individual demand for higher education, *Journal of Higher Education*, 46, 623–52.

Jaschik, S. (1991) State funds for higher education drop in year; first decline since survey began 33 years ago, *Chronicle of Higher Education*, 6 November, 1, 38–40.

Lee, B.A. (1983) Faculty trends and projected needs, *New Directions for Institutional Research*, 10(40), 37–8.

Leslie, D.W., Kellams, S.E. and Gunne, G.M. (1982) *Part-time Faculty in American Higher Education*. New York, Praeger.

Loozier, G.G. and Dooris, M.J. (1987) Is higher education confronting faculty short-ages? Paper presented at the Annual Meeting of the Association for the Study of Higher Education.

McGuire, M.D. and Price, J.A. (1989) Faculty replacement needs for the next 15 years: a simulated attrition model. Paper presented at the 29th Annual Forum of the Association for Institutional Research, May.

McVicar, D.M. (1992) Carothers urges massive overhaul at URI, *Providence Journal-Bulletin*, 18 January, A1.

Marcus, J. (1992) University to cut more programs, *New Bedford Standard-Times*, 25 September, B5.

Martin, J. and Samels, J.E. (1993) *Merging Colleges for Mutual Growth.* Baltimore, Johns Hopkins University Press.

MGT Consultants (1990) *Survey of Space and Utilization Standards and Guidelines in the Fifty States.* Sacramento, CA, CPSEC.

Mishel, L. and Bernstein, J. (1992) *Declining Wages for High School and College Graduates: Pay and Benefits Trends by Education, Gender, Occupation, and State, 1979–1991.* Washington, DC, Economic Policy Institute.

Mortimer, K.P., Bagshaw, M. and Masland, A.T. (1985) *Flexibility in Academic Staffing: Effective Policies and Practices.* ASHE-ERIC Higher Education Report No. 1.

National Center for Educational Statistics (1991) *Digest of Education Statistics, 1991.* Washington, DC, Government Printing Office.

National Governor's Association (1992) *Fiscal Survey of the States.* Washington, DC, NGA.

New England Board of Higher Education (1992) *Regional Conference on the Financial Crisis Facing New England Colleges: Mutual Problems and Solutions. Selected Articles and Press Clippings.* Boston, Mass., NEBHE.

Newson, J. and Buchbinder, H. (1988) *The University Means Business: Universities, Corporations and Academic Work.* Toronto, Garamond Press.

O'Brien, K.B. (1990) *The Dynamics of Postsecondary Expansion in the 1990s: Report of the Executive Director.* Sacramento, CA, CPSEC Report 90–12, 5 March.

O'Connor, J. (1973) *The Fiscal Crisis of the State.* New York, St Martin's Press.

Office of the Chancellor of Higher Education (1987) *Commitment to New Jersey's Future: a Five-year Agenda for Higher Education,* Revised draft, 29 June.

Office of the Commissioner of Higher Education (1986) *Issues in Montana Higher Education: a Report Requested by the Montana Board of Regents of Higher Education,* October.

Office of the Commissioner of Higher Education (1987) *Report of Colorado Commission on Higher Education's Program Discontinuance Responsibility,* July.

Piore, M. (1971) The dual labor market: theory and implications, in D.C. Grodon (ed.) *Problems in Political Economy: an Urban Perspective.* Lexington, MA, D.C. Heath, 90–4.

Piore, M.J. and Sabel, C.F. (1984) *The Second Industrial Divide.* New York, Basic Books.

Policy Working Group (1992) *Planning to Plan: a Proposal for Trustee Action.* Boston, University of Massachusetts.

Reich, R. (1992) *The Work of Nations: Preparing Ourselves for Twenty-first Century Capitalism.* New York, Alfred A. Knopf.

Ristine, J. (1992a) SDSU plans to mail 190 pink slips, *San Diego Union-Tribune,* 6 June, 1.

Ristine, J. (1992b) Faculty urges day to spare SDSU jobs, *San Diego Union-Tribune,* 12 June, B1.

Roche, B.J. (1992) State college seeks liberal arts niche, *Boston Globe*, 26 July, 21.

Roemer, R.E. and Schnitz, J.E. (1982) Academic employment as day labor: the dual labor market in higher education, *Journal of Higher Education*, 53(5), 515.

Rush, S.C. and Johnson, S.L. (1989) *The Decaying American Campus: a Ticking Time Bomb*. Prepared for the Association of Physical Plant Administrators of Universities and Colleges.

Russell, G.F. (1992) Worcester State to focus on biotech, *Boston Globe*, 21 October, 31.

Scott, B.A. (1983) *Crisis Management in American Higher Education*. Westport, CT, Praeger Press.

Strobel, C. (1992) Campus required to slice budgets. *UCLA Summer Bruin*, 6 July, 1.

Thomson, J.J. and Sandalow, T. (1978) On full-time non-tenure-track appointments, *AAUP Bulletin*, September, 267–73.

US Department of Education (1990) *Projections of Education Statistics to 2001: an Update*. Washington, DC, Government Printing Office.

US Department of Education (1991) *Digest of Education Statistics 1991*. Washington, DC, Government Printing Office.

US Department of Labor (1991) *Bureau of Labor Statistics, CPI: Detailed Report*. Washington, DC, US Department of Labor.

Western Interstate Commission for Higher Education (1988) *High School Graduates: Projections by State, 1986–2004*. Boulder, CO, WICHE.

11

Higher Education as a Form of Labour Market Reform

Kerry Barlow

Introduction

In Australia, as in many other OECD countries, the focus of economic policy-making has been at the micro-level, and there are two reasons for this. First, the growing internationalization of capital flows has meant a consequent inability of national governments to pursue workable macro-economic policies. Second, the economic crisis has been theorized by many as a crisis of Fordism; that is, a crisis of mass production techniques. The solutions to the crisis are seen to lie in the elimination of 'rigidities' in production techniques, labour utilization patterns and management approaches – the increased 'flexibility' solution, which Nielsen (1991) claims is neo-classical economic in origin.

One of the key Australian responses to the perceived crisis of Fordist production methods is the award restructuring process (Curtin and Mathews 1990). However, in Australia, unlike some other countries, the labour force is formally implicated in the success (or otherwise) of the 'adjustment' process.

The 1983 tripartite (federal government, peak union council and peak business council) wages accord in Australia has made the focus on labour productivity seem both 'rational' and possible. The accord has not only delivered reductions in real wage costs, but enabled a consensus of national purpose across union and business lines. In the period of less than a decade, under the processes of the accord, the Australian industrial relations framework has been drawn into the task of not only distributing the productivity gains of production, but creating them. This is the logic of award restructuring which has become the central mechanism in Australia's industrial relations and industrial restructuring processes.

This chapter gives a brief description of the award restructuring process and its philosophical underpinnings, before turning to a fuller analysis of the implications of the process for academic workers. It will be shown that award restructuring makes dual demands on academic work: first, in its

demands for changes to the higher education system to enable the preparation and certification of the future 'post-Fordist' employee; second, in its
demands for changes in academics' work 'practices' to enable increased
productivity to emerge.

These demands on academic workers are placed in the context of government higher education policy documents and wider training agendas,
and the chapter concludes with a discussion of some of the contradictory
tendencies inherent in both the award restructuring process (as it affects
academics) and the government's higher education policies.

Award restructuring rationale

In return for anything more than a minimum wage increase, Australian
workers now have to enter into bargains with employers to trade 'productivity' enhancing changes for pay increases. It is at workplace level that key
labour market issues such as skills formation, job regrading and reclassifi-
cation, performance pay and the like are being negotiated, for a share in
the productivity that might follow from such restructuring techniques.

Support for the award restructuring process has been given by the accord
tripartite major groups but for differing reasons. According to Burgess
and Macdonald (1990) the federal government needs to demonstrate its
managerial competence. The Australian Council of Trade Unions (ACTU)
has been keen actually to set the agenda for workplace reform. However,
as many commentators point out, the manufacturing unions have been the
strongest supporters and the model of award restructuring adopted seems
to be based on secondary rather than tertiary industry notions of productivity. Peak employer groups like the Business Council of Australia and
Confederation of Australian Industry have long pushed for some of the
types of 'reforms' now being bargained for at workplace level (e.g. EPAC
1989).

Post-Fordist and human capital influences

The federal government and ACTU model of award restructuring has been
informed in part by an optimistic post-Fordist notion of work and industry.
This particular version of post-Fordism focuses on the creation of a multi-
skilled workforce, on decision-making that is decentralized, on cooperative
rather than hierarchical workplace organization, and on organizational
decision-making practices about product development and resource allocation that have been democratized (Boreham n.d.). The paradigm incorporates a particular view of the nature of work that emphasizes the need
for a cooperative employer–employee relationship (Davidson 1990). It also
postulates that the main source of productivity lies in the workplace, in
employees' desire willingly to contribute above and beyond what they were
formally required to in more hierarchical (Taylorist) settings. There is the

potential, under such a paradigm, to overcome labour's alienation and the lack of recognition of its real contribution, seen to be inherent in Fordist forms of work organization (Carmichael 1990).

These particular post-Fordist understandings of the new nature of work and the productivity potential of employees' workplace practices are progressive and potentially liberating, from the trade union perspective. They explain the ACTU's support of that part of the award restructuring agenda which promises to develop the 'new' worker.

Award restructuring is also informed by human capital understandings of skill and productivity. In the current economic context, investment in individual workers' education and training is seen as a source of improved productivity because it can add to the repertoire of workers' skills (multi-skilling) and at the same time improve their intellectual skills of problem-solving, analytic ability, initiative, creativity and decision-making. Investment in human capital, via mass provision of tertiary education and higher levels of training, is perceived by many to be the key to meeting the demands of the 'postindustrial' society.

The view of knowledge as a key economic resource legitimates government policies which encourage higher post-compulsory education participation rates, since the more 'knowledge' employees hold, the 'smarter' they will be able to work. It also legitimates calls for closer business–education links so that the institutions which produce this key resource can develop it in forms that are more immediately useful to economic interests.

Creation of the flexible worker under award restructuring

The dominance of post-Fordist and human capital theories about work and skills formation has made the notion of the 'flexible' worker a desirable and, indeed, necessary entity. The logic of new production paradigms is that they demand new types of workers. Thus, in the new age of 'flexible specialisation' (Mathews 1989) and 'flexible accumulation' (Jessop *et al.* 1991), what is required is the 'flexible worker'. The construction implies a number of things. First, it implies workers who willingly upgrade their skills or credentials to match the shifting shape of job designs within firms; who have the flexibility of knowledge and skills to act as both leader and led in teamwork and can respond rapidly to production problems and make improvements in its design and organization (Boreham n.d.). Second, it implies workers who can develop new competencies which are transferable from job to job and which are necessary to meet the structural adjustments of the economy (Bluer and Carmichael 1991). These are the human capital dimensions. It also implies workers who are able to be contracted for change-able worktimes under changeable wage conditions. In effect the term 'flexible worker' acts as a catch phrase, with the meaning differing according to which group is using it. The ACTU has placed emphasis on functional flexibility (multi-skilling), with demands for career-pathing and associated training opportunities; employers, on the whole, have pushed for wage and numerical flexibilities in the form of changes in work hours and on-labour costs, and increases in part-time, casual and contract work (Burgess and Macdonald 1990; Junor *et al.* 1994).

The strategy of award restructuring is to confine issues of productivity to the individual efforts of employees at the workplace level. Thus the focus of workplace agreements is on the types of worker flexibilities that will result in so-called productivity gains. In Australia many workplace agreements have incorporated initiatives that allow for the development of performance indicators, against which performance can be measured or 'appraised'. The meeting of specific targets, for example, is used to gauge the increased productivity of workers in some industries. Such performance appraisal systems are seen by some as a way of enhancing productivity via their incentive effect. But these systems rely on indicators which are often narrowly based on job description documents that fail to capture the full dynamics of the workplace and the invisible labour of many workers (Junor *et al.* 1994).

As an industrial intervention that operates at the level of the workplace, award restructuring acts to individualize the relationship between employer and employee, and has the effect of making the individual worker, rather than the total organizational relationship, responsible for productivity gains. This is a problematic position for all workers, but especially for teachers because productivity is a total factor relationship. The outcomes from teachers' work are just as dependent on the class, gender and racial nature of the student population, the availability of quality teaching resources, support of parental groups, general morale and so on as they are on individual teachers' level of training, ability to plan and deliver lessons and so on. In teaching, the award restructuring process will make individuals responsible for educational outcomes over which they really have very little control.

There are thus emerging tensions between the rhetoric and the reality of the post-Fordist 'flexible' worker. It is important to map these tensions at their various sites, and especially crucial to do so at the site of education, which is so thoroughly implicated in the production of the 'flexible' worker and in the human capital investment process.

Demands of award restructuring on higher education

The career-pathing, multi-skilling and flexibility-enhancing intentions of the award restructuring process implicate higher education institutions and their workers. The process has dual ramifications for academic workers. On the one hand it demands the restructuring of educational curricula (defined in the broadest sense to include content, teaching methods, assessment and credentials) to meet the needs of the workforce reform agenda.

On the other it makes industrial demands. As workers, academics must restructure their own work 'practices' in return for productivity gains and hence pay increases. The sorts of tensions between post-Fordist models and workplace realities already alluded to have pertinence for academic workers, because the dual demands of award restructuring on their work can pull them at times in very different directions.

Added to the award restructuring demands are other policy changes related to higher education, notably the federal government's White Paper, *Higher Education: a Policy Statement* (Dawkins 1988), which at times is contradicted by the thrust of the award restructuring agenda for higher education; and the Training Guarantee Act of 1990, which requires most firms to spend a minimum of 1 per cent (in 1990–1; 1.5 per cent from mid-1992) of payroll on training. The act has stimulated demand for higher education courses, which are seen to enhance the skills and credentials of some professional workers.

To understand the compexities of award restructuring for academic workers, let us consider the dual demands of the process on their work.

The demand for system change

In the first instance, changes to curriculum content, teaching methods, credentials and assessment are seen to be important for the fundamental 'paradigm' shift required of higher education institutions to meet the award restructuring agenda. The institutions are seen by the government, many unionists and many in the business community as fossils of an earlier age, providing a reified learning environment, away from the 'real' world of work. The unions especially are keen to move many of them away from provision for an elite to being a fundamental part of the public education system (ACTU 1991).

One of the requisite curriculum changes is seen to be a more diverse range of both general and professional courses to allow for the sort of career-pathing flexibility envisaged under post-Fordist production. Bridging courses and stand-alone modules are seen to be needed for building credit towards career paths. Upgraded management training courses are also a perceived requirement to prepare management for the new forms of work organization promised by post-Fordism. It is believed that curriculum content must reflect leading-edge research and enable the development of creative thinking and problem-solving.

One of the key mechanisms which could take the control over curriculum out of the hands of academics will be the National Training Board's Competency Standards Framework. Under the process each industry will identify those sets of skills needed to be competent in a specific job. Each competency is translated into behaviourially based performance indicators, and the 'implementation process for identifying the competencies and agreements on performance indicators involves tripartite consultation between unions, government, and employers, with training providers having observer status' (Cooper 1992: 19). If what Cooper says is true for academia the curriculum content (increasingly expressed as modular programmes) and assessment will become more directly industry-driven rather than being left to the discretion and interests of academic curriculum developers.

Teaching methods (or, as they are rapidly coming to be called, delivery systems) must become more diverse, to include open (including TV) systems, cross-utilization of other systems (like technical and further education, TAFE) and off-campus institutions (e.g. industry); a mixture of teaching modes is seen as desirable.

The related areas of credentialling and assessment are seen to be in need of renovation, to enable truly flexible career pathways to develop. The Competency Standards Framework will probably be the main mechanism which will push higher education institutions, as educators for the professions (levels 7 and 8 of the Board's eight-level framework), to develop new approaches to their own credentialling and assessment. Since the focus under the competency movement is on measurable outcomes, that is measurement in terms of what people can do rather than what they know, in many cases academics may be required to modify their own existing forms of assessment, which are completion of task rather than outcomes oriented. In some professions, notably nursing and welfare, definition of competency based standards has already progressed, while in others, like teacher education, it is just beginning. These processes are having spill-over effects in faculties which do not directly produce professionals.

This emphasis on outcomes creates a 'train the trainers' role for higher education as well, since many TAFE and other industry trainers see the need to reassess their own approaches to modular planning and assessment of outcomes, and look to higher education to equip them for the task.

Award restructuring has a two-fold implication for access to higher education. First, award restructuring requires expanded opportunities for mature age entry, so that retraining and up-skilling of older workers and career-pathing is possible. This pressure on the institutions is in addition to that placed on them by the increased post-compulsory education participation rates, which have seen vastly increased numbers of young people entering the system. Second, entrance requirements will need to change. They will need to select on broader criteria than they currently do to allow for more diverse career paths. This will ruffle the feathers of the more elite institutions, which have always maintained fairly strict academic entry criteria in an effort to preserve what the cultural elitists call 'high standards'.

In summary, compliance with the needs of the award restructuring process entails quite significant changes to those curriculum components which directly serve industries that are restructuring their career paths and setting competency based standards.

The demand for change in work 'practices'

In the context of the higher education White Paper, restructuring, and the amalgamations of approximately 70 universities and colleges of advanced education into 40 'new' institutions, academic workers found that new working cultures were being forged at the same time that their industrial conditions were being revised.

Cultural changes

The amalgamation of two quite distinct working cultures has resulted in serious tensions between staff, in some cases located on the same campus. The colleges of advanced education (CAE) staff had been funded mainly for teaching, with only limited research funding for a minimal number of staff, and had historically a closer, more vocational connection with employers and the business sector. Universities, on the other hand, had been funded for teaching and research activities, a reasonable proportion of which were not directly related to business or vocational needs. The dominant model of the 'new' university professional is now based on elements of both work cultures. It is based in part on the 'old' university one, incorporating the notion of an all-round researcher, publisher and teacher, and includes aspects of the vocational–business culture links as well. In the absence of adequate government and corporate funding for research, and the recession taking its toll on publishing outlets for many areas of academic research, however, the 'new' professional model is one that cannot be emulated by all. Those most likely to be in a position of meeting the demands of this newly emerging hegemonic model of the professional will be experienced researchers located in those federal government national priority areas which also meet the business community's perceptions of relevant research and teaching activities.

Industrial changes

Two elements of the award restructuring agenda, the career-pathing dynamic and the notion of the post-Fordist worker, have brought notions of professionalism more clearly on to centre stage. Career development is seen, at least by the government and the unions, to be the key incentive for workers to undergo training and retraining. In the professions questions about the most appropriate forms of training are currently being raised. However, in the case of teaching, the parameters of the debate are being limited by the increasingly narrow definition of teacher's work.

Ashenden (1990: 11) sees the most appropriate training for teachers to be 'deep-skilling' rather than 'multi-skilling', in the technical aspects of the job: 'Their training would concentrate not on multi-skilling but deep-skilling, in both knowledge of curriculum areas and in teaching and learning methods and strategies.'

While discussion of the increasingly technical construction of the professional teacher has mainly been confined to school teaching (Seddon 1991;

Robertson and Trotman 1992) the same concerns must be raised for higher education teaching. As in school teaching, 'professionalism' in academic teaching will increasingly be defined in terms of expertise in preparing and organizing learning tasks and in their 'delivery', and their assessment in terms of outcomes. Cultural and socio-political concerns, which there have always been room for in academic teaching, will be increasingly marginalized as the forces of educational commodification and the moves to technical notions of professionalism intensify.

There is also a growing focus on the development of 'professionalism' among academic teachers (as there has been among their school and TAFE colleagues) and researchers so that they can competently produce 'post-Fordist' employees. The types of changes to the system, previously outlined, are seen to be one way of enabling academics to meet the training needs of the new post-Fordist employee, and thus to be 'professional' in their work. The other way, within the logic of the award restructuring process, is to 'tighten up' their own working arrangements so that their workplace becomes more 'productive'. To this end academics entered into lengthy negotiations with employers in order to comply with the industrial imperative of workplace change.

Academics had, by May 1990, negotiated a draft award restructuring agreement which incorporated major changes to their job classification, to promotion, to probation and to staff development arrangements, in return for a 3 per cent pay increase. The finalized version of this agreement was reached in January 1991. This was only after lengthy disputes between the employers' representative body, the Australian Higher Education Industrial Association (AHEIA), and academics, who had resorted to stop-work action over proposed performance barriers to incremental progression, lack of regulation on the incidence of contract and casual employment, and extensive use of salary 'packages' and over-award payments. The final agreement included a broad-banded five-level salary and classification structure with mechanisms for internal promotion between each level to be developed by individual institutions. A three-year or less probationary period for all but the lowest level of new appointments (who have a five-year or less period) and, most significantly, a system-wide ceiling of 30 per cent on untenured (contract and casual) staff numbers were negotiated. Under the agreement, institutions have been set tenure targets for 1993, including an establishment of approximately 30 per cent of staff at the lowest level to be tenured, and a minimum of 10 per cent to be untenured at the middle level (previously senior lecturer level). These targets represent an improvement in career possibilities for the lowest level academics, whose current rates of tenure at approximately 10 per cent are significantly lower than 30 per cent. But the 10 per cent minimum untenured establishment at the middle level, where a great proportion of academic staff (especially in the older universities) are located, means a significant increase in the actual numbers of untenured middle level staff than had previously been the case. The fact that this is a minimum target means that some institutions may move beyond that figure, resulting in a diminution of the career-pathing possibilities of a higher proportion of staff on those campuses. Because the overall 30 per cent ceiling itself is a system-wide target, there will also be disparities between institutions, with some offering better career-pathing opportunities, in terms of tenured establishment numbers, than others.

The target of 70 per cent of all academic staff in tenured positions by 1993 represents a containment of the recent rush to casualization and contractualization of academic labour at more junior levels, and to some extent curtails the employers' use of numerical flexibilities at those levels of appointment. At the same time, however, employers have had an increase in the numerical flexibility of the bulk of their staff, that is those in the middle level. This group is probably the most multi-skilled of academics, in terms of the broad range of duties they can perform under the new broad-banded classification. To be able to employ a minimum of 10 per cent of this group on casual or fixed-term contract also gives the institutions enhanced functional flexibility.

Disagreement between the unions and the AHEIA over a proposed staff appraisal scheme was resolved temporarily by agreement between them to a twelve-month trial (beginning in mid-1992) of compulsory appraisal for staff development purposes, with normal increments to be paid during the period. Employers had sought summative staff appraisal linked to the salary structure, which in effect meant that staff would only receive salary increments if they had met appraisal criteria, a system known in other sectors as performance-based pay. This type of pay system is seen to enhance wages flexibility for employers. However, in a number of cases where performance-based pay schemes operate, it has been found that owing to budget restraints employers limit the proportion of employees actually given their incremental increase, and may in some cases have 'revised' staff appraisal results to be within budget limits (OECD 1989). Higher education unions have so far sucessfully attempted to link staff appraisal to career development, rather than to performance indicators for pay purposes.

Further worktime, wage and numerical flexibilities are being currently sought by employers who are pushing for an abolition of the 17.5 per cent annual leave loading for academics, longer institutional hours and terms, including 'summer terms', and staff appraisal for disciplinary purposes. It is proposed that these be bargained for salary increases on an institution by institution basis, which in actuality could create disparities between institutions at a time when the new salary and classification structure is supposed to give broad national standards for the first time in the history of higher education in Australia. The issue of market salary loadings has not been resolved, although it seems, at this stage, that only a small proportion of staff are currently receiving them.

In summary, the overall thrust of higher education employers' demands to date have been for numerical, worktime and wage flexibilities. The unions' agenda, career-pathing options, will be somewhat diminished by the increases in percentage of untenured middle level positions and possibly by the outcome of the staff appraisal trial, if a punitive rather than staff developmental model is ultimately adopted.

Outcomes of these dual demands

System changes

Some of the changes required of the system to meet the award restructuring agenda have already taken place, but, on the whole, they have been *ad hoc*. Most higher education administrative personnel and academics have been too busy attempting to negotiate the work practices agenda, the White Paper, the Training Guarantee Act and other policy developments to have had the time systematically to digest and plan for the imposed system changes arising from award restructuring.

From those administrative and academic staff just beginning to realize that the brave new world of post-Fordist education is upon them, the responses have been mixed. The economic entrepreneurs among them seem to be responding in ways which could enable the changes in curriculum required to proceed in some segments of their institutions. Some of the more culturally elite institutions and/or faculties have given the impression that they are not interested in changes which are driven by 'training' models of teaching and learning, and which take control of curriculum even further out of their hands. A third type of response has been a more ambiguous one. It incorporates a critique of the overall thrust of award restructuring, but an understanding that some progressive gains may be possible if it allows the opening up of higher education institutions to democratic scrutiny. Such scrutiny may reveal some of the corruption of some institutions' administration and the structural inequalities which persist despite lip-service to anti-discrimination legislation.

Because the system is not really a unified one and the responses to award restructuring are so diverse, the implementation of system changes will not proceed smoothly or exactly as planned. But the momentum for the award restructuring process lies elsewhere, in the restructuring of job designs and workplaces, and higher education institutions will have no real choice in the matter of participation. The deciding factor regarding the full implementation of system changes will be the state of the economy and, in particular, the political and financial will of employers and unions (or individual employees) to negotiate career-pathing, retraining and up-skilling of workers, utilizing the higher education sector to do so.

Changes to 'practices'

Award restructuring also implies a change in the nature of work itself, as academics negotiate their own productivity trade-offs for career-pathing and pay rises. This industrial intervention into academia targets the work of teachers (Seddon 1991) and forces them to comply with notions of efficiency and productivity derived from craft/manufacturing production.

Therein lies the source of a key conceptual problem for service providers. Notions of productivity currently being used are vague because the concept emanates from the manufacturing sector and doesn't translate easily into the service sector. Although some work has been done on ways of defining and measuring productivity in the service sector (see, for example, Committee of Heads of Australian Public Service 1991), qualitative goals and long-term equity goals are not easily incorporated into the input–output framework which dominates most productivity modelling.

As has been the case in recent secondary industry productivity bargaining outcomes, the terms 'efficiency' and 'productivity' have been used synonomously in the service sector, with the result that most negotiated changes have been for increased efficiencies rather than real (qualitative) increases in productivity. As Marginson (1991) points out, the reasons why this is the case have to do with the fact that input/output costs are easier to measure than qualitative changes, the administration of firms and institutions is usually hierarchical, which impedes cooperative agreement on productivity goals, and from some political quarters there is pressure for short-term survival efficiencies rather than real productivities. In an attempt to intervene in the teaching award restructuring agenda, Marginson (1991: 212) claims: 'educational policies and practices would benefit considerably if productivity goals were the driving force, rather than efficiency goals. The key to productivity advance lies in cooperation around productivity goals.' In the higher education sector many of the longer-term goals (like equity, which would be an important productivity goal) are being supplanted by the shorter-term financial survival strategies designed to chase corporate monies. This juggling of what may, in fact, be conflicting productivity goals makes the task of cooperative agreement very difficult.

As in other sectors, the award restructuring process has attempted to produce the flexible worker, but in higher education the main type of flexibility that has been negotiated to date has been numerical flexibility. A ceiling of 30 per cent untenured workers is fairly high and this form of flexibility obviously allows institutions more readily to increase or decrease their labour force as demand dictates, but the industrial position for the staff thus employed is usually less than satisfactory. The majority of untenured academics are women in the lower grades whose tenuous and often exploited position bolsters the career progression of the core labour market academics, who in the main are male. The employment of casual and part-time academics, especially, enables career path academics to remain active on the conference circuit, take up more consultancies and contract research, and take regular overseas and study leave. Because the old apprenticeship model of academic training no longer operates, and only 30 per cent have to be given tenure, these lower level part-time and casual academics now tend to remain in the secondary labour market, with limited chances of obtaining access to the career-pathing promised by award restructuring.

In academia, as in other sectors of the economy, flexibility trade-offs for career-pathing and up-skilling have been given and gained by different groups (Junor *et al.* 1994). Women, as the majority of casual, part-time and contract academics, have given the numerical flexibility, while the core senior labour market academics (mainly male) have maintained their opportunities for upgrading and career-pathing. The effects of the White Paper's national priority research and teaching funding on career opportunities will reinforce this model (Barlow 1989).

Coalescing of forces of change

As well as these award restructuring processes there are other strong forces coming together in the current period to change radically the structure of higher education. A redefined (private) model of public management is being applied to higher education institutions, even within the contradictory framework of collegial traditions (O'Brien 1990). This corporate managerial model is seen by government to be the most effective means of managing fewer resources to meet multiple and speedy outcomes (Yeatman 1987), and, according to Henry and Ross (1991: 83), 'its general shape appears to have been solidly endorsed within the white paper proposals.'

The key measures of the White Paper are designed both to make education itself a commodity and to realign academic work to more market-driven activities, like consultancies and contract research for private companies. Thus the management style, the curriculum form and the teaching and research directions are all changing as a result of such forces. There are tensions and contradictions between the major forces shaping higher education at present, but there is also an important coalescing of the award restructuring, corporate managerial, White Paper and general commodification processes that mean the momentum is unmistakably market-driven. While the tensions and contradictions about to be outlined may mean that the various outcomes from tripartite policy-making may not be realized in their anticipated form, the impact on higher education in Australia will none the less be widespread and detrimental to democratic processes.

There are a number of contradictions, both in the rhetoric of the different policy agendas and in the realities of their working through. First, the award restructuring process implies the valuing of all forms of human capital investment, since such investment enhances skills and therefore productivity. But the federal government's White Paper specifically targets certain types of human capital as being more valuable for economic growth purposes. By declaring business and administrative studies and the applied sciences and technology areas for national priority funding, and playing down the role of the behavioural and social sciences, the White Paper implies that investment in specific forms of human capital rather than in human capital in general is conducive to economic growth.

Second, the award restructuring rhetoric of post-Fordist human capital formation implies the requirement of cutting-edge, state-of-the-art infrastructure and teaching/research culture. The reality of White Paper funding cutbacks and cost efficiency drives is, in many cases, run-down, obsolete, overcrowded infrastructure and a burnt-out, low morale teaching/research culture.

Third, there is a major contradiction between the corporate managerial model of 'leadership' now operating in institutions and the award restructuring requirement for academic curricula to develop in students (as future employees) a 'culture of productivity'. The implementation of staff appraisal procedures as part of the award restructuring process coalesces with the type of corporate managerialism operating on most campuses. As Henry and Ross (1991) point out, corporate management denotes a devolution of accountability to the individual department, with autonomy and control maintained at the centre. The employers' award restructuring model of staff appraisal and performance indicators really replicates the same process at the workplace level. But both these models are in conflict with the post-Fordist management model, which implies joint cooperation and shared problem-solving between management and workers. Thus, according to that element of award restructuring which demands institutional changes to enable the production of the post-Fordist worker imbued with the 'culture of productivity', management models must be democratic. The corporate managerial model is far from democratic (Bessant 1988; Henry and Ross 1991), and the staff appraisal procedures currently being pursued by employers under award restructuring are also undemocratic.

Fourth, the White Paper's expansion of higher education to give wider access to tertiary education could be in conflict with the realities of access to higher education gained under award restructuring agreements. As Hall (1991) and others have argued, there is a gendered pattern to the type of flexibility trade-offs different groups have made under award restructuring. To date, core labour market male workers have been the ones gaining functional flexibility (multi-skilling) agreements which imply further education and training. Women, on the whole situated in the secondary labour market, have 'gained' numerical and work-time flexibility, which doesn't imply up-skilling, retraining or further education as part of the agreements. Thus, further down the track, if award restructuring does forge ahead, higher education institutions will increasingly become the preserve of core labour market male students. This reality is in tension with the White Paper's stated objective of improved access to a wider number of groups in the community.

Finally, one of the key contradictions, as far as academics are concerned, is that the demands on curriculum change and research directions required to comply with the general award restructuring agenda may not allow a proportion of current academics to develop their own negotiated career paths. This may come about because their own research and teaching interests lie in areas (like general philosophy, cultural sociology, etc.) outside those curriculum areas likely to be demanded by general award restructuring. As already stated, if the career-pathing element of award restructuring does grow in importance, it will be the needs of those restructured industries which will be increasingly served by higher education curriculum.

Conclusion

The award restructuring process is not the only force shaping higher education institutions in Australia, but it is a crucial one. The full ramifications of its effects on curriculum can only be understood if one takes into account the up-skilling and retraining realities of industry restructuring. In industries where the negotiated restructuring requires increased training and education levels for a high proportion of the current staff, and where firms are willing to release staff for training periods, such agreements will result in increased demand for relevant courses and for articulation between courses.

The competency frameworks movement, closely related to the award restructuring process, will proceed whether or not major industrial restructuring takes place. The movement focuses on learning/training outcomes rather than processes, but does not necessarily require significant industry restructuring to forge ahead. A flow-on effect, even to those faculties not directly preparing for the professions, will occur, as industries continue to formulate competency standards.

The industrial dimensions of award restructuring will have long-term effects on the nature of academic work. In a context increasingly characterized by corporate managerial models of administration and financial austerity, the mechanisms of performance appraisal and numerical flexibility will consolidate anti-democratic trends that contradict the possibilities of the post-Fordist academic.

References

ACTU/TDC (1987) *Australia Reconstructed: ACTU Mission to Western Europe.* Canberra, AGPS.
Ashenden, D. (1990) Award restructuring and productivity in the future of schooling, Text of the 1990 Frank Tate Memorial Lecture, Victorian Institute of Educational Research, Melbourne.
Australian Council of Trade Unions (1991) For an educated, high competence society, Draft Policy on Education, August.
Barlow, K. (1989) The White Paper and restructuring the academic labour market, *Australian Universities' Review*, 32(1), 30–7.
Bessant, B. (1988) Corporate management and the institutions of higher education, *Australian Universities' Review*, 31(2), 10–13.
Bluer, R. and Carmichael, L. (1991) Award restructuring in teaching, *Unicorn*, 17(1), 24–30.

Boreham, P. (n.d.) The politics of production from Fordism to flexible specialisation?, Paper presented at the Australian Sociological Association Annual Conference.

Burgess, J. and Macdonald, D. (1990) The labour flexibility imperative, *Journal of Australian Political Economy*, 27(November), 15–35.

Carmichael, L. (1990) Over-view: work organisation, skills analysis, training, entry points, career paths, Workshop papers from Award Restructuring Workshop, Realising the Potential: Women and Award Restructuring. Office of the Status of Women, Department of Prime Minister and Cabinet, Canberra.

Committee of Heads of Australian Public Service Agencies (1991) Improving productivity: a challenge for the Australian public service, Discussion paper prepared for the Minister for Industrial Relations, September.

Cooper, T. (1992) Qualified for the job: the new vocationalism, *Education Links*, 42, 18–22.

Curtin, R. and Mathews, J. (1990) Two models of award restructuring in Australia, *Labour and Industry*, 3(1), 58–75.

Davidson, J. (1990) The road to functional flexibility: white collar work and employment relations in a privatised public utility, *Sociological Review*, 38(4), 15–35.

Dawkins, J. (1988) *Higher Education: a Policy Statement*. Canberra, AGPS.

Economic Planning Advisory Council (1989) A better way of working, Discussion paper 89/02, prepared for the Business Council of Australia.

Hall, P. (1991) Award restructuring and the quality of working life, Unpublished paper, Commonwealth Department of Industrial Relations, Canberra.

Henry, M. and Ross, B. (1991) Managing academia, *Discourse*, 11(2), 78–97.

Jessop, B., Nielsen, K., Kastendiek, H. and Pedersen, O. (eds) (1991) *The Politics of Flexibility*. Aldershot, Edward Elgar.

Junor, A., Barlow, K. and Patterson, M. (1994) *Measuring Service Productivity: Part-time Women and the Finance Sector Workplace*. Canberra, Commonwealth Department of Industrial Relations.

Marginson, S. (1991) Productivity and efficiency in education, *Australian Journal of Education*, 35(2), 201–14.

Mathews, J. (1989) *Age of Democracy: the Politics of Post-Fordism*. Melbourne, Oxford University Press.

Nielsen, K. (1991) Towards a flexible future – theories and politics, in B. Jessop *et al.* (eds) *The Politics of Flexibility*. Aldershot, Edward Elgar.

O'Brien, J. (1990) Privatising state workers: the case of academics, *Australian Universities' Review*, 33(1 and 2), 30–7.

Organisation for Economic Cooperation and Development (1988) *Recent Trends in Performance Appraisal and Performance-related Pay in the Public Sector*. Paris, OECD.

Robertson, S. and Trotman, J. (1992) A spoke in the wheels of professionalism, *Education Links*, 42, 23–9.

Seddon, T. (1991) Restructuring teachers and teaching: current Australian development and future prospects, *Discourse*, 11(2), 1–23.

Yeatman, A. (1987) The concept of public management and the Australian state in the 1980's, *Australian Journal of Public Administration*, 46(4), 339–53.

12

The Gendered Management of Equity-oriented Change in Higher Education

Anna Yeatman

Restructuring and management for change in higher education

The discourse of restructuring is often taken by both its proponents and its opponents to refer only to economic and managerialist aspects of restructuring. However, it is clear that contemporary restructuring agendas are a response to substantive and value-oriented agendas for change as much as they are a response to making national economies more 'competitive'. Examples of the former include the following: a post-colonial politics of acknowledgment that formerly colonized and/or conquered peoples have a right to self-determination; a multicultural politics of acceptance that cultural diversity has become an irreducible feature of social life; and a post-patriarchal politics of acceptance that, in principle, women have rights of personhood which require respect. While all these substantive aspects of restructuring are fiercely contested in respect of what they are to mean, it is this contestation which can be taken to be the harbinger of new contours of political debate.

In Australia the adoption and implementation of affirmative action legislation in 1986 may be seen to form part of the dynamics of restructuring. All higher education institutions in Australia are required by national law to have developed affirmative action plans whereby these employers adopt 'systematic means. . .of achieving equal employment opportunities for women' (Affirmative Action Resource Unit 1985: 1). The agendas of restructuring, to be sure, are presently dominated by market-oriented economic cultures of action. Among other things, this revival of *laissez-faire* ideology is championing the notion of enterprise-based employer–employee contracts where regulative norms constraining these contracts are to be minimized, and, at least in the New Zealand setting, collective bargaining is to be replaced by individual contracts if employers deem this to be in their interest. It is quite clear that these employer-oriented agendas of restructuring, designed as they are to minimize constraints on employers in the effective, economic and efficient exploitation of their workforces, are in general inimical to all equal employment opportunity initiatives.

Conceding that these are the dominant agendas of restructuring when conservative parties such as the Thatcher or Bolger governments are in power, these are not the only agendas of restructuring. Even staying inside the instrumentalist-functionalist discourse of restructuring, we can find an awareness that governments and complex organizations of all kinds, including universities, have to develop organizational cultures and employee capacities to respond effectively to ongoing socio-cultural change and complexity. These agendas work to complicate the simple, reductive agendas of market-oriented, employer-dominated restructuring (a similar point is made by Sue Middleton 1992 for the restructuring of schooling in New Zealand).

Examples of what I have in mind here are the following. It is clear that national societies such as Australia are becoming internally more rather than less culturally complex, and that this dynamic is not likely to level off as Australia becomes more identified with its Asian neighbours. At the same time, Australian organizations – including universities – are now having to orient their performance and products to 'export' as well as domestic (Australian) markets. In higher education, this means efforts to attract fee-paying overseas students and, over the next few years, it is likely to mean the elaboration of cross-national educational programmes (of which Erasmus in Europe and the twinning arrangements shared between Australian and Malaysian universities may be taken to be examples). All these developments add up to demands on academic managers, academics and general staff for increased tolerance of socio-cultural complexity in general, and for skills in intercultural communication in particular. These are demands on substantive organizational development, which is not likely to occur without organizational investment in staff development. It is arguable that there are intrinsic links between policies and practice which encourage intercultural communication and those which are concerned with equal employment opportunity objectives.

As we transit into the twenty-first century there seems little likelihood that demands on capacities for management of change are likely to diminish. All organizations confront a context in which established visions and cultures of expectation no longer hold. In particular, they confront a time when the certainties of modern Western society are subject to fundamental challenge. Among other things, this is a post-colonial time, meaning not that the exploitive relationships of colonization are a thing of the past, but that they no longer command legitimacy. This loss of legitimacy is a profound dynamic of contemporary change. It affects the standing and status of the core values of modern Western civilization, including those on which the very idea of a university rests. It is no longer possible to invoke these values as the foundations of civilization in general, for questions are now asked. Whose civilization? And, more pointedly, if these values are core values of modern, Western civilization, do they operate to reproduce the unequal relationship of colonizer and colonized? In contemporary New Zealand, many Maori see these values as 'Pakeha' values, i.e. values specific to the white settler colonist culture and without any more general and shared value.

This is a difficult challenge. I am among those who wish to argue that the core values of a university are central to a democratic society and that a professionally autonomous culture of rational enquiry is a condition of civic virtue. The circular character of this argument is readily appreciated when it is viewed through the eyes of those who would see all these values – democratic, rational, professional autonomy, civic virtue – as the core values of a modern, Western, colonizing enterprise. This is not an unfamiliar problem territory for feminist academics, who have to find their way in relation to the paradox that these core values are both patriarchal *and* a condition of feminist critique of them.

There can be no doubt that these core values are thoroughly implicated in the modern colonizing and patriarchalist enterprise. At the same time, it is equally clear that those who would criticize these values as they have been instituted in modern Western institutional practice derive the very terms of their critique from these values. Claims of injustice are phrased in terms of the egalitarian culture of modern society. Claims directed at showing how modern scientific enquiry is conducted according to a patriarchalist binary ordering of reason and its other, those who come to stand for the exigencies of embodiment – an ordering that excludes women from the business of reason – depend for their power and cogency on norms of rational enquiry. In short, the terms of the critique fall not outside but inside the objects of critique. It is this which permits contemporary efforts by democratic theorists of difference to reframe norms of justice and rational enquiry so that they operate to work *with* rather than *against* gender and cultural difference.

If the terms of the critique fall not outside but inside the objects of critique, it is clear that change agency is complex. One may argue – as I am about to do – that those who represent the excluded terms in these patriarchal binaries are the recruiting base for the initiator/innovator aspects of change agency. It is also clear that the those who represent the privileged terms in these binaries – disembodied reason – are positioned by their own rational/ethical claims to respond positively to this initiative, while, at the same time, they seek to conserve the privilege conferred on them by this binary order of values. This model of change agency is considerably different from the older agonistic models of revolutionary change, which pit one class interest against its other, and assume there is a zero-sum relationship between their respective strategic claims and achievements.

What tasks arise in relation to understanding and brokering the complexities of these fundamental challenges to the core values of the university? This is a question I have been asking in the context of the University of Waikato, which stands on land to which the Tainui tribe lay claim, and which for this and other reasons is answerable to Maori claims on a bicultural university education. Just what a bicultural university education means and should mean is a question requiring careful discussion and debate. What I observe occurring in this context is an avoidance of this debate, a not unlikely outcome in the context of the social and cultural polarization that attends a history of settler colonization of an indigenous people. At present this university has evolved no institutional procedures to permit safely a considered discussion and debate of the issues where disagreement can be aired and respected. My own diagnosis of this present lack is that the academic leaders/managers of the institution – white, middle class, male – however well-intentioned, are unprepared by their background and experience to work with these issues. These citizens of the university have inherited its culture and core values as their birthright. With the exception of class dissonance in the case of male academics with working-class origins, there is nothing in their situation to permit them to distinguish between how these values *have* been instituted in patriarchalist and racist ways, and how they *could* be instituted. Thus, when they confront radical critique of the core values of the university, their response has to be *either* a conservative reiteration of these values as they have known them *or* (what amounts to the same thing) a paternalistic concession that these values may not be adequate to the needs of particular disadvantaged groups.

The first response leads these managers of change to remain silent in the face of Maori or feminist demands for justice in the university. The second response leads these managers of change to institute Maori or women's studies in ways which do not have to be subject to the same criteria of academic rigour and scrutiny as the mainstream, proper heartland of the university has to be. In its early stages, this second response generates these new components of the university as low-cost units staffed by academics whose qualifications and experience position them low in the academic pecking order. In due course, the inadequacies of this arrangement become evident, and the university invests more in the academic expansion and upgrading of these units. In the current climate especially, such investment is perceived in resource allocation terms as occurring at the expense of the mainstream parts of the university. Academic leadership in this process tends to be abnegated, with the allocational decisions made by executive fiat rather than subject to collegial discussion and debate. Again, this reproduces the binary ordering of the university as the contrast between its proper and its interloper components. One effect of this is to position those women who are identified in institutional equity change agency roles as highly vulnerable to modes of resistance to change which are unaccountable to collegial standards of discussion and debate.

It is arguable that post-colonial and post-patriarchal claims on justice evoked, as they are by the very universalism of modern Western culture, pose unprecedented demands on the substantive management of change. Undoubtedly, they are requiring universities as other institutions to enter into a steep learning curve where we can be sure that the early stages of responding to these challenges are beset by inexperience on all sides. This inexperience concerns not just those who are privileged within the patriarchal rational ordering of the university. At the present time, the claimants on justice – Maori and feminist – tend too often to advance their claims in disregard of the due process that belongs to an an academic professional culture of policy-making.

It is a short-term strategy at best to respond as the neo-liberal conservatives are doing, namely to let the market sort out the winners and losers. Within universities, this means that units which cannot compete effectively for research funds and students will be resourced poorly. This does not change the current situation for the equity-oriented components of the university – women's studies, aboriginal studies, Maori studies, etc. – for they are already defined as small or marginal resource claimants. It remains the case that universities as other institutions have entered a long-term, substantive crisis of legitimacy in the face of these post-colonial and post-patriarchal claims on justice. This crisis is not going to go away. If anything it is likely to grow. As it grows, it is likely to fuel both populist and conservative attempts to reign in universities, diminish if not destroy their professional autonomy and thereby threaten their cultural base. These threats raise anew the question as to whether universities' current leadership/management culture and recruitment base are adequate to the task of conserving core values through formulating new vision.

So far in Australia it has been a national Labor government (1983 to the present) which has brokered the agendas of restructuring and ensured that there is an up-front, equity-related component of them. In this I think we can generalize to Australia Cynthia Cockburn's (1991: 30) remark of Britain: 'Not only in passing supportive legislation but also. . .in introducing positive action for sex and race equality at local level, the state under Labour Party administration has been a significant factor.' Thus, with the passing of the Affirmative Action Act in 1986, Australian universities, like other organizations with over 100 employees, are subject to affirmative action legislation. A conservative government in the future might dilute or remove the force of this legislation, while it proceeds in general to enhance employer prerogatives at the expense of employee-related equity. Such policies amount to control agendas. They remove employee security of tenure, union supports and collectively transparent award-based pay and conditions; and instead use the whip of performance pay, individual contracts, short-term contracts for higher proportions of staff, part-time, casualized contracts for substantial numbers and, last but not least, bring the executive, divisional and middle levels of academic management into a culture of employer prerogatives with suitable material rewards accruing to the personnel in these levels. The incentives in this imaginative piece of institution design work to create academic managers who control rather than collegially work with the academic staff for whom they are responsible. The former are positionally and materially placed so as to lose identification with the latter, while these become increasingly demoralized and marginalized citizens of this institution.

However, it is significant that in Australia it has been a Labor government which has set the agendas for restructuring in higher education. This has conduced an intelligent adaptation of university management structures and cultures to the contemporary dynamics of restructuring. I am compelled to add that my university experience in both Australia and New Zealand indicates considerable intelligence and imagination on the part of most (not all) universities in adapting the restructuring agendas to fit the needs and culture of a university. This is likely to ensure that the worst features of the neo-liberal simplistic carrot-and-stick approach are diluted and mediated within university settings.

This is still at a high cost of morale and, arguably worse, the capacity of the university to respond to contemporary societal challenges with a considered and proactive vision for justice. If the neo-liberal agendas of restructuring develop social polarization *within* the university, so that there is a small band of relatively highly paid academic managers, a middling group of academics whose conditions are vastly improved by effective commercialization of their activities, and a larger pool of semi-proletarianized academics, it is difficult to see how the university can sustain this capacity for vision. Yet without such capacity it is arguable that a university cannot sustain its critical insistence on the distinctions between knowledge and information, and between academic excellence and academic competency.

The role of equity in the substantive management of change

If the social value of the professionally autonomous university is to be sustained, an equity-oriented vision is a necessary condition of management of change in higher education. By professional autonomy, I mean that the university is essentially a self-managing entity enabled to respond to demands for financial and social accountability in ways which fit its distinctive value orientation. This concerns the promotion of a culture of critical, rational enquiry which fosters systematic scepticism as to the grounds of all claims on truth. This scepticism is rationally oriented because it insists that truth claims are falsifiable if they cannot meet evidential and logical criteria. Just what these criteria should be is currently subject to sustained debate inside the university. This debate represents the demise of a monorational culture of scientific enquiry and its cession to a universe of contested and contestable truth claims where consensual closure to debate is no longer possible (see Yeatman 1992). This culture of rational enquiry – old as new – depends on academics being granted a conditional autonomy to practise within it, the conditional component residing in demands on them for high quality performance in this practice.

An equity-oriented substantive vision for the academic development of the university is not likely for the reasons argued above to come from the university's traditional academic leaders and managers. Instead it is more likely to come from academics who are placed as marginals in relation to this traditional culture of academic leadership and management. The core marginals in a binary hierarchical ordering of reason and embodiment are women. This is why (usually white and English-speaking background) women are used in organizations as equity change agents.

It is true that there is no guarantee against white women's racism and classism. Women, however, are positioned as embodied subjects in a way that men are not. This means that women are more likely than even racially marginalized men to understand the issues for equitable policies which arise from challenging the patriarchalist binaries of mind/body, reason/ emotion, protector/protected (etc.). In Cynthia Cockburn's important book *In the Way of Women: Men's Resistance to Sex Equality in Organizations* (1991: 67), she says of two of her organizational case studies: 'Of only two or three men out of the thirty I interviewed in the [public] Service [agency] would it be possible to say they were self-motivating and pro-active on equality issues. It has to be added that ethnic minority men were no less negative than white men about positive action for sex equality in the Service and High Street Retail.'

To put this somewhat differently, Cockburn adapts Carole Pateman's (1988) argument that a fratriarchal sexual contract underwrites the structuring of the modern public domain. Cockburn (1991: 62) distinguishes two clauses in this contract: a domestic clause and a workplace clause. The domestic clause 'is an understanding that in ideal circumstances each man may have authority over the person and labour of a wife as housekeeper, child-rearer and sexual partner in the home.' However, capitalist employers are interested in exploiting the labour of these men's wives precisely because their domestic involvements compromise their effective labour market capacities, and thus ensure their status as a cheap labour supply. Employers develop serious contradictions in the domestic clause of the sexual contract by bringing women into the workplace. This is where the workplace clause of the sexual contract comes into play: 'Men guarantee each other rights over women in paid employment and in the organizations in which they work' (Cockburn 1991: 62). This is achieved through two fundamental strategies. As far as possible, women's work is segregated from and awarded lower value than men's work (Cockburn 1991: 63). Where women achieve an effective claim on promotion or senior positions, either they are placed in supervision over other women (as in women's studies units) or their executive management role is identified with the 'feminine' aspects of the organization's work, equity policy for example. Cockburn (1991: 64) remarks of these senior women managers: 'They will become the personnel managers and public relations officers rather than the production managers, staff rather than line.'

We seem to confront a neat double-bind here. Women are the equity change agents in an organization; equity policy roles signify a sex-segregated domain for women at the senior levels of the organization. If this is so, it is a double-bind in which both women and organizations are developing some experience. For what appears from one angle as a double-bind can from another appear as a powerful and creative site of dynamic contradictions in the organization.

It is at this point that we need to be reminded that both equity change agents and organizations have developed about ten years worth of experience in equal employment opportunity type policies and practices in universities. Cockburn's capacity to research the resistance of men in organizations to these policies and practices depends on this fact. So does her important reminder that we have passed beyond the first phase of putting equal employment opportunity policies on the agenda, with necessarily a good deal of the energy involved going into legitimizing the necessity of such policy in the first place and into conceptualizing these policies in ways which anticipated their opponents' efforts to sweep them off the agenda (see Ronalds 1990, on the affirmative action legislation). The policies are 'up' now, and, as Cockburn (1991: 227) proposes, 'as more organizations declare themselves "equal opportunity employers", the first wave will shift emphasis from policy-making to implementation and monitoring.'

It is worth reflecting on what such implementation may entail. Among other things, it must entail within universities a substantive commitment to developing an equitable vision within academic curriculum and scholarly process. For this to occur, it is clear that the institution has to recruit many more women, and not just English-speaking background and/or white women, within its ranks. In particular, for this to occur the leadership of the university needs proactively to anticipate how the sexual contract is reasserted in changed circumstances, and to attempt to head this off at the pass. For example, it is clear that universities are developing something like an internal market. If an academic or, more likely, a group of academics can effectively commercialize their activities – let these be research activities – they can buy their way out of intensive lower-level teaching efforts, and contract these out to part-time, casualized academic workers. The latter will find it very difficult to complete their doctoral dissertations under these conditions, not least because that intangible factor of senior colleague encouragement and esteem is withdrawn from the very terms of their employment contract.

The university is not likely to want to lose the commercial value and academic repute of this research effort. Accordingly, it may be difficult for it to challenge root and branch this emergent division of labour between privileged researchers and proletarianized teachers, a division of labour that is clearly gendered. What it can do is insist on accountability of these teachers' employment contracts to equal opportunity objectives. This may mean that a percentage of the research funds generated is put in an equity pool to fund research leave entitlements for contract academics completing doctoral dissertations. It may also mean that research teams are required to recruit women both as full, senior members and as the research students apprenticed to these teams.

It is all too likely that marketable research which pulls in big dollars will become the new patriarchal heartland of the university. A Waikato colleague a year out from the Canadian university system tells me that in Canada academic management has become feminized while research has become masculinized. This pattern, I suspect, is already becoming evident in Australian universities with a policy of elected departmental headships. There are a number of academic staffing policy issues arising in relation to the professionalization of academic management which can be proactively identified and aligned in relation to equity considerations. For example, if senior academic managers are on term contracts, where are they to go and how is this role transition to be supported when the contract runs out? How may they be supported to recover research and teaching identities? These questions need to be broached if (a) academic management is to be located within the collegial culture of academic professionalism, and (b) good people are to be attracted into senior academic management.

It is arguable that the academic managers of the institution will come to stand to its researchers as do those who keep the household ticking over to those who succesfully avoid household labour. It is also arguable that the researchers, like most men in households, will do all they can to show they are unfit for generic academic administrative/management tasks even if they are proving to be adept in managing a research project team. Demonstrated aptitude of *this* kind will be used to establish claims on vice-chancellorships, with an avoidance of the middle (departmental head) and divisional (deanship) management roles. Since it is these management roles which are likely to become feminized over time, care needs to be taken in ensuring that these management contributions do not compromise the career opportunities of those who make them. Feminization, of course, means that the men who fill these good householder roles in the institution are symbolically associated with the feminine side of those patriarchal binaries.

Women as front-runners for equity-oriented restructuring

Senior women who are tagged as equity change agents in universities are currently in a vulnerable position where it is all too easy for them to become condensed targets for resistance to change. This tagging can occur in various ways: to be one of two women vice-chancellors in a national university system where this is the one associated with the less established, or in British parlance more redbrick, of the two universities concerned and, thus, lies outside the protective range of the male academic establishment; to be a professor of women's studies; to be the only women dean of a country's law schools, where this law school is identified with the university's bicultural and gender equity objectives and seen to be pioneering a 'law in context' approach; to be a pro-vice-chancellor responsible for foreign students, student welfare and equal opportunity. At this point of time, there simply are not enough such women to provide the individuals concerned with the powerful support of their own network, and with what may be termed the cultural impact of a powerful cohort effect.

Nor is the experience of equity type objectives mature enough in universities to ensure that the senior male colleagues of these women strategically anticipate and counter resistance to their change agency. Senior men, many of them, are genuinely sympathetic to equity objectives because (a) their institutional positioning affords them some understanding of the centrality of these objectives to the institution's growth and development, and (b) their own institutional placement makes these few women's advancement into senior positions unthreatening to them. At this point of time, the fratriarchal social contract of which Pateman speaks encourages the senior/ executive level male academic managers tacitly to ask the one or few women senior academics who are identified with equity change agent roles to take the flak. By so doing, these men distance themselves from equity agendas. They do so more by sins of omission than sins of commission. Instead of lending active strategic support creatively to anticipate men's resistance to sex equality in organizations (Cockburn 1990) and to provide leadership that would both challenge and channel this resistance, they indicate that they still belong to and will uphold a fratriarchal social order within the institution.

I have suggested that it is semiotically prescribed that women are associated with the institutional roles of equity change agency. I have also suggested that the cultural and ethical demands of restructuring now make these roles diffuse, a diffusion evidenced in the increased participation of albeit very small numbers of women in generic or mainstream senior academic positions. In comparison to the past, some women will be accorded much faster advancement in the new performance-oriented and competitive environments of restructured higher education. Such women are valuable to all the restructuring efforts of the institution. Precisely because of their positioned lack of loyalty to the established ways of doing things – and to the established masculine elite of the institution – those of them who show management and policy talent become highly valued managers for change in the new environment. Classically they are used as 'front-runners' by chief executives at the corporate level and deans at the divisional level. They are encouraged to use their outsider positioning, their task rather than status orientation, and their vested interest in new ways of doing things to 'call' all the fustian, patriarchal inefficiencies of the old institutional culture. They are used as the institutional 'breath of fresh air'. Change agency is an intoxicant for those who are congenitally attracted to innovator roles. It is, however, a guarantee of burn-out unless it is well supported by the executive and senior levels of management of the institution.

There is currently sufficient information about the patterns of gender stratification in academia for there to be effective, proactive anticipation of how the dynamics of restructuring in universities are likely to affect and reshape these patterns. There is also sufficient information and analysis of how gender at work works. Both Cockburn's work and that of Game and Pringle (1983) show how deeply entrenched the sexual contract is in the structuring and culture of work and organizations. Acknowledgment of this by the management and leadership of universities is the first step in the development of an effective and proactive equity policy for the institution. One of the difficulties facing those few senior women academic managers is precisely the lack of this acknowledgment. The men of good will are clearly committed by way of individual intentions to change – at work if not at home – but their fratriarchal loyalties lead them to deny how deeply entrenched the sexual contract is in the organization. Such denial effects a kind of disingenous innocence about men's resistance to sex equality in organizations, an innocence that leaves the women change agents unprotected and vulnerable.

Equity-oriented change management, which is informed by academic professional collegiality, is oriented to the place of all women academics and students in the institution. Since their place is not separable from the place of women within the general staff career structures of the university, equity-oriented change management of this kind has to be oriented to the issues arising for women general staff as well. The terms of this argument require that the university continues to be structured within a collegial culture of policy discussion and debate. Collegiality is the academic version of industrial democracy, and it provides constraints on the extent to which an unbridgeable gulf opens up between the semi-proletarianized ranks of contract teachers, on the one hand, and the reasonably well-paid and relatively secure academics who can experience the joys of research-led teaching, on the other.

Current managerialist rhetorics notwithstanding, universities are not like business firms. If they are to be universities, these organizations have to work in ways which encourage a critical culture of rational enquiry. Such a culture will not survive unless it becomes genuinely responsive to contemporary post-colonial and post-patriarchal demands on justice. Among other things, this means making the staffing and student profiles of the university as 'representative' as possible. This must be done in ways which are aligned with academic objectives. There is much in the process of the amalgamations of Australian higher education institutions to suggest ways in which this can be done: for example, generous time release to ensure that ethnically or racially marginalized male and female academics can undertake doctorates in ways which ensure effective mentoring and support for these academics.

All this involves a complex and difficult process of change. I have tended to construct this process here from the standpoint of senior women at an historical point where the use of them as institutional front-runners is insufficiently supported in substantive policy and programme implementation.

It is not entirely clear to me how the male senior managers will construe the next steps, particularly if they find their senior women moving on or burning out. It is very important that 'pressure from the bottom' be both sustained and developed. It is crucially important that women doctoral students undertake research on the impact of the restructuring of higher education on women, where they ask whether this impact is different depending on the race/ethnic status of the women concerned. Research of this kind is central to the design and monitoring of equity-related policy and its implementation.

In conclusion, there are both substantive aspects of as well as opportunities in contemporary restructuring agendas. These include the fact that equity change management strategies in universities, as in other organizations, are entering stages of maturation which demand of these institutions more serious and proactive support for the women who are asked to play the role of equity change managers. I have argued that this kind of support is in the university's interests if it is to re-envision its core values in ways which fit contemporary demands for justice. If universities do not re-envision their core values in this way their survival cannot be guaranteed within the complex processes of cultural and social change which the dynamics of restructuring connote.

References

Affirmative Action Resource Unit, Office of Status of Women, Department of Prime Minister and Cabinet (1985) *Affirmative Action Implementation Manual: Higher Education Edition.* Canberra, AGPS.

Cockburn, C. (1990) *In the Way of Women: Men's Resistance to Sex Equality in Organizations.* London, Macmillan.

Game, A. and Pringle, R. (1983) *Gender at Work.* Sydney, Allen & Unwin.

Middleton, S. (1992) Equity, equality and biculturalism in the restructuring of New Zealand schools: a life history approach, *Harvard Educational Review*, 62(3), 301–24.

Pateman, C. (1988) *The Sexual Contract.* Cambridge, Polity Press.

Ronalds, C. (1990) Government action against employment discrimination, in S. Watson (ed.) *Playing the State.* Sydney, Allen & Unwin.

Yeatman, A. (1992) The place of women's studies in the contemporary university, Inaugural lecture, University of Waikato, 23 June.

Index

The Society for Research into Higher Education

The Society for Research into Higher Education exists to stimulate and coordinate research into all aspects of higher education. It aims to improve the quality of higher education through the encouragement of debate and publication on issues of policy, on the organization and management of higher education institutions, and on the curriculum and teaching methods.

The Society's income is derived from subscriptions, sales of its books and journals, conference fees and grants. It receives no subsidies, and is wholly independent. Its individual members include teachers, researchers, managers and students. Its corporate members are institutions of higher education, research institutes, professional, industrial and governmental bodies. Members are not only from the UK, but from elsewhere in Europe, from America, Canada and Australasia, and it regards its international work as amongst its most important activities.

Under the imprint *SRHE & Open University Press*, the Society is a specialist publisher of research, having some 45 titles in print. The Editorial Board of the Society's Imprint seeks authoritative research or study in the above fields. It offers competitive royalties, a highly recognizable format in both hard- and paperback and the world-wide reputation of the Open University Press.

The Society also publishes *Studies in Higher Education* (three times a year), which is mainly concerned with academic issues, *Higher Education Quarterly* (formerly *Universities Quarterly*), mainly concerned with policy issues, *Research into Higher Education Abstracts* (three times a year), and *SRHE News* (four times a year).

The Society holds a major annual conference in December, jointly with an institution of higher education. In 1991, the topic was 'Research and Higher Education in Europe', with the University of Leicester. In 1992, it was 'Learning to Effect' with Nottingham Trent University, and in 1993, 'Governments and the Higher Education Curriculum: Evolving Partnerships' at the University of Sussex in Brighton. Further conferences include in 1994, 'The Student Experience' at the University of York.

The Society's committees, study groups and branches are run by the members. The groups at present include:

Teacher Education Study Group
Continuing Education Group
Staff Development Group
Excellence in Teaching and Learning

Benefits to members

Individual

Individual members receive:

- *SRHE News*, the Society's publications list, conference details and other material included in mailings.
- Greatly reduced rates for *Studies in Higher Education* and *Higher Education Quarterly*.
- A 35% discount on all Open University Press & SRHE publications.
- Free copies of the Precedings – commissioned papers on the theme of the Annual Conference.
- Free copies of *Research into Higher Education Abstracts*.
- Reduced rates for conferences.
- Extensive contacts and scope for facilitating initiatives.
- Reduced reciprocal memberships.

Corporate

Corporate members receive:

- All benefits of individual members, plus
- Free copies of *Studies in Higher Education*.
- Unlimited copies of the Society's publications at reduced rates.
- Special rates for its members e.g. to the Annual Conference.

Membership details: SRHE, 344–354 Gray's Inn Road, London, WC1X 8BP, UK. Tel: 071 837 7880
Catalogue: SRHE & Open University Press, Celtic Court, 22 Ballmoor, Buckingham MK18 1XW. Tel: (0280) 823388

THE MANAGEMENT OF CHANGE IN UNIVERSITIES
UNIVERSITIES, STATE AND ECONOMY IN AUSTRALIA, CANADA AND THE
UNITED KINGDOM

Henry D.R. Miller

This book presents an account of the management of changes in universities new
and old in Australia, Canada and the United Kingdom. Recent developments in the
system of higher education are described with particular reference to the change
from a binary to a unified system in Australia and the United Kingdom. Changes in
states and economies during the 1980s and 1990s are examined in terms of their
affects on universities and their management. One hundred interviews in twenty
universities, with academic managers and staff representatives across Australia, Canada
and the United Kingdom provide the basis for an analysis of how change is being
managed. Henry Miller points out that managerialism and the language and methods of the market are permeating the structure and culture of universities and that
this raises questions about what are and should be the purposes of universities and
how they should be governed.

Contents
*Developments in higher education in Australia, Canada and the United Kingdom – The state
and the universities – The economy and universities – Management in Universities – Case
study: Aston University – Management and academic work – References – Index.*

192pp   0 335 19089 8 (Hardback)